D0820342

REIMAGINING EQUALITY

Reimagining Equality

A New Deal for Children of Color

Nancy E. Dowd

NEW YORK UNIVERSITY PRESS

New York

NEW YORK UNIVERSITY PRESS
New York
www.nyupress.org

An earlier version of Chapter 0 was previously published as "Straight Out of Compton: Developmental Equality and a Critique of the Compton School Litigation," in 45 *Capital University Law Review* 199 (2017). Copyright 2017, Capital University; reprinted with permission.

An earlier version of Chapter 6 was previously published as "John Moore Jr: *Moore v City of East Cleveland* and Children's Constitutional Arguments," in 85 *Fordham Law Review* 2603–13 (2017). Copyright 2017, Fordham University, reprinted with permission.

Some material from the book is adapted from an article previously published as "Black Boys Matter: Developmental Equality," in 45 *Hofstra Law Review* 47–116 (2016). Copyright 2016, Hofstra University, reprinted with permission.

References to Internet websites (URLs) were accurate at the time of writing. Neither the author nor New York University Press is responsible for URLs that may have expired or changed since the manuscript was prepared.

Library of Congress Cataloging-in-Publication Data
Names: Dowd, Nancy E., 1949– author.
Title: Reimagining equality : a new deal for children of color / Nancy E. Dowd.
Description: New York : New York University Press, [2018] | Includes bibliographical references and index.
Identifiers: LCCN 2017054999 | ISBN 9781479893355 (cl : alk. paper)
Subjects: LCSH: Children of minorities—United States—Social conditions. | African American boys—Social conditions. | Equality—United States. | Children's rights—United States. | Children—Legal status, laws, etc.—United States.
Classification: LCC E184.A1 D69 2018 | DDC 323.3/520973—dc23
LC record available at https://lccn.loc.gov/2017054999

Manufactured in the United States of America
10 9 8 7 6 5 4 3 2 1
Also available as an ebook

To Paul

CONTENTS

Introduction

[T]he question of how one should live within a black body,
within a country lost in the Dream, is the question of my
life. . . .
—Ta-Nehisi Coates

The American Dream is one of equality and opportunity; the ability to succeed and be whoever and whatever one wants to be, limited only by one's own drive and talent. But for Black boys, this is not the reality. As Ta-Nehisi Coates so eloquently explains in *Between the World and Me* (2015), his letter to his then seventeen-year-old son, the overriding reality is danger to the body, literally the threat to one's life, filling him with fear for his son. Grounded in his own experience growing up in inner-city Baltimore, it is a no less justified fear for his son raised amidst relative wealth and privilege. Coates writes about being stopped in his car by the Prince Edward County police while he was in college. He had done nothing but was acutely aware that meant nothing in this dangerous moment when anything could happen to him, and be justified. Quite literally, you hold your breath as you read this passage; you know his fear is warranted. Nor is his fear for his son misplaced. Indeed, his letter to his son was triggered by his son's reaction to the refusal to indict the Ferguson police officer who killed Michael Brown. But, Michael Brown was neither the first nor the last young Black man or boy to lose his life to private or state violence. Every new death reinforces that this is unexceptional. The fear for the body, for life itself, is real for every Black boy and man.

But this fear is only the tip of the iceberg. Beyond the danger to the bodies of Black boys and men is the reality that as children or as adults, if they survive, most will fall far short of realizing the American Dream. This book confronts that larger reality and aims to change it. Allowing this reality to persist violates fundamental principles of law, of moral-

1

ity, of humanity. In this book, I confront this reality and articulate a groundbreaking strategy for change. I propose developmental equality as a model to accomplish children's equality. Using developmental scholarship grounded in the lives of children of color and other outsider children, I aim to infuse and shift the law's perspective on development and harness developmental insights to achieve equality. A developmental equality model would be the basis for policy and litigation strategies to identify and dismantle structural discrimination, prevent ongoing replication of inequality for children, and provide affirmative support for *all* children's opportunity to develop.

I make the case for the developmental equality model by looking to the life course of Black boys from birth to age eighteen. In this book, I gather and distill the social science research on the development of Black boys. This information is important in its own right, because Black boys matter: they deserve our focus and attention as a group. The data also serve to expose structural discrimination that fosters not only the inequality and subordination of Black boys but also inequalities generally for children linked to their identities. It should require that we ask other questions: Who else is at the bottom? What similar or distinctive developmental barriers do they face? This deep look into the lives of Black boys from birth until legal adulthood informs the model of developmental equality, and that model, as applied to their lives, points to structural factors and the role the state plays in children's continuing inequalities.

My analysis is not intended to create a hierarchy of harm or need. I do not claim that Black boys matter more, or Black girls matter less (Crenshaw and Ritchie 2015). Nor do I claim that Latino, Asian, or Muslim children are less affected. And this perspective is equally applicable to children outside of the United States. Roma children, for example, are at the bottom in every country in which they live. Children of Muslim immigrants, similar to children of immigrants elsewhere, do poorly on every metric and suffer from discrimination. In every country that I have examined, hierarchies exist among children that typically rest on identities (Farkas 2014; Coursen-Neff 2015; Eddy 2015; Masi 2015; UNI-CEF 2005).

The life course of Black boys is an exemplar, not a claim of priority. It demonstrates the centrality of developmental equality to all children who face unequal developmental hurdles tied to the intersection of identity (or identities) and state-supported structures. And while my focus is on children subordinated and challenged in normative development due to identity, this same model might be used as well to unravel how privilege is created and reinforced for some children, advantaging them unfairly and reproducing hierarchies among children (Flagg 1993; McIntosh 2013; Rush 1999; Rush, Feagin, and Johnson 2000).

Developmental equality identifies the structural components of inequality created and sustained by the state that generate hierarchies among children. Exposure of structural inequality and the state's role should trigger an obligation on the part of the state to dismantle, reorganize, and reorient those systems. As President John F. Kennedy stated, "Simple justice requires that public funds to which all taxpayers of all races [colors, and national origins] contribute, not be spent in any fashion which encourages, entrenches, subsidizes or results in racial [color or national origin] discrimination" (U.S. Department of Justice 2017). The state should take evidence of bias seriously, whether linked to policies and practices, to people, or both. Beyond dismantling barriers to development, an affirmative approach would require state action to ensure equality of development and opportunity.

This book is divided into three parts. In Part I, I examine the life course of Black boys from birth to age eighteen based on social science research specifically focused on them and their development. I divide this into early childhood (Chapter 1), entering school (Chapter 2), and adolescence (Chapter 3). This scholarship exposes steep developmental challenges. These challenges arise not from individual families or communities, but rather from conditions designed by the state or known by the state to harm particular families and communities. The individual pattern of exacerbated developmental challenges is reinforced by identity-based policies affecting families and communities in a cycle that perpetuates inequality. Structures and cultural norms of the state create substantial negative developmental hurdles that differentially affect identifiable groups of children based on identity. This is a complex pattern of the interaction of race and gender that is differentiated, but not immunized, by class. Undermining development generates potentially lifelong subordinating consequences that are difficult or impossible to overcome. I focus in particular on the poverty, educational, and juvenile justice systems, and the lack of a comprehensive system of support in early childhood (Chapter 4).

In Part II, with these developmental patterns in mind, I evaluate the use of a developmental frame in legal analysis and public policy and outline a developmental equality model. Typically, the developmental perspective imagines the child as neutral: race-less, gender-less, class-less (Chapter 5). Using such a frame in the guise of progressive policy is fundamentally flawed. Even worse, it reinscribes inequalities rather than attacking them, while claiming a more child-centered, progressive approach. After critiquing the neutral child of those models, I suggest reframing the legal developmental lens to a "developmental equality model" (Chapter 6). This model incorporates insights from social scientists who have focused on the development of children of color, in particular the work of Margaret Beale Spencer and Cynthia García Coll. The developmental equality model is a powerful tool to make the promise of equality real. It can be used (1) to expose and dismantle barriers to equality; (2) to recognize and celebrate positive racial identity development; and (3) to create concrete benchmarks to achieve real equality by maximizing potential and development for *all* children. I add the insights of theory to enrich this model (Chapter 7), using critical race and feminist theories, vulnerabilities theory, economic inequalities analysis, and children's rights theory. These theoretical perspectives reinforce the importance for developmental equality of (1) focusing on identities, singly and intersectionally, in evaluating children's hierarchies and identifying necessary structural and cultural reforms; (2) articulating the state's responsibilities as those of a responsive state that serves all its children; (3) recognizing the interconnectedness of multiple systems in sustaining inequalities, and the responsibility for complex restructuring to achieve equality; and (4) identifying the unique claim of children to a right to develop to their full potential.

Armed with the developmental equality model, in Part III I explore strategies to implement the model to support the equality not only of Black boys, but of *all* children. Beyond dismantling what currently harms and discriminates among children, a developmental equality framework could be the basis to construct affirmative policies, structures, and culture that support all children and youth. Such affirmative obligations must be constructed with great care, to maximize family autonomy and integrity, given the history of destructive, counterproductive interventions into the lives of families of color, the poor, and others at the bottom of social hierarchies.

The discussion of strategies in Part III includes both litigation and policy. From a litigation perspective, a developmental equality model might expand the scope of the landmark case brought against the Compton Unified School District (*P.P. v. Compton Unified School District* 2015) (Chapter 8). In *Compton*, the litigants used developmental research and the ACEs (Adverse Childhood Experiences) framework to argue that the school district must implement schoolwide trauma-informed policies in order to fulfill its statutory duties to educate the children in its system. I argue that ACEs must be critically evaluated and considered not solely as a basis to build resilience but also to require structural change. Second, I explore potential constitutional litigation (Chapter 9). Using the landmark case *Moore v. City of East Cleveland* (1977), I consider what claims the child at the center of that lawsuit, seven-year-old John Moore Jr., might bring using a developmental equality model. Current doctrine suggests this is not an easy project, however much it reflects foundational constitutional principles. I argue for the necessity of recognizing children's positive rights, including robust equality rights, as essential constitutional pathways.

A policy initiative offers a more viable way to achieve children's developmental equality. A developmental equality model could be implemented in systems that currently block rather than support developmental growth and opportunity, and be the basis as well to create an affirmative system of children's rights and support. What is needed is a comprehensive New Deal for Children (Chapter 10). It is far from an idealist vision. I link this New Deal to comprehensive reforms previously undertaken as well as to the absolute necessity of such comprehensive change if we are to ensure the full development of future generations essential to our country's strength and future, as well as its moral compass. Focusing on the example of Black boys, a New Deal for Children would transform their development from a pathway littered with challenges and dead ends to one reflecting a fundamental guarantee of individual support and opportunity, and meaningful equality. Making Black boys matter is a path to embrace a commitment to developmental equality that benefits all children currently treated as less than full and equal persons. Ensuring developmental equality for all children to achieve their developmental potential is an essential beginning to equality throughout the life course for all.

PART I

Black Boys

1

Black Boys

Why focus on the lives of Black boys? Because their lives starkly illuminate how developmental inequality functions and replicates hierarchy among children. The high likelihood of negative life outcomes and the funneling of their lives toward subordination show us how it is done. And, they lead us to ask the other question: "Who else?" (Matsuda 1991). When we do, we more specifically look for other identities and intersectionalities linked to inequalities of gender, race, ethnicity, class, and immigration status that expose similar patterns.

I began this research in the juvenile justice system. It is overwhelmingly populated by boys, and disproportionately boys of color. That system exposes not only a sharp pattern of racial and ethnic disparities but also the overwhelming failure of the system, for all boys and for society, to produce positive outcomes (in addition to its mismatch and distinctive failures for girls) (Dowd 2011a, 2015). The racial configuration of juvenile justice, however, is particularly disturbing, and in exploring that pattern, I began to look earlier in the lives of Black boys, the most disproportionate group in the system. One of the pipelines into the juvenile justice system is schools (Gagnon and Barber 2011; Nance 2015). But schools not only feed the juvenile justice system, they also produce unequal educational outlines along race and gender lines. Pushing back further, the link to negative achievement outcomes is evident on day one of kindergarten; even on day one of preschool (Mead 2012). Inequality begins with the context into which Black boys are born. This developmental story, from birth, is essential to understanding the inequality of Black boys and why developmental equality is critical for all children.

Study of the lives of children of color has been limited, submerged under a developmental norm grounded in the study mostly of white children, or when directed at children of color, it has focused on questions that presume deficit and deviance. Despite the unevenness and underdevelopment of the research, however, several clear themes emerge from the available scholarship regarding the development of Black boys.

First, racialized patterns of development emerge early, literally at birth and in early childhood, traceable to several factors: the impact of poverty; lack of support of Black families and communities; the impact of early racial awareness; and the poor quality of child care and prekindergarten. While economic circumstances strongly affect the environment of early childhood, children born into middle- and upper-class families nevertheless face significant, distinctive challenges that are not erased by increased wealth. Second, this racialized pattern becomes an intersectional race and gender pattern, to the disadvantage of Black boys, once they reach school. As Black boys engage with the world outside their families and communities, they face stark stereotypes and significant cognitive bias, particularly at school. These patterns transcend their economic circumstances: they are present in public schools as well as the most exclusive private schools. Third, adolescence, as critical as the early years of development to neurological growth and overall development, generates further challenges for all children but particularly for Black boys. All adolescents experience a confusing and challenging array of physical, emotional, cognitive, and other changes at this stage, and move from dependency to emerging identity as adults. For Black boys, to that volatile mix is added the necessity of constructing a racial identity. This identity is both a strength and a danger. One of the keys to success for Black males is a strong racial identity. But that very identity can trigger dangerous reactions, particularly from police and other authority figures. Discipline and policing policies, in schools and on the streets, affect their lives, and exacerbate their risk of interface with the juvenile justice system. The importance and danger of a strong racial identity is present for all Black teenage boys, irrespective of neighborhood or circumstances. Fourth, resistance to oppression and stereotypes emerges in this context that constrains and funnels Black boys toward failure. Those Black boys and youth who succeed resist and build a persona of strength. They draw their strength from grounding in strong family relationships, a developed racial identity, and the positive impact of racial socialization.

The dualism of the developmental patterns of Black boys, of the effects of subordination as well as positive, empowering, resistance and success, cautions that the developmental data not be read either as a deterministic mark of failure, inadequacy, and inferiority, nor as an identification of a resilient path that simply needs to be followed by all. Too often in the analysis of Black boys, Black families, and Black communities, any evidence of what is perceived as a negative is read quickly against a persistent script of racial inferiority and blame of family and communities, rather than confronting the strength and persistence of racism, its structural manifestations, and state culpability (Moynihan 1965). The pattern of dualism instead suggests the importance of removing the obstacles to developmental success and adult opportunity, while recognizing and sustaining unique and positive cultural strategies.

In the balance of this chapter and the two chapters that follow, I present the interdisciplinary research that substantiates these four patterns. This developmental picture suggests a series of developmental challenges that undermine the ability of Black boys to achieve their inherent developmental potential, and thus profoundly affect their equality. This pattern is not unique to Black boys; it is characteristic of children at the bottom of hierarchies among children. It therefore necessitates reconceptualizing equality in developmental terms. In Part II, I take on that task, and argue for a model of developmental equality as every child's right. I use the developmental equality model (1) to identify the role of the state in constructing inequality and (2) to generate strategies for change. The data that follow about Black boys offer an example, not an argument for uniqueness, exceptionalism, or priority. It is a window into the creation of hierarchy among our children that begins at birth.

Early Developmental Patterns, Poverty, and Racial Awareness

From birth to age three is a period of critical development when the context of children's families (neighborhood, work, economic circumstances, wealth, and stability) has a huge impact on children reaching developmental benchmarks (Zero to Three 2016; Bronfenbrenner 1979). Indeed, even before birth, the impact of maternal circumstances and health on the developing fetus is significant (Zero to Three 2016). From birth to age three, there is an explosion in neurological growth. Positive support or interventions to facilitate early development at the familial level can have tremendous impact (U.S. Department of Health and Human Services 2013; Dallas 2015). Conversely, trauma has significant developmental effects. While trauma is a part of life for virtually all children, toxic levels of trauma generate significant developmental consequences. Chronic stress for Black boys emanates particularly from two sources: economic disadvantage, including violence associated with poverty; and racism, rooted in the consequences of historical racism in the current lives of their families and communities, as well as current manifestations, including daily microaggressions and structural barriers. Poverty and racism generate stress, and stress challenges children's development in a very significant way. Indeed, although there are few posttraumatic stress disorder (PTSD) studies of African American adults or children, the level of stress, and its constancy, is arguably comparable to that which generates PTSD (Hunt, Martens, and Belcher 2011; Stopford 2015; Hill and Madhere 1996; Gump 2010).

Nearly 40 percent of African American children are born into poverty (Birckhead 2012a). As of 2013, the poverty rate for African American children was 38.3 percent, *four times the rate of poverty for white children*, holding steady even as overall poverty rates for children have dropped to 20 percent (Patten and Krogstad 2015). In the United States, the rate of child poverty is high and runs deep. Poverty affects the opportunity structures that impact parental well-being, family formation, and parent-child bonds, thereby potentially rendering toxic the most critical ecology for children in their early years—their family. The developmental setup here is the interaction poverty will foreseeably create between children and school, as well as how poverty compromises the ability of parents to provide support for their child's development and education (Edin and Nelson 2013; Huntington 2014). Poverty exacts a terrible price on development, particularly the development of very young children (Ready 2010). It is associated with consequences for physical, intellectual, and emotional development. It affects where children live and how they live, including nutrition, family well-being and interaction, safety, and community well-being (Birckhead 2012a; Hobbs and Baity 2006).

The positive support of families is especially critical to foster children's attachment, which is linked to warm and responsive parenting. Secure attachment affects school readiness and behavior (Dexter et al. 2013). What affect parents most strongly, and derivatively their children, are context and socioeconomic status (SES) factors (Tudge et al. 2006). While racial differences in early childhood frequently are framed as differentials in parenting, to the contrary, those differences are more often linked to SES factors (Dexter et al. 2013). At the same time, although race and SES are often related, they function differently and independently in children's development (Fouts et al. 2012). Those factors, in turn, are significantly linked to state-created environments and structures that lead to, and perpetuate, poverty.

Poverty has a significant impact on family forms (Cahn and Carbone 2010; Edin and Nelson 2013). The dominant family form for African American children is a single-parent, mother-headed family. The proportion of single-parent families has remained at roughly two-thirds of African American families for the past five years (Kids Count Data Center 2015). Single parents generally are not well supported; this is especially true of nonmarital single parents (Dowd 1997; Edin and Nelson 2013; Huntington 2014; Maldonado 2005, 2014; Fragile Families and Child Wellbeing Study 2015). In addition, there are strong negative stereotypes about women of color and their role as mothers. The classic critique is that of Daniel Patrick Moynihan (Moynihan 1965; see also Roberts 1994, 2012). Moynihan blamed Black mothers and mother-headed families for the poor outcomes of Black children. Maternal education level, family income level, maternal age, neighborhood quality, and family structure can all negatively impact school readiness (Baker 2014b). Although mothers often function within networks of support, they are subject to ongoing stress—and maternal stress has a negative impact on child development (Baker and Iruka 2013). There are particular maternal behaviors that have been correlated with better school achievement: maternal warmth, for example, correlates with better reading, and home learning stimulation links with math skills (id.). Supporting mothers, and helping them to avoid maternal depression and stress, can have a strong positive impact on children and their school readiness at kindergarten. Without that readiness, by kindergarten, under existing systems, the gaps widen.

Fathers have a significant developmental impact as well:

> Fathering is a dynamic, multidimensional construct that has direct links to children's health, education, and social-emotional development. Early childhood research suggests that fathering may be particularly important during the first 5 years of life, when children are rapidly acquiring cognitive skills that can contribute to early school success. . . . [T]here is very

little literature on the specific ways in which African American fathers contribute to their children's early academic achievement and readiness for school. (Baker 2014a, 19)

Sustaining father involvement is particularly important given the patterns of family and residence for children and their biological parents (Edin and Nelson 2013). Low-income fathers engage significantly with their children, but poverty and fathers' lack of opportunities and hopelessness, as well as the impact of mass incarceration coupled with a punitive child support system, make parenting for some fathers difficult and conflicted (Cunningham-Parmeter 2013; Hatcher 2013).

It is critical to emphasize that policies that undermine poor families and parents, and that fail to provide opportunity for parents or their children, are a public policy choice, structurally carried out, that consigns poor children to the likelihood of failure. The links between parental poverty and outcomes for children are clear. "[P]overty and economic loss diminish the capacity for supportive, consistent and involved parenting and render parents more vulnerable to the debilitating effects of negative life events, . . . [generate] psychological distress deriving from an excess of negative life events, undesirable chronic conditions, and the absence and disruption of marital bonds, [and] . . . adversely [affect] children's socioemotional functioning in part through its impact on the parent's behavior toward the child" (McLoyd 1990, 311). The correlations between poverty and children's socioemotional development include poor school outcomes (such as low achievement and higher drop-out rates), teen parenthood, substance abuse, gang involvement, and violence (Barbarin 1993). Family, instead of being a resilience factor, becomes a risk factor.

This begins in infancy (Burchinal et al. 1997). One of the ironies of advances in neonatal care is an increased survival rate of low-birth-weight babies but a higher number of infants with impairment (Perenyi et al. 2011). Black women are twice as likely to deliver low-birth-weight babies, irrespective of their class status (Catov et al. 2015). Infants are incredibly malleable, and there are identifiable positive interventions that work to foster their development. "[M]ore optimal patterns of cognitive development [are] associated with intensive early educational child care, responsive stimulating care at home, and higher maternal IQ. . . . [C]hild care experiences [are] related to better cognitive performance in part through enhancing the infant's responsiveness to his or her environment" (Burchinal et al. 1997, 935). The issues that arise for children once they begin school have already emerged by three to five years of age (Moiduddin 2008).

Especially important is the support of cognitive development, as the potential impact of poverty on cognitive development is well known: "The cognitive development of children reared in low-income families is generally characterized by average performance on standardized tests during infancy, *followed by gradual declines during early and middle childhood* for U.S. children in general and for African American children specifically" (Burchinal et al. 1997, 935, emphasis added). This is a critical point to emphasize: children begin their lives at relative cognitive equality. Inequality emerges in the first few years. Cognitive development is correlated with social competence, which includes emotional regulation and impulse control (Brown, Barbarin, and Scott 2013; Scott, Barbarin, and Brown 2013). Supporting cognitive skills in higher order thinking increases the ability to self-regulate and creates less behavioral issues for children once they begin school. This link between cognitive skills and behavior continues through fifth grade (id.).

This consequence is particularly important for Black boys: "Cognitive skills during kindergarten and first grade are especially important in the positive emotional functioning of Black boys throughout childhood" (id.). Black boys are often scrutinized and evaluated under stereotypes assuming that they will behave poorly and may experience harsh discipline to counter this perceived stereotypic behavior (Scott, Barbarin, and Brown 2013). The very articulation of norms of emotional regulation and externalizing behavior conventionally has been defined by white middle-class children, in racial comparisons of young children (Supplee et al. 2009). For Black boys, "the cast for the patterns may have been set as early as kindergarten" (Brown, Barbarin, and Scott 2013, 183). The perfect storm creating negative consequences for Black boys as they enter kindergarten combines poor support of their parent(s); a cognitive skills gap despite equal cognitive capacity; intersecting socioemotional gaps linked to their cognitive development; and a raced and gendered standard of behavior differentially applied due to the cognitive bias of teachers.

Cognitive skills also directly impact academic achievement. The achievement gap appears very early, by eighteen months, and widens by age three, reflecting differences in resources in families and neighborhoods that impact development. "[T]he relative disadvantages in aspects of neighborhood (social disorganization), family (less income, more authoritarian attitudes, and less verbal stimulation), and schooling (teachers with lower expectations of Black children compared to white children) may account for differential attainment and achievement between the two" (Burchinal et al. 2011, 1405–6). These linkages return us to contextual factors in infancy and toddlerhood (id., 1416–17).

Prekindergarten is important to development across race and class (Gormley et al. 2005). But because of the impact of context on families, child care and prekindergarten systems are more important for poor children and children of color than for higher income children as possible sources of resilience and support not provided directly to their families and communities that could close developmental gaps that emerge from birth to age five. Yet, child care in the United States generally does not reflect a high level of care, and low-income parents are less likely to have access to high-quality care (Kreader, Ferguson, and Lawrence 2005). So children with the greatest needs have limits on access to the least resourced systems. This includes the absence of supports in early childhood as well as the piecemeal programs inadequately funded such as Head Start. Early childhood education, from age three to five, is even less universal and is of uneven quality.

In addition to the impact of poverty on early development, pervasive racism impacts children of color across class lines beginning very early in their lives. Racial awareness emerges at a young age in all children and has an impact on self-awareness as well as the perception of others. Cultural and social cognition of discrimination and stereotypes is evident by age three and is the foundation for racial awareness in children as they begin kindergarten. "The first years of elementary school have been identified as a 'critical period' in the development of young children" (Caughy et al. 2006, 1221). Children act on the basis of learned stereotypes, as well as sensing how they are viewed. Young children learn to sort and separate the meanings of such differences, from social and cultural clues embedded in stereotypes.

[B]y age 10, children can recognize discriminatory actions that are both overt . . . and covert . . . , understand that these actions may be caused by

others' social stereotypes, and use contextual information to make decisions about whether discrimination is likely to have occurred. (Brown
and Bigler 2005, 535)

The perception of discrimination is "likely to affect individuals' identity formation, peer relations, academic achievement, occupational goals,
and mental and physical well-being. Perceiving other individuals . . . to
be the victims of discrimination is likely to affect these domains as well,"
so this impacts all children with messages of subordination, privilege,
or both (id., 533). To combat the negative impact of racial awareness,
parents of children of color engage in conscious racial socialization, defined by one scholar as including cultural socialization, preparation for
bias, and promotion of mistrust (Caughy et al. 2006, 1220), and parents
must start this process at a very young age with their children. Parents
are preparing their children for one or more cultures: both for the dominant culture but also for their place within the affirmative values of their
cultural group (Tudge et al. 2006). Racial socialization helps children in
both cognitive development and engaging less in behaviors that trigger
behavioral issues. This process of racial awareness and racial socialization intensifies in middle childhood, from six to twelve, when children
to a greater degree move beyond their family and engage in the process
of identity formation (Cooper et al. 2005; Way et al. 2013).

Racial socialization is essential across class lines, as the challenges of
racism confront all children of color, even if they may be differentiated
in kind and intensity by class. Even for those children raised in middle-
and upper-income families, race generates developmental issues and
real-world danger. Black families have not translated economic success
into comparable benefits for their children (Pattillo 2005). Instead, enduring barriers of race in housing, which can dramatically affect school
choices, continue to pose a major problem. And regardless of schools
chosen, challenges remain for Black parents to prepare their children
for implicit bias and stereotypes that devalue their children in school
(Brewster, Stephenson, and Beard 2013; Hannah-Jones 2016). For example, one set of parents who succeeded in placing their son in an elite
private New York City school chronicled the challenges faced by their
son and his friend (Brewster, Stephenson, and Beard 2013). The two boys
were automatically categorized as "at risk" and "deficient," as well as sub-

jected to stereotypes and implicit bias, bullying, over-disciplining, and stereotype threat. The school's construction of the two boys as "problems" deflected scrutiny of the school's culture and biases. The boys' eventual success, the parents argue, was not because of the school, but in spite of the school, and rested on their own strengths overcoming the aggravated challenges at this "good" school that hardly made the learning environment equal for all students (id.).

Nor does class privilege insulate Black boys from racial profiling or police bias. In the wake of the scrutiny of the Chicago police over the shooting of Laquan McDonald, a video was released of the Tasering of Philip Coleman, a thirty-eight-year-old University of Chicago political science graduate, who subsequently died (St. Clair, Mills, and Lighty 2015). The brutal and inhuman treatment of Coleman in no way reflected any class privilege. Another example is the incident involving the son of Charles Blow, a prominent *New York Times* columnist, who was detained at gunpoint by a college police officer after leaving the library at Yale (Jaschik 2015).

Both race and poverty, separately and in combination, generate major developmental challenges for a disproportionate number of children of color. The state's role in creating and perpetuating this context is strong. As detailed more fully in Chapter 4, state policies create and perpetuate structural causes of poverty, fail to provide support to families and communities to move out of poverty, and fail to provide resources sufficient for families of whatever form to provide critical developmental support to their children. The state remains deeply entrenched and responsible for sustaining the culture and concrete effects of racism. All of these state actions collectively generate deep developmental consequences for Black communities, Black neighborhoods, Black families, and therefore Black children (Bryan and Martinez 2008; Piketty and Saez 2013; Saez and Zucman 2016). "Reducing racial/ethnic economic disparities will not only improve economic conditions for millions of lower-income parents, but will also benefit children" (Povich, Roberts, and Mather 2014, 13).

After family, the primary critical environment for children is school. As the next chapter explains, the early developmental challenges of poverty (which continue throughout childhood) are not addressed or equalized once children begin school. Rather, inequality is exacerbated, and this is particularly the case for Black boys.

2

School, Cognitive Bias, and Stereotypes

A significant proportion of Black boys begin school hampered by the context of poverty and its ongoing effects on their development. "Socioeconomic status (SES) differences in children's reading and educational outcomes are ubiquitous, stubbornly persistent, and well documented. Economically disadvantaged children acquire language skills more slowly, exhibit delayed letter recognition and phonological sensitivity, and are at risk for reading difficulties" (Aikens and Barbarin 2008, 235; Jarrett 1997). This in turn links to fewer books at home, parents being less involved with their children's education, children being less likely to be read to by their parents, and children having fewer resources to draw upon in schools and communities. Poor communities have the risk of "low quality child care, poor and distressed schools, and economically depressed neighborhoods" (Jarrett 1997, 227; Armistead, Forehand, et al. 2002; Armistead, Jones, et al. 2002; Bolland et al. 2007; Li, Nussbaum, and Richards 2007). Instead of psychosocial competence, based on self-regulation and resources from family and peers, which can be used to manage stress, Black boys experience barriers, not supports, in school environments that exacerbate the effects of poverty (Armistead, Jones, et al. 2002; Barbarin, Chinn, and Wright 2014).

Added to the effects of developmental hurdles already placed in their path is the likelihood that Black boys will be subject to significant stereotyping and cognitive bias from teachers and other school personnel once they begin school. This results in differential and declining school achievement, disproportionate diagnosis for learning disabilities, and disproportionate discipline that excludes them from school (by suspension or expulsion) (Johnson 1998; Graham and Lowery 2004; Baccara et al. 2014). Exclusion rarely leads to rehabilitation and reincorporation into mainstream education, and in the absence of familial and community supports can translate into dropping out, failure to complete high school, and lifelong disempowerment (Wright, Standen, and Patel 2010).

School then means for many Black boys that their racial disadvantage is sharpened by gender disadvantage. As one scholar points out, three realities intersect: an educational system that does not perform well in areas of concentrated poverty and of concentrated children of color; exacerbated inequality when children are out of school (after school and school vacations, especially the long summer vacation); and the intersectional disadvantage of gender and race (Johnson 2014). The gender/race intersection falls most harshly on Black boys, and functions also independently of intersections with economic disadvantage (id., 345; Becares and Priest 2015).

Black boys confront strong negative stereotypes at school. These reflect the persistence of historically negative stereotypes in media and culture more generally (Hutchinson 1996; Rome 2004). One of the strongest stereotypes about Black men is that they are dangerous, associated with evil and threat, and likely to be criminals (Howarth 1997). Elijah Anderson has compared the cases of Emmett Till and Trayvon Martin, noting the persistence of negative racial stereotypes that create what he calls the "iconic ghetto," a definition that is linked to all Blacks in public when they are "out of place" (Anderson 2013). James Forman Jr. argues that class is a huge factor in defining what portions of the Black community and other communities of color are affected by stereotypes and stigma (Forman 2012). Class privilege, nevertheless, does not erase racial effects.

Race/gender stereotypes are triggered for Black boys early, when they begin to grow from toddlers into young boys. The costs of stereotypes are significant and profound, beginning in childhood and extending through adulthood (Bertrand and Duflo 2016). "Black students as young as five are routinely suspended and expelled from schools for minor infractions like talking back to teachers or writing on their desks" (Rudd 2014). Recent research underscores the misperceptions and danger perceived by very young children. One recent study confirms that perceived threat and cognitive bias were linked to images of Black boys *as young as five* (Todd, Thiem, and Neel 2016). A second study notes that Black boys as young as ten are routinely perceived as older and "guilty," rather than benefitting from the "assumption of innocence" attached to white children of the same age (Goff et al. 2014). Culpability, and less need for protection, is linked to dehumanizing stereotypes (id.). "Dehumanization is the route to moral exclusion, the denial of basic human protections to a group or group member" (id., 527). It is precisely such dehumanization that could justify the brutal murder of fourteen-year-old Emmett Till based on a false accusation by a white woman in some way offended by his behavior in a country store. The same dehumanization framed twelve-year-old Tamir Rice, on a playground, as so dangerous that police officers drove up to within ten feet of him and immediately shot to kill.

We construct childhood for Black boys in a way that quickly transforms them into men subject to discrimination (Dumas and Nelson 2016). Rather than school being a "site of discovery and joy; protection of bodies and spirits; allowing nonconformity" (id., 38), Black boys are "imagined not as real children but as suspect Black bodies for whom the broader public need have little compassion or connection" (id., 34). Moreover, as one scholar suggests, the thread of sexual threat of Black boys to white girls in integrated schools may also affect the disproportionate discipline and removal of Black boys from schools, echoing historic calls after race segregation was declared unconstitutional for sex-segregated schools as a means to combat the threat perceived by whites of potential cross-race friendship and intimacy (Irby 2014; Mayeri 2006).

Stereotypes function in a dual way: they directly impact children as well as serve as the foundation for implicit bias exercised by others toward them. Claude Steele's work on stereotype threat is particularly helpful to understand the impact of stereotyping on children's development, and how it confounds their achievement in school. Steele focuses on the impact of stereotypes on their objects. As Steele points out, competence is not something that simply *is*, but emerges from social relations and the sense of one's ability (Aronson and Steele 2005). Competence is fragile:

> [I]ntellectual competence is not just something inside a person's head. Rather it is quite literally the product of real or imagined interactions with others. How a student construes the way he or she is viewed and treated by others matters a lot: how welcomed or excluded, how respected, how tuned in to others' difficulties and triumphs—these perceptions can exert a profound influence on intellectual competence, on motivation, and ultimately upon a student's academic self-concept. Competence is fragile, then, because it is transacted within a web of social relations. (id., 437)

Stereotypes impact academic performance, engagement, and self-concept because of their impact on the perception of the target as well as on teachers, parents, and peers. With respect to peers, they impact friendships as well (Barth et al. 2013). This is despite evidence that Black boys arrive at school with comparable socioemotional maturity as white boys, and socioemotional competence is a foundation for academic achievement (Barbarin 2013b):

> When a negative stereotype about a group that one is part of becomes personally relevant, usually as an interpretation of one's behavior or an experience one is having, stereotype threat is the resulting sense that one can then be judged or treated in terms of the stereotype or that one might do something that would inadvertently confirm it. (Steele, Spencer, and Aronson 2002, 389)

Stereotype threat (the worry that one will conform to a stereotype) creates pressure on students not to fail; yet, ironically, stereotype threat undermines performance (Aronson and Steele 2005). So, for example, the classic experiment of Steele and Aronson compared white and Black college students with matched SAT scores taking the same test, but in two different scenarios (Steele and Aronson 1995; Steele 1988). In one, students were told the test measured intellectual ability; in the other, that it was simply a lab test. The intellectual ability information triggered stereotype threat for the Black students of conforming to stereotypes of inferiority—and they underperformed. On the other hand, in the lab test scenario, with no stereotype threat trigger, Black students performed as well as equally skilled whites (id.).

This effect has been replicated with privileged groups, including white males at top universities, in experiments by Steele and his colleagues (Aronson and Steele 2005). As Steele explains, all of us have social identities. Some cue lets us know that one of our identities may trigger a negative reaction in that setting, and that feels threatening, affecting our experience in that setting. According to Steele, "There are two primary triggers that can turn the performance of challenging cognitive tasks into a stereotype-threatening situation—ability evaluation, and the salience of a social identity that is stereotyped as inferior in the ability domain" (id., 447). Threat is felt strongly by those who care about doing well and those with strong racial/ethnic identity (id., 447–48). Steele and his colleagues conclude that stereotype threat is a major factor in the achievement gap when other factors are held constant (for example, differences in SES, schools, and the quality of teachers) (Steele 1997, 2003; Steele and Davies 2003; Steele and Sherman 1999; Steele and Aronson 2004).

Steele's analysis, with experiments done primarily on college students, places into perspective the tricky interpretation of data about achievement: on the one hand rejecting the story of damage, deficit, and blame, but also seeing the pattern as one of damage but also resilience—the ability to resist the threat, and the implementation of means to counter the threat (Steele 2004a). Steele uses the example of the doll studies of Kenneth and Mamie Clark, famously used to justify the decision in *Brown v. Board of Education* (id., 62). The studies were used to argue that segregation damaged Black children. Other social scientists, however, saw more harm from integration, but for a long while the deficit model prevailed. Steele emphasizes that African Americans have not been passive victims of stereotype threat; to the contrary, he characterizes their response as one of "resilience and creativity" (id., 65). Stereotype threat can be counteracted with specific strategies, so the positive message of Steele's work is that things can change, rejecting the notion of permanent deviance or defect as the takeaway of his work (Steele and Aronson 2004; Inzlicht and Schmader 2012).

Stereotypes are not only a challenge for the objects of the stereotype but also the basis for implicit bias. Cognitive bias/implicit discrimination is the subject of a deep body of literature, demonstrating how discrimination functions, and how it is possible to hold egalitarian views but also to discriminate (Richardson and Goff 2014; Richardson 2015). More recently, research on implicit racial *favoritism* has added to this understanding. In addition to negative bias disfavoring people of color, positive bias favoring whites operates simultaneously. And even the absence of negative bias toward Blacks does not mean race neutrality: positive bias continues to be associated with the favored racial group, whites (Richardson 2015; Russell-Brown 2017). Neuroscience has added to this body of work, reinforcing that bias is learned and malleable, not hardwired. The pervasiveness of discrimination is well established by this literature (American Psychological Association 2001, 2012a, 2012b;

Anderson 2013; Greenwald and Krieger 2006; Kahn 2008; Krieger and Fiske 2006; Krieger 1995).

Jerry Kang, one of the most prolific and powerful writers about cognitive bias, advocates specific strategies for dismantling cognitive bias but stresses that implicit bias is a problem that can be resolved (Kang 2005). As Kang notes, strategies must correlate with the depth and extent of the problem:

> (1) [T]he magnitude of implicit bias toward members of outgroups or disadvantaged groups is large, (2) implicit bias often conflicts with conscious attitudes, endorsed beliefs, and intentional behavior, (3) implicit bias influences evaluations of and behavior toward those who are the subject of the bias, and (4) self, situational, or broader cultural interventions can correct systemic and consensually shared implicit bias. (Kang and Banaji 2006, 1064)

Kang identifies *racial mechanics* as how race "alters intrapersonal, interpersonal, and intergroup interactions contrary to our sense that we function rationally" (Kang 2005, 1493). Most of us have bias linked to stereotypes and negative attitudes, but we do not acknowledge it because we lack the insight to be aware of our bias. This is the interplay of mapping, schemas, and triggers, all constructed and malleable. These are mechanisms that presently reinforce biases, according to Kang, but could be used to change implicit thinking. Kang and Banaji have applied implicit bias research to reframe affirmative action (Kang and Banaji 2006). Others as well emphasize that empathy, and same-race identification of greater empathy, is a learned behavior, not an inevitable cognitive turn (Sheng and Han 2012; Blasi 2002; Blasi and Yost 2006).

Stereotypes and implicit cognitive bias render competent children and youth less competent, their potential for achievement undermined by their processing of how they are viewed by others as well as bias in how they are treated by teachers and others. This has a significant impact on their educational experience, and as they mature and separate more from their parents, or encounter more of their community and the broader world, it creates a major identity challenge in adolescence, as well as the threat of harm from others, which creates an adolescence full of risk. Scholars have identified strategies to deal with stereotypes and cognitive bias, emphasizing that these realities are constructed, not innate, and their operation to undermine equality similarly can be confronted and addressed.

Schools fail to support achievement, and overly discipline and exclude. Schools also underperform, providing less to students, based on the same foundation of stereotypes and cognitive bias, as well as fewer resources, creating different opportunities by class. A recent story profiling an innovative middle school math camp designed to draw children of color, as a strategy to increase the representation of underrepresented groups in math and finance, exemplifies this pattern of underperformance (Harmon 2017). The story describes the supportive ecology for middle- and upper-class "math geeks/math wizards" that begins in elementary school. The middle school children of color invited to this camp lacked this ecology and therefore were playing catch-up with their white peers, despite the enrollment of some in well-regarded charter schools. The special nurturing of their talent simply was absent from their schools.

Racism not only affects achievement, self-concept, and discipline at school but also has a powerful impact on mental health. Surprisingly little has been done to study the impact of discrimination upon children's development (Fisher, Wallace, and Fenton 2000; Nyborg and Curry 2003; Scott and House 2005). The overall impact of racism is underestimated, understudied, and unacknowledged. Williams and Williams-Morris identify at least three effects of racism:

> First, racism in societal institutions can lead to truncated socioeconomic mobility, differential access to desirable resources, and poor living conditions that can adversely affect mental health. Second, experiences of discrimination can induce physiological and psychological reactions that can lead to adverse changes in mental health status. Third, in race-conscious societies, the acceptance of negative cultural stereotypes can lead to unfavorable self-evaluations that have deleterious effects on psychological well-being. (Williams and Williams-Morris 2000, 243)

The available research indicates that the impact of racism on mental health and well-being is deep, chronic, and potentially debilitating. There are mental health issues for all children, but this adds to the challenges for children of color. A completely inadequate mental health system for children is also least likely to be used by children of color (Katner 2015; Smith-Bynum et al. 2014). Resistance to racism requires powerful resources when marshaled by adults; this resilience is far more difficult to muster by children. African American boys in particular are likely to underuse mental health services if they seek help at all (Lindsey, Joe, and Nebbitt 2010). Masculinity norms of denying and avoiding mental health issues further diminish the likelihood of seeking treatment (Dowd 2010; Glennon 2002; Johnson 2010).

Racism correlates with stress, depression, and the lack of a healthy sense of self and well-being (Fisher, Wallace, and Fenton 2000; Latzman et al. 2011; Simons et al. 2002). "The psychological cost of striving to maintain a positive sense of self while facing frequent exposure to discriminatory experiences can tax youths' coping resources, resulting in disillusionment, depression, and anxiety" (Brody et al. 2006, 1183). Children of higher SES and youth of color may be more stressed because of their greater exposure to racism and need to be prepared to deal with it (Bogart et al. 2013). Racism acts as a chronic stress, with severe challenges for well-being:

> Racism can traumatize, hurt, humiliate, enrage, confuse, and ultimately prevent optimal growth and functioning of individuals and communities. While, within the context of racism, there have always been abundant examples of resilience, strength of character, capacity for love and giving, joy, fulfillment, and success, there remain far too many examples of despair, dysfunction, isolation, hopelessness, destructiveness, and spiritual depletion. (Harrell 2000, 42)

Stress emerges from "episodic stress . . . , daily hassles . . . , and chronic strain" (id., 45; see also Robinson 2008).

In terms of mental health and psychological behavior, much of the research on Black boys, and children more generally, has focused on externalizing responses versus internal reactions (Grant, Lyons, et al. 2004). It is well to remember that there is a high rate of conduct disorder diagnosis for Black boys, and that in comparison to white boys with a similar diagnosis, Black boys are less likely to receive mental health treatment and more likely to be steered into the juvenile justice system (Atkins-

Loria, Macdonald, and Mitterling 2015). Diagnosis as conduct disorder may mask assessment that the symptoms are "untreated affective disorders, Posttraumatic Stress Disorder (PTSD), or substance abuse" (id., 433). Internal reactions tend to be ignored, and that omission renders what is happening to kids more invisible. This is particularly true about depression. Depression in children generally was rarely studied before the 1970s, based on the assumption that children do not get depressed; but modern studies show a significant correlation between depression and race discrimination (Simons et al. 2002) as well as indicating that depression is common among adolescents, ranging from 20 percent to 40 percent of all adolescents (Repetto, Caldwell, and Zimmerman 2004, 468). Anxiety is also a neglected area of study for African American children but is related to interaction with stress and racial socialization (Neal-Barnett 2004). Boys are more likely to report depression than girls, and the symptoms increase over time and link to academic deficits (Kistner et al. 2007). One indicator of the depth of unaddressed mental health issues is revealed by suicide data on elementary school children. According to one study of data from 1993 to 2012, while the overall suicide risk was level, the rate for white children declined, while the rate for Black children increased, with the most significant increase for Black boys (Bridge et al. 2015).

Stereotypes, cognitive bias, and mental health stress occur dominantly, although not exclusively, at school (Wong, Eccles, and Sameroff 2003). Policies that structure academic achievement, codes of conduct and discipline, teacher education, and concepts of what each child is entitled to from public education currently permit the continued functioning of challenging, even crippling, educational systems, to the detriment of Black boys—accepting their failure and criminalization as normative. This undermining of developmental success from state-created structures and policies is further heightened in adolescence, exacerbating the foundational problems created earlier.

3

Adolescence, Racial Identity, and Resistance

Adolescence is a critical developmental phase, for different though equally complex reasons as early childhood. The core task of adolescence is the development of identity and separation from one's parents (Kroger 2004). This occurs amidst physical changes and neurological maturation that is a work in progress, not completed until early adulthood (National Institutes of Health 2001). Often this is a period of intense experimentation, not always well thought out, characterized by bad judgment and strong peer influence. For boys, due to the influence of masculinities, it carries the risk of hypermasculinity and hypervulnerability (Dowd 2010). For Black boys, it is even more volatile because they are most at risk for being perceived as dangerous just as they adopt an identity, including a racial identity, which is critical to their success (McMahon and Watts 2002; Brittian 2012; Bryant 2011; Harper, Terry, and Twiggs 2009; Pahl and Way 2006; Thomas, Townsend, and Belgrave 2003; Wong, Eccles, and Sameroff 2003; Roberts et al. 2011; Seaton et al. 2008).

"Adolescents not only 'make bad decisions,' they 'make decisions badly'" (Miller-Wilson 2006, 322; Haggerty et al. 1994; Cunningham 1999). Indeed, it is common to have an antisocial/aggressive period into young adulthood (Rabiner et al. 2005). This is normative in late teens, peaking at age seventeen, after which teens desist from this behavior by early adulthood. The relationship between inward emotions and outward violence is often not what it seems (Sullivan et al. 2010). Much of the research on adolescents focuses on white males and externalizing behavior; far less focuses on kids of color, and if they are studied, it is almost exclusively in low-income urban settings (Grant, Lyons, et al. 2004).

Masculinities have a huge impact on all male adolescents, as young men adopt the identity of being a man. Aggressiveness is often a sign of hypervulnerability (Aronson, Whitehead, and Baber 2003; Cassidy and Stevenson 2005; Roberts-Douglass and Curtis-Boles 2013; Seaton 2007). In high-crime neighborhoods where violence is a constant risk, the presence of PTSD among young Black men is a reaction to traumatic stress (Smith and Patton 2016). The combination of race and gender factors makes masculinity especially risky for Black males. "Being Black and male is surreal. You are desired and you are despised" (Stevenson 2004, 59). As one scholar notes, one response to this perception is "reactive coping": "[b]eing missed, dissed, and pissed presents the struggle of constructing identity within a quicksand of false Black male images and is as vulnerable as one can get. . . . Racial profiling of Black males while they drive, walk, shop, talk, stand, and gather in groups has reached epidemic proportions" (id., 61). This extraordinarily difficult context makes nearly every identity move dangerous (Rios 2009, 2011). Bravado is particularly the response in high-risk neighborhoods for self-protection (Cunningham and Meunier 2004; Gunn 2004). This makes masculinity and development distinctive for Black boys (Harris 1992, 1995; Price 2000; Wade and Rochlen 2012). It also is a complex identity, bicultural in the sense that identity is framed differently in the community and in the dominant culture (Hunter and Davis 1992).

The classic work on how masculinities play out for Black boys in school is the work of Ann Ferguson (Ferguson 2000). She identifies two dominant stereotypes about Black boys that pervade schools: their criminal nature and their deficiency, such that they are "endangered." Most significantly, they cannot claim the protection of the common view that "boys will be boys," that is, that boys are natural and inevitable rule breakers linked to what is viewed as simple and essential masculinity.

> African American boys are not accorded the masculine dispensation of being "naturally" naughty. Instead the school reads their expression and display of masculine naughtiness as a sign of an inherent vicious, insubordinate nature that is a threat to order that must be controlled. Consequently school adults view any display of masculine mettle on the part of these boys through body language or verbal rejoinders as a sign of insubordination. (Ferguson 2000, 86)

Black boys are also viewed as likely to fail, which affects both assessment by teachers and discipline. The response of Black boys, according to Ferguson, is to construct themselves in response to this perception of them in a way that gives them a sense of worth, by using three strategies: heterosexual power, classroom disruption, and fighting (id., 171). They are invested in being tough and not behaving like girls (Phoenix 2003). As one researcher notes, "Young [Black] men are both loved and hated in and out of school. They set the standards for what is cool, hip, exciting and risky while at the same time they are experiencing disproportionate levels of punishment and academic failure" (Davis 2006, 302).

Pedro Noguera, who has written so eloquently about education and young Black boys (Noguera 2008), describes the struggle for identity of his teenage son:

> As he grew older, Joaquin felt the need to project the image of a tough and angry young Black man. He believed that in order to be respected he had to carry himself in a manner that was intimidating and even menacing. To behave differently—too nice, gentle, kind or sincere—meant he would be vulnerable and preyed upon. I learned that for Joaquin, part of his new persona also involved placing less value on academics and greater emphasis on being cool and hanging out with the right people. (Davis 2006, 293, quoting Noguera)

The fraught challenges of masculinity against the backdrop of deeply negative ecologies for adolescents in school and on the streets pose unique challenges in this volatile developmental phase (Ross 2004; Majors and Billson 1992). This should not obscure the positive identities Black youth create, including positive masculinities, but rather demonstrates that the challenges of masculinities for all boys and men create distinctive, difficult hurdles to negotiate the hierarchical demands of masculinities in relation to other youth and men, as well as in relation to women (Dowd 2010; Hammond and Mattis 2005; Neal 2005).

The link between masculinity and violence is strong, but as James Garbarino argues, violence is the predictable outcome of risk factors that make boys feel shame (Garbarino 2000; Gilligan 2001). The "lost boys" whom Garbarino writes about, boys who have killed, are predominantly Black. As he points out, "Sociologists have long recognized that the experience of racial discrimination provokes feelings of rage and shame, which play a potent role in stimulating violence" (Garbarino 2000, 11). Shame is the key emotion in his analysis.

Violence is present for Black adolescents in several ways, first because of the likelihood that a significant number are growing up in poor neighborhoods. "[T]he journey has become *mission impossible*—resulting in problems and outcomes so devastating that recovery into adulthood of self-sufficiency and marriage, let alone any broader societal participation, is out of question. . . . [This promotes] a culture of disengagement" (Edelman and Ladner 1991, 1, emphasis added). Violence is present in poor neighborhoods and is directed at Black boys. Violence per se has a strong negative impact on development because it triggers aggression in response, and that triggers both peer and state violence. Violence is also a reaction to Black youth as themselves. This has been played out all too persistently and publicly since the death of Trayvon Martin, although it was always present but less public. In numerous killings of young Black youth and men, it is because they are perceived as dangerous, but often found without weapons, or killed with a level of violence that far exceeds any actual or perceived threat. A recent example is the death of Laquan McDonald in Chicago, shot sixteen times as he was walking in the middle of a street, with no apparent aggressive move toward police and armed only with a knife (Cooper 2015; McGinley 2015). The leading cause of death for Black youth and young men ages fifteen to thirty-four is homicide (Rich 2000). So the role of violence connects to the structural conditions of poverty but also to the cultural norms and stereotypes attached in particular to Black boys and men (Cooper 2013; McGinley 2015; Gilligan 2001; Fitzpatrick 1997; Hammack et al. 2010; Howard 1996; King 1997; Patton and Johnson 2010; Randolph et al. 2000; Tolan, Gorman-Smith, and Henry 2003; Yakin and McMahon 2003).

There is voluminous evidence of the pattern of police harassment, profiling, and oversight of the daily lives of Black teens and young men. They are stopped and arrested more often, and this generates mistrust and suspicion of police (Brunson and Miller 2006; Rios 2011; Jones 2014). Frequently these interactions are groundless, as borne out by the racially charged stop-and-frisk policy of New York City police that was eventually halted by the courts (New York Civil Liberties Union 2014; Gelman, Fagan, and Kiss 2007). The interaction of race and gender operates on both sides of this dynamic, in the actions and reactions of teenagers to the particular masculinity of police culture, training, and bias (Cooper 2006, 2015; Harris 2000). Teenage risky behavior and aggressive responsiveness, understood and minimized for white boys, are dangerous and risky, even life-threatening, for Black adolescents. The pattern of Black youths as young as eight or ten not being seen as children is exacerbated by the time they reach their teens. They are not allowed the innocence of childhood or the stupid mistakes of white youth (Nunn 2002; Feld 1999). In every arena—school, employment, policing, juvenile justice—"less affluent Black males pay a disproportionate price for enacting masculinity norms in comparison to white males" (Royster 2007, 153).

Racial Identity

Within this context, even outside of poor communities, the adolescent task of constructing identity requires another essential task for Black boys: constructing a racial identity, an entirely unique developmental task and one fraught with peril. President Barack Obama's memoir of his early life is a high-profile example of this critical construction of identity (Obama 1995). The importance of racial identity is due to several factors. First, it is the universal developmental piece of adolescence to create one's identity (Pahl and Way 2006; Billson 1996; Evans et al. 2010; Hall, Cassidy, and Stevenson 2008). Second, coexistent with the difficulty of this task is the affirmative story of racial identity. Racial identity, grounded in a strong identity of valuing culture and community, provides resilience. It is a strength. This is a distinctive factor in the lives of Black boys, responsive to and descriptive of the distinctive dangers that they face. It also invites comparisons with the generating of racial identity among white boys. Constructing identity is reactive coping in one sense, but also involves pride. Racial identity is diverse and creative; it is not singular or confined to an ideal (Cooper 2006). There is no one meaning to being a Black man (Neal 2005; Mutua 2006). Racial identity is plural. Finally, and ironically, racial identity is important because racial identity may trigger danger. So, one's very strength triggers challenges.

Racial identity is not an integral part of child development theory—it is only studied for children of color—so the developmental piece of racial identity has been marginalized (McMahon and Watts 2002; Williams et al. 2012). The process of constructing racial identity begins in middle childhood, and is linked to racial awareness, which emerges in early childhood (Altschul, Oyserman, and Bybee 2006). Racial awareness begins as early as six, and by middle childhood, children have an awareness of both racial identity and its consequences (id.). Early middle childhood, roughly second to fourth or fifth grade, "is an active period for meaning-making as children [describe] ethnic identity to include ideas such as language, physical appearance, pride, relative social position, and culture" (Rogers et al. 2012, 99). At this developmental stage, abstract thought capability emerges, so children clearly understand social identities.

One group of scholars identify three aspects of racial identity: connection to one's racial group, awareness of racism and negative attitudes, and awareness of whether one's group succeeds (Altschul, Oyserman, and Bybee 2006, 1156; Thomas, Townsend, and Belgrave 2003). Phinney breaks down ethnic identity into "self-identification, sense of belonging, and pride in one's group" (Phinney 1993, 73–76). According to her, it is a gradual process of unfolding (id.; Pahl and Way 2006; Phinney and Ong 1989; Seaton, Maywalt Scottham, and Sellers 2006; Yip, Sellers, and Seaton 2006). It is also critically connected to racial socialization, the key role of parents and constructing a non-Eurocentric identity. Self-esteem is linked to positive racial socialization (Stevenson and David 2004).

Racial identity is positively correlated to school achievement, providing resilience to discrimination experienced in school (Butler-Barnes et al. 2013; Rivas-Drake et al. 2014; Friend, Hunter, and Fletcher 2011; Smalls et al. 2007). There is little scholarship on exactly how this works (Butler-Barnes et al. 2013; Pahl and Way 2006). Racial pride contributes to a feeling of control and ability to accomplish, as well as self-acceptance (id.). It is protective, especially for so-called "at-risk" youth, and contributes to their positive coping and behavior (McMahon and Watts 2002; Neblett, Rivas-Drake, and Umana-Taylor 2012). Interestingly, in one study, in low SES neighborhoods high racial pride was associated with high GPA; in more advantaged neighborhoods, however, one study found that high pride correlated with lower GPA (Byrd and Chavous 2009). Having a strong identity can be motivating and can act as a buffer, but in suburban neighborhoods, where Black boys may have only token representation, the interface of identity with the racial context of school is different (Bulotsky-Shearer et al. 2012).

Carla Shedd's remarkable ten-year study of teenagers in four Chicago high schools provides unique insights into the complex construction of identity (Shedd 2015). The teenagers in her study included those who remained in their highly segregated South Side neighborhood, as well as those who traveled across neighborhood and racial boundaries to attend predominantly white schools elsewhere in the city that offered better educational opportunities. The students who engaged in these daily border crossings were exposed to contexts and ecologies that diametrically contrasted with their home neighborhoods. Their exposure to these differences most commonly left them feeling subordinated and unequal. The contrast between the worlds they lived in versus those where their schools were located reinforced their sense of injustice, particularly with respect to comparing both schools and police behavior. It also dramatically and viscerally demonstrated the connection in their communities between schools and the carceral state. The price of opportunity and awareness was a sense of devaluation. In contrast, those students who remained in their South Side neighborhood had a more limited worldview, but a stronger sense of self and security.

> What emerges from my detailed interviews in all four schools is the central role of race and place in shaping students' worldviews. While some of them find their homogenous world claustrophobic, others find it comforting. But whether or not these students realize it, the breadth or narrowness of their frame of reference will have profound consequences for both their experiences and their interpretations of those events. (id., 58)

We can hardly envision what it would be like to imagine neighborhood schools as equal and boundary crossing as exploration rather than subordination. What is made clear to these teenagers instead is their place in a racial hierarchy and its steep challenges, and the price of achieving a different place.

Making it through the tricky phase of adolescence, difficult for any child, is thus an enormously more complex and risky, even life-threatening, developmental phase for Black boys and young men. The risks they face arise from a complex array of systems created and operated by the state, particularly the continued inequalities of the educational system, the persistence of the effects of poverty, and the combined impact of policing their behavior in school and on the streets. In addition, they are likely to come into contact with the juvenile justice system at this stage, by school referral or in relation to their behavior out of school. Just as they are exploring identity by functioning beyond their families and communities, they are subject to interactions with police at school and on the streets that increasingly translate fear and threat into system constraint and incarceration. Adolescents as a group commonly engage in behavior that violates the law, but many, if not most, are never arrested or, if they are, are diverted from serious consequences (Dowd 2011a, 1–3). Black boys, on the other hand, are disproportionately system-involved and disproportionately likely to face increasingly severe consequences, including incarceration at the deepest end of the system (id., 3–4). They are disproportionately referred to the adult criminal justice system, a system that makes no effort at rehabilitation. The failure of the juvenile system to ensure public safety or the well-being and rehabilitation of a substantial portion of children committed to its care, disproportionately Black boys, means that this system powerfully arrests development and imposes long-term consequences for adult opportunities due to direct and collateral consequences (Bell 2015; Burrell 2015).

Finally, Black boys as adolescents face the potential that they will be victims of violence. We have a litany of deaths that keeps adding new tragedies from private or public violence: Trayvon Martin, Laquan McDonald, Freddie Grey, Jordan Davis, and Tamir Rice are only a few. Black teenagers' risk of death is higher than that of any other demographic group (Dowd 2011b, 46). No matter what the range of teenage behavior is, this group distinctively risks never living beyond their teenage years. No piece of data could more graphically illustrate the stacked developmental deck. And if they survive their adolescent years, the possibility of significant developmental strikes against them—lack of education, criminal justice involvement, and lack of opportunity—is very high, resulting from the very identity that ultimately can be their strength, if they survive.

Resistance and Resilience

The challenges to development and negative correlations of Black boys' context are cumulative and daunting. But, the racial identity research exposes resistance and positive outcomes as well which have been underresearched and poorly understood. One illuminating piece of data given the challenges to identity is that contrary to the prediction of low self-esteem levels for Black boys, and for Black children and youth in general, their self-esteem levels when measured are quite high (Gray-Little and Hafdahl 2000; Owens, Stryker, and Goodman 2001). Self-esteem is developmentally important as it reflects past experience and has an impact on future success (Luster and McAdoo 1995). Not only do Black children not suffer from low self-esteem, but research shows they have higher self-esteem than other racial groups, and among Black children, boys have higher self-esteem than girls (Gray-Little and Hafdahl 2000; Greene 1994; Major et al. 2002; Whitesell et al. 2006; Twenge and Crocker 2002). According to scholars, several factors that contribute to high self-esteem are racial socialization and development of a strong racial identity (Gray-Little and Hafdahl 2000). Segregated schools and communities also have a positive impact by generating a feeling of belonging and support, and group identity (García Coll and Szalacha 2004).

Racial socialization is critical, and families are the core of providing this support. Racial socialization provides support against personal discrimination but less so for institutional discrimination (Saleem and Lambert 2016). Racial socialization is protective for anxiety and stress, and positively affects school achievement (Banerjee, Harrell, and Johnson 2011; Evans et al. 2012; McCabe, Clark and Barnett 1999). Family is an important factor in studies on the factors that correlate with successful Black boys (id.). The presence of a strong family, not of a particular form of family, is critical (Hrabowski, Maton, and Greif 1998). Parents are important in a distinctive way in the development of all Black children because they must prepare their children for a world still framed and pervaded by racism. They must give their sons strategies to counter stereotypes that can trigger deadly responses (Dow 2016). The literature recognizes this additional and challenging parenting task (Gray, Carter, and Silverman 2011; Hines and Holcomb-McCoy 2013; Vazsonyi, Pickering, and Bolland 2006). This task must be achieved by parents who themselves continue to face the stresses of race in their own lives. Yet, racial socialization sometimes is blamed or criticized for socializing kids in a defensive way that then is argued to negatively affect kids in school and the greater society.

Although developmental responses of opposition or resistance are normative for adolescents, the exacerbated challenges of Black boys can create patterns of resistance and rebellion that are frequently misconstrued, used to blame Black boys for their subordination. One of the enduring contributions to the racial identity literature, but perhaps the least well understood, is the concept of oppositional culture, sometimes called "the burden of acting white," frequently interpreted as rejection of majority culture and behavior necessary to succeed because it is racially identified as white (Cooler and McLoyd 2011; McHale et al. 2006; Murry et al. 2010; Payne and Brown 2010; Anderson 1998; Biafora et al. 1993). Related to this is the importance of "respect" as a means of survival for Black youth (Rich and Grey 2005; Rios 2011; Bohnert et al. 2009; Bruce 2000; Drummond, Bolland, and Harris 2011; King 1997; Wilkinson, Beaty, and Lurry 2009).

Signithia Fordham and John Ogbu's classic work argues that subordinating context generates collective responses to oppression that are not "oppositional" in the sense of a recalcitrant child, but rather are in opposition to dehumanization (Fordham and Ogbu 1986). Their work echoes W. E. B. Du Bois's idea of "double consciousness" (Du Bois 1903). Important to their analysis is the concept of collective identity, which "refers to people's sense of who they are, their 'we-feeling' or 'belonging'" (Ogbu 2004, 3). "Collective identity usually develops because of people's collective experience or series of collective experiences" (id., 3). It is historically grounded in slavery and postslavery construction of Black Americans as separate—generating collective identity tied to oppression and exploitation (id., 8). Labeling behavior as "oppositional" ignores the construction of the category and the context that creates the response; labeling it resistance to oppression reframes it and should focus on the frame that generates the reaction, as well as whether a single culture or set of standards is required (id.; Carbado and Gulati 2013).

Fordham describes identity as complex and oppositional in a variety of ways (Fordham 2008). For her, the "burden of acting white" is the necessity to comply with, as well as resist, white norms; to act white in order to succeed as defined in white terms; and also to remain true to one's community: "[I]n exchange for what is conventionally identified as success, racially defined Black bodies are compelled to perform a white identity by mimicking the cultural, linguistic, and economic practices historically affiliated with the hegemonic rule of Euro-Americans" (id., 234). At the same time, this challenges identity within one's community:

> [E]very American of African ancestry who opts to perform whiteness, even episodically, is forced to fight to retain citizenship in the Black community while concurrently seeking acceptance by the hegemonic white society. This compulsory dual citizenship, with one segment being the site of privilege and the other a sign of stigma, produces the phenomenon I defined as acting white. (id., 231)

In her work, Fordham "found that all Black students were alienated by the mismatch between the culture of their community and that of the school" (id., 243). They saw their choices as to resist and fail, or to comply and lose their voice. Each path requires loss; each imposes burdens.

There have been critics of Fordham and Ogbu, arguing that there are other readings of their data (Spencer and Harpalani 2008; Farkas, Lleras, and Maczuga 2002; Harper and Davis 2012). First, there is a long history of the African American community valuing school as a means to succeed (Spencer and Harpalani 2008). Second, deploying the charge of "acting white," to critique and limit youth, is disputed as not a fundamental component of Black culture. Spencer and Harpalani view the reactions of students as a "reactive coping strategy," to be expected of adolescents exploring identity in the face of a hostile majority culture. "If Black youth perceive a classroom, school, or any setting as a context where they are devalued, they may reactively cope by defining the expectations of this context as 'acting white'" (id., 232). This reaction is normative, a reflection of "struggling to cope adaptively—to attain success in this society without assimilating and compromising their racial and cultural identities" (id., 235). The responsibility for change, then, lies not in Black youth or Black communities, but in making schools more equitable and supportive. Other researchers argue low achievement is due not to opposition but to underdevelopment of academic skills (Harper and Davis 2012).

Duality of identity is important to recognize because it links to a final important framing of the developmental pathway of Black boys. It is easy, and dangerous, either to let a single piece of their developmental pattern lead to determinism (Black boys are so harmed, broken, or scarred as to be unsalvageable) or to seize on positive identity as an easy solution (support Black boys' development of strong racial identity and that will be sufficient for them to withstand developmental challenges and succeed). Racial identity is tempting to see as the "cure" or an affirmative factor that belies any need to address developmental inequality. Care must be taken to recognize and acknowledge strength and empowerment in the face of adversity without providing an apology or justification for inaction. Racial identity in fact points to structural factors that make such identity critical, as well as illuminating family and community strengths.

Summary

In summary, what do the patterns for Black boys tell us about the arc of their development, particularly their ability to achieve their full individual developmental potential? These three chapters detailing their lives from early childhood through adolescence make clear several patterns for Black boys as a group.

First, their overall development is funneled toward developmental challenge and failure, rather than success and opportunity. Black boys' cognitive, physical, and emotional development occurs within a context of challenge and threat, undermining their sense of competency, self, future, and hope. Their trajectory from birth is one of exacerbated challenges and outright barriers. What is normal in early childhood is made more difficult, and separation and subordination begin very early.

Second, that pattern is accomplished through the presence of key state structures that disserve them, particularly the educational and juvenile justice systems, as well as policing of them in school and in the community. These systems negatively affect their development and preparation to be productive adults by failing to support their achievement and disproportionately punishing them and guiding them toward a future of incarceration rather than adult accomplishment and citizenship.

Third, their outcomes are also significantly shaped by inadequate systems, particularly the absence of effective systems to deal with poverty. Limited income supports, an inadequate and damaging foster care system, and the lack of health and educational supports to ensure that poverty is not intergenerationally fostered are largely absent. Their most immediate systems of developmental support, their families and communities, are not only inadequately supported but also affirmatively stressed and undermined, with predictable impacts on their development.

Fourth, they are impacted by the absence of essential supports, most notably in early childhood. Therefore, not only are their families functioning under stress, but critical well-being and developmental support, such as high-quality child care and early childhood education, in addition to robust health care, are noticeably absent. The developmental differentiation begins early; indeed, the predictability of challenge and subordination is present at birth.

The pattern is one of compounded inequality linked to systems that interconnect to minimize, undermine, or simply fail to support their development. In addition to this structural locus is the cultural pattern of both the persistence of these structural outcomes along with the recognized presence of implicit bias and stereotype. This is directed against Black boys in particular. Nevertheless, this is not a pattern of exclusivity; rather the pattern of Black boys is one that should lead us to ask which other children are similarly affected, and what other patterns we should be asking about. Thus, the example of Black boys is neither extraordinary nor unique. It is not a claim of, nor should it be understood as, Black male exceptionalism (Carbado 2000) or Black male dysfunctionality, although it reflects the historically negative, particular discourses around Black boys and men (Brown and Donnor 2011).

Because the pattern of Black boys' development is race- and gender-differentiated, that means a disproportionate impact on the community within which they are located, having the result of replicating intergenerational racial subordination and the particularized gender pattern of racial subordination for Black boys. It is a pattern linked to structural and cultural factors that are largely controlled by or significantly contributed to by the state, by their "tilt," negatively impacting Black boys; by their inadequacy, leaving them, their families, and their communities without support; or by their absence, knowing the negative consequences because of the interconnected disadvantages likely to be present due to historical causes or present ongoing structural and cultural discrimination. The role of the state is exercised primarily through race- and gender-neutral policies, and therefore the impact of those policies, vividly illustrated for the life course of Black boys, is not specifically geared to them alone, nor is the impact on them alone. In the next chapter I explore further some of the primary structural and cultural factors that impact the life of Black boys.

4

Structural and Cultural Barriers

The developmental data and patterns of Black boys tell us that race and gender matter in their development. The risks likely to be encountered by Black boys are state-created, reinforced, and recognized. The systems of risk interact not only to thwart development, but to generate the predictable outcome of this intersection of developmental challenges and barriers as involvement or incarceration in the juvenile and then adult criminal justice systems.

> African American men figure so prominently in the correctional system that the number of African American 4-year-old males can be used to model the number of people who will be incarcerated 15–20 years in the future. . . . Of the approximately six hundred thousand 4-year-old African American males growing up in the United States in 2008, prisons are being planned to house 28,134 of them by 2029. (Barbarin 2010, 81)

Three structural factors—the state's creation of, response to, and perpetuation of poverty; the public educational system; and the state juvenile justice system—particularly function to create developmental hurdles for Black boys. The evidence of this is starkly apparent in the developmental scholarship on Black boys summarized above. It is captured succinctly in three pieces of data that describe, for Black boys as a group, their outcomes within these systems. At birth:

- One in three will be born in poverty
- One in two will not graduate from high school
- One in three will be incarcerated in his lifetime; and if he is born into the lower end of socioeconomic circumstances, his risk of incarceration doubles (Dowd 2013a)

Cultural factors—biased actors within those systems and bias in the structure of systems, as well as broad societal bias and discrimination that is tolerated, ignored, or facilitated by the state—powerfully impact Black boys on individual, familial, and community levels. State policies and practices that permit and arguably support the perpetuation of those cultural norms translate into state complicity in a culture of denigration, fear, and subordination. Student protests at public and private universities have driven home the point that the literal construction of universities and the wealth of donors immortalized by the names of buildings at elite colleges rest on a foundation of slave labor, white supremacy, and a history of exclusion of students of color (Hartocollis and Bidgood 2015; Deere and Addo 2015; Rein and Bernstein 2015; Stanley-Becker 2015; Wong and Green 2016).

The first system that impacts Black boys' lives is the poverty system, as over one-third of all Black children are born into poverty. Any policy regarding poverty (income support, housing, employment), or the lack of such policy, has a significant impact on the Black community as a whole because such a large proportion of the community is affected, infringing on the life course of the individual, the person's family, and the community as a whole (Patten and Krogstad 2015). Historically the perpetuation of Black subordination has been, and continues to be, economic. Slavery connects to Jim Crow connects to current inequalities in wealth, work, housing, and community resources (McKernan et al. 2013; Rothstein 2015; Wilson 2011a). Housing patterns particularly are shaped by historical practices of outright segregation, differential access to mortgages, and redlining, as well as ongoing resistance to movement into white neighborhoods (Freund 2016). As William Julius Wilson has noted, the interlocking policies of housing and employment discrimination are the origin of the current concentration of chronic poverty, coupled with poor schools and the outmigration of middle-class families (Wilson 1987). Most recently, the 2008 recession had a deep impact on poor communities, with the weight or "load" of exacerbated poverty especially apparent in health statistics (Chen and Foshee 2015) and continuing stagnation even as wealthier areas moved out of the recession (Schwartz 2016). Poverty undermines full participation in citizenship, and thus the opportunity to effect change and influence policies, structures, and culture (Alexander 2010).

Poverty policy and systems do little to help children, and much to reinforce the impact of poverty and sustain its effects. As Dan Hatcher has powerfully demonstrated, abuses of power within the poverty structures that currently exist siphon off resources even from the limited benefits available (Hatcher 2016). But more importantly, the existing structures to deal with poverty are inadequate. Welfare is limited and inadequate to lift a child's family into even a marginal ability to sustain basic life needs. "Welfare payments are not sufficient to keep people out of poverty" (Sethi 2010, 6). Poverty links to poor housing, inadequate schools, high crime rates, lack of basic safety and security, and a disproportionate police presence that infuses everyday life with the risk of criminal justice consequences. Lisa Pruitt calls this set of consequences "spatial inequality" (Pruitt 2010, 15–23). Although Pruitt's work has focused on rural poverty, her concept equally applies to concentrated, identified urban neighborhoods with similar characteristics. In such contexts, even those youth who try to succeed and use opportunities are often undermined by the lack of support for their goals and the undertow of the needs of their families and neighborhood. In other words, a narrow focus on youth but not on their ecologies ignores that they function within a context. A ten-year study of youth in Baltimore found that they were actively resisting the perils of the street and seizing postsecondary educational and work opportunities. They nevertheless were frequently exploited rather than supported in trade schools and community colleges, and disrupted from their goals by families, neighborhoods and peers (DeLuca, Clampet-Lundquist, and Edin 2016). The will to succeed, the "grit," is there; but mobility out of poverty is not.

Indeed, the rate of intergenerational mobility is quite low in the United States, lower than in comparable countries (Alexander, Entwisle, and Olson 2014). According to the 2016 Innocenti Report Card, for which income inequality data for forty-one countries is collected, including the Organisation for Economic Co-operation and Development (OECD) countries that the United States compares itself to, there is a broadening gap between the poorest children and those at the median (UNICEF Office of Research 2016). The United States ranks in the lowest third of countries in terms of income inequality, with its child poverty rate plus the high proportion of children with half the income of children at the median. In European Union countries, the gap is closed significantly by social transfers; not so in the United States (id.). Persistent, rather than episodic, poverty has the deepest impact on intergenerational transmission of disadvantage (Dickerson and Popli 2012). Recent research confirms the low rate of intergenerational mobility, its variability across the country, and its correlation to racial segregation, income inequality, school quality, social capital, and family structure, all factors that translate into racial disadvantage for children of color (Chetty et al. 2014; Chetty et al. 2016).

Housing is particularly problematic: three-quarters of families who qualify for housing assistance do not get it because there is not enough to go around, while one in four poor families devote 70 percent of their income to housing (Desmond 2016). Housing inadequacies rest on a long history and continuing evidence of racial discrimination (Freund 2016; Sharkey 2013). The disproportionate poverty of African Americans and their continued geographic segregation are linked to deliberate state policies overtly racially defined or facially neutral policies with known and foreseeable racial impacts. These historical patterns have been further exacerbated by our most recent recession and the unevenness of recovery (Schwartz 2016).

The absence of early childhood supports reinforces the impact of poverty on very young children by the lack of an integrated policy for family supports, health care, child care, and early childhood education. Instead, poverty stresses families, triggering child welfare interventions at a disproportionate rate for Black families, even when taking their rate of poverty into account (Roberts 2001). Theoretically designed to help children escape from abuse and neglect, the child welfare system frequently makes matters worse instead of better, due to an inadequate foster care system and policies that ignore evidence-based practices that would suggest a far better outcome for children if they remained with their families or, better yet, if affirmative interventions proactively provided support to their families before they were deemed in crisis (Harris 2011; Birckhead 2012a; Huntington 2006). A poor child welfare system disproportionately disserves Black children.

These are systems that are inadequate, linked to historical and current "neutral" policies that reinforce historical disadvantage and discrimination. They also reflect a preference for explaining poverty as individual failure or dysfunction, sometimes writ large to blame communities or culture. Our macrosystem dialogue about poverty, coupled with our devotion to individualism, gets in the way of analysis of structural issues, and abandons children to the circumstances of their birth.

The poverty system casts a pall on the lives of all poor children, disproportionately children of color. This impacts their lives throughout their development. An additional factor in early childhood is the remarkable *lack* of systems and policies to support the critical period of early childhood development prior to the beginning of school. The systems that might be present would include not only income support but also high-quality prenatal and postnatal health care; high-quality child care; universal, high-quality early childhood education; paid parental leave; sick leave to care for sick children; parental education; and support such as a universal visiting nurse framework. Instead, a minimalistic patchwork of limited services of uneven quality means that children born with equal capacity but unequal circumstances experience highly differential developmental supports, with the predictable result that inequalities emerge early, take root, and are widening by preschool and kindergarten.

The subordination imposed by poverty might, potentially, be outweighed by the education system. Education might provide a means to mobility and opportunity, and a leveling of economic inequality. In order to do so, in the absence of early childhood support, it would have to take account of the unequal supports and predictable unequal school readiness for many children of color. To the contrary, however, education perpetuates the separation of children by class. Sean Reardon's work at the Stanford Center for Education Policy Analysis presents the evidence of class inequality and achievement gaps in education (Reardon 2011). Indeed, some researchers argue that class is an even more powerful determinant of opportunity than race (id., 99–100; see also Dowd 2011a). But in addition, education is where race and gender patterns of inequality emerge, with the greatest disadvantage to Black boys. School is where discrimination that combines race and gender appears: in the pattern of low achievement, high rates of discipline, high rates of exclusion through suspension and expulsion, and high rates of tracking by intellectual and emotional disability occur. Overall, Black children enter school, and preschool, at a disadvantage, *and the achievement gap widens and differentiates by gender once they get in school.* In other words, school makes matters worse.

As Pedro Noguera points out, the negative outcomes for Black boys in school are so pervasive that they are normative (Noguera 2008; see also Harper 2015). By middle school their disciplinary rates skyrocket, and by high school high rates of dropping out occur, leading to their low rate of completion of high school (id.). Black boys have high rates of suspension and expulsion, magnifying the possibility that they will not complete high school (Nance 2016). The high school graduation rate is abysmal, and shockingly low and disproportionate for Black boys (Dowd 2011a). School is constructed by systems of financing, curriculum, and policies legally created and enforced. The differential resources and outcomes are a persistent, well-recognized outcome of this system. As a system, education fails to serve Black children at a very high rate; race disadvantage is compounded with gender disadvantage for Black boys, however, as they stand out negatively on parameters of achievement and discipline. They also stand out as more likely to be assigned to special classes that may exclude them from mainstream education (Noguera 2008). Finally, school does not simply fail to educate them; it sends disproportionate numbers of them into a system sure to guarantee and exacerbate failure, the juvenile justice system (Nance 2015, 2016).

The poverty and education system interaction is geometrically reinforced by the structure, policies, and outcomes of the juvenile justice system (Birckhead 2012b). School discipline issues are treated as delinquency, and pipelined to the courts (Nance 2016; Banner 2015). Despite critiques of zero tolerance and the criminalization of school discipline, these policies persist and disproportionately impact Black boys (Dowd 2016a). On the streets, Black boys are excessively targeted and implicated by the system, heavily influenced also by disproportionate policing patterns that put them in the crosshairs of the system (Dowd 2011a; Rios 2011). Black boys are disproportionately represented at every stage of the juvenile justice system, and the rate of disproportion increases as the consequences become more serious (Bell and Ridolfi 2008; Rios 2011; Stevens and Morash 2015). In 2016, New York City released its Disparity Report, comparing outcomes for the city's youth by race and class for the prior decade (New York City Office of the Mayor 2016). While school suspensions and rates of felony and misdemeanor arrests overall were down, they were up for Black males by 36 percent. The felony arrest rate for Black males under sixteen was thirty times higher than for white males; the likelihood of juvenile detention for Black males under sixteen was thirty-five times higher than that for whites (id.).

Juvenile justice system involvement and its consequences are not insignificant events, but have lifetime consequences, as well as being strong predictors of adult criminal justice involvement (Burrell 2015). Mass incarceration does not begin at adulthood; the groundwork for this pernicious and harmful practice begins much earlier, in the juvenile justice system. The rate of juvenile incarceration in the United States is the highest in the world, far beyond any other country (Mendel 2011). This is a system that by its history has responded to the inclusion of Black boys within its purview with increasingly harsh and counterproductive punitive, rather than rehabilitative, policies (Ward 2012; Rios 2011; Dowd 2011a, 2015).

Policing brings into play another system, intertwined with the education and juvenile justice systems, that does not function fairly or equally, does not protect from harm, and, in the worst cases, is a threat to the very existence of Black boys (Cooper 2009, 2013; Richardson 2015). Training, field policies, and practices all contribute to this, as does the failure to address bias in policing. This is a state-funded, state-created, legally defined system just as are the poverty, educational, and juvenile justice systems.

These structural components—the poverty system, the educational system, and the juvenile justice system in conjunction with policing—have a powerful impact on the lives of Black boys, by collectively erecting significant barriers to their normative development. State undermining of families and communities not only compromises "normal" developmental supports but also undercuts the ability to counteract the extraordinary hurdles and cultural devaluation placed in their path (Editorial Board 2015). The state plays an enormous role in the creation and sustaining of those obstacles (Edin and Nelson 2013; Huntington 2014). The law perpetuates this role of the state. Not only are Black boys disserved, but this systemic subordination also elevates others while reinforcing hegemony based on race, gender, and class.

Nor is this negative impact limited to Black boys. So, for example, the developmental drag of poverty, which has such an enormous impact on Black boys, similarly impacts all children who are poor, and all communities of poverty. Low achievement linked to schools with limited resources and harsh disciplinary systems linked to negative school cultures affect all children in those schools. So for example Black girls' achievement is lower than that of white girls, and they are disproportionately disciplined for gender-specific infractions similar to Black boys (Archer-Banks and Behar-Horenstein 2012). The juvenile justice system, filled primarily with boys, disserves nearly all who end up incarcerated. It serves neither their well-being nor the community's safety. Rather than being a rehabilitative second chance, it becomes the entry point for the adult system and its even more crushing lifetime consequences.

The level of subordination and the intersecting structural forms of inequality evident in children's hierarchies but particularly clear in the example of Black boys are so stark that they suggest comparisons with facial, blatant examples of discrimination: anti-Semitic ghettos and extermination, South African apartheid, misogynist subordination of women and girls, heterosexist homophobic actions, anti-Asian separation and internment. While these are unique and broad-ranging patterns, the similarity among them, I would argue, is in the acceptance of inequality as normative rather than as a contradiction of basic principles. The role of the state in all of those cases is unmistakable. The responsibility of the state to dismantle the architecture of developmental inequality should be similarly inescapable. Adopting a developmental equality model is critical to expose the state's role in *creating* developmental challenges and *subordinating* some children while privileging others. Each of the systems identified here that produces such disproportionate negative outcomes for Black boys is state created and sustained, with knowledge of the patterns that it creates and perpetuates.

So where do we go from here? In Part II, I develop a model for change; in Part III, I explore particular strategies.

In Chapter 5, I detail the power and potential of a developmental lens to address inequalities among children and youth. That lens, however, must clearly focus on the developmental realities for children of color and other children at the bottom of children's hierarchies. I detail that essential framing of the developmental lens in what I call a developmental equality model in Chapter 6. That model can both expose hurdles and challenges that render children unequal, and illuminate what is necessary for true equality of opportunity for all children. In Chapter 7, I further explore what we need to pay attention to in order to achieve developmental equality. I add further theoretical insights including attention to identities, particularly race, gender, and class, to ensure that substantive equality is meaningful. Policy cannot be color-, gender-, or class-blind, without risking reinscribing inequality. Tools to help us with race and gender identities come from critical race theory and multidimensional gender theory. They remind us in particular to pay attention to intersectionality, to ask the other questions, and to keep our eye on structural change. Second, we can use vulnerabilities theory to keep us focused on structure, and to articulate a theory for a responsive state, owing positive duties to all children. Additional structural theories, particularly focused on economic inequalities, can further emphasize the interconnected nature of the systems involved in children's development. We can use children's rights to articulate the specific claim of children on the resources of society through the mechanism of the state.

In Part III, I focus on strategies. First, I consider using existing legislation, focusing on the *Compton* litigation attempting system-wide change using developmental data and the ACEs framework (Chapter 8). Second, I explore an alternative litigation strategy of constitutional arguments (Chapter 9). Finally I propose a public policy strategy in Chapter 9, a New Deal for Children. Inherent in that comprehensive public policy is a vision of what developmental equality would mean: what is needed, what outcomes would be visible, what structural dismembering and reform are required, as well as what structures need to be created and what family and community supports must be present, including how to build resilience for those children and youth already partway on their path to adult development. It is a tall order; but it is also a vision that is designed to ensure equality and full development not only for Black boys but for all children.

PART II

Developmental Equality

5

A Developmental Model

A developmental model or perspective in law is critical both as a theoretical, strategic vision for children, and as a metric to hold the state accountable to dismantle existing barriers and to ensure developmental support for all children. Such a perspective imagines the state as responsive and dedicated to the equality of its citizens (Cooper 2015; Dowd 2013a; Fineman 2008). It is crucial that this developmental perspective be informed by an intersectional race and gender model, rather than a "color-blind," gender-neutral approach. A developmental *equality* model ensures that the power of the developmental perspective is harnessed to achieve equality for children, rather than inadvertently or deliberately used to reinforce hierarchy among children.

In this chapter, I describe and critique the existing developmental model assumed in current legal frameworks. I then explore the work of two social scientists, Margaret Beale Spencer and Cynthia García Coll, who put children of color at the center of their analysis, and expose the impact of identities and structural discrimination. Using their work, and fusing it with legal principles of equality and our obligations to children, in Chapter 6, I construct a model of developmental equality. This model can be used to identify barriers to equality from birth and provide support for real, substantive equality of opportunity for all children. The life course example of Black boys, explored in Part I, validates and necessitates a developmental equality model to expose the role of identity factors in state-created structural barriers to development. The model points the way forward not only for Black boys but for all children.

Development and Law

Developmental research has been a powerful tool to reorient legal rules and social policy related to children and youth. This approach is epitomized by Justice Kagan's majority opinion in *Miller v. Alabama* (2012):

Our [prior] decisions rested not only on common sense—on what "any parent knows"—but on science and social science as well. In *Roper* [*v. Simmons*], we cited studies showing that "'[o]nly a relatively small proportion of adolescents'" who engage in illegal activity "'develop entrenched patterns of problem behavior.'" And in *Graham* [*v. Florida*], we noted that "developments in psychology and brain science continue to show fundamental differences between juvenile and adult minds"—for example, in "parts of the brain involved in behavior control." We reasoned that those findings—of transient rashness, proclivity for risk, and inability to assess consequences—both lessened a child's "moral culpability" and enhanced the prospect that, as the years go by and neurological development occurs, his "'deficiencies will be reformed.'" (id., 2464–65)

Roper and *Graham* emphasized that the distinctive attributes of youth diminish the penological justifications for imposing the harshest sentences on juvenile offenders, even when they commit terrible crimes (*Roper* 2005; *Graham* 2010; see also *Montgomery v. Louisiana* 2016). The Court reaffirmed this view in its most recent summary dispositions vacating and remanding to state courts five juvenile life-without-parole cases (*Purcell v. Arizona* 2016; *Najar v. Arizona* 2016; *Arias v. Arizona* 2016; *DeShaw v. Arizona* 2016; *Tatum v. Arizona* 2016). Justice Sotomayor, concurring in those dispositions, restated the importance of developmental considerations and meaningful developmental inquiry by the courts:

This Court explained in *Miller v. Alabama* that a sentencer is "require[d] . . . to take into account how children are different, and how those differences counsel against irrevocably sentencing them to a lifetime in prison." Children are "constitutionally different from adults for purposes of sentencing" in light of their lack of maturity and underdeveloped sense of responsibility, their susceptibility to negative influences and outside pressure, and their less well-formed character traits. Failing to consider these constitutionally significant differences, we explained, "poses too great a risk of disproportionate punishment." In the context of life without parole, we stated that "appropriate occasions for sentencing juveniles to this harshest possible penalty will be uncommon." (*Tatum*, slip op. at 1)

Indeed, one might argue that a developmental lens has begun to fundamentally reshape family law and juvenile justice. Developmental arguments have been particularly effective toward reframing juvenile justice to reflect the immature and incomplete brain development of adolescents that affects their judgment, risk taking, and susceptibility to peer influence (*Miller v. Alabama* 2012, 2464–68; *Safford Unified School District No. 1 v. Redding* 2009, 375–79). The consequence has been to dismantle harsh sentences for juveniles on the basis that they are different from adults, not yet fully neurologically or emotionally developed and, therefore, are less culpable while also having greater potential for rehabilitation (*Miller v. Alabama* 2012, 2464–68). Many harsh aspects of juvenile incarceration remain, however, including the practice of solitary confinement (American Civil Liberties Union 2015; Bilchik 2011; Ross 2012). Nevertheless, the potential exists to extend this developmental understanding throughout the juvenile justice system.

Conversely, the same scientific evidence has been important to determine capability and maturity in the reproductive rights realm (*Hodgson v. Minnesota* 1990; *City of Akron v. Akron Center for Reproductive Health*, 1983; *Bellotti v. Baird* 1979; *Carey v. Population Services International* 1977). Many teenagers are sufficiently mature to make decisions about their reproductive choices (Rebouché 2011). The consequences if youth are not allowed this choice, coupled with recognition of their capability to make their own decisions in a setting that permits time and reflection, suggest that maturity and capability may be defined differently in different situations, at different ages, and based on the specific experience and capabilities of particular youth.

These two seemingly opposing positions, recognizing immaturity and poor decision making versus respecting sufficient maturity and capability to make major life decisions, suggest that the use of the developmental lens needs to be nuanced and careful so as not to infantilize children and youth, but at the same time to recognize the fluid developmental dynamic that affects behavior and relates to legal concerns of capability and capacity. As children's rights scholar Barbara Woodhouse has so eloquently written, adolescents in particular need to be supported in their opportunity to develop, including their opportunity to make mistakes (Woodhouse 2008a).

One final example of an area where the developmental perspective has been helpful has been with respect to issues of custody and shared parenting, particularly to differentiate between the needs and support of children at different ages and over time (California Courts 2015). Florida, like many states, recognizes developmental information as a relevant factor in determining the best interests of the child in devising parenting plans (Florida Statutes § 61.13(3) (a)–(m) (2006)). In addition, guidance and sample plans of the courts expressly differentiate between the needs of infants versus those of middle school children and older teenagers (Oregon Judicial Department 2016). As distinguished from juvenile justice and reproductive rights, here the developmental data are used as a guidepost to formulate individualized plans that adjust over time congruent with normative developmental stages. In addition to change over time that must be a part of many parenting plans, divorcing parents also deal with the impact of the divorce on their children, which varies by age in terms of immediate impact as well as long-term implications for development and socialization (Kelly and Lamb 2005).

The use of developmental scholarship in law commonly conceptualizes development as linear, represented most familiarly in the developmental charts from infancy to adulthood that organize physical, cognitive, emotional, and other aspects of development according to age-linked norms. Common developmental stages and indicators are used to evaluate children and to provide guidance to parents (Centers for Disease Control and Prevention [CDC] 2015a). The linear view reminds us that children are a moving target, with unique needs at various ages and stages. So, for example, normative adolescent needs and behavior are far different from those of newborns. At six months some of the benchmarks are sitting up with support, rolling over, and saying two-syllable words (id.). By adolescence, goals include separation from parents, independent work habits, dealing with sexuality, and identity development (CDC 2015c). This linear progression also highlights particular periods as especially critical: infancy and adolescence are the two most dynamic periods of development.

An ecological development model, grounded in the work of Urie Bronfenbrenner and most strongly advocated in legal analysis by Woodhouse, provides a more complex picture that situates the individual's linear development within an ecology, capturing the impact of multiple environments on the child and the dynamic interaction of various aspects of the ecology with individual aspects of the child (Bronfen-brenner 1979; Woodhouse 2005, 2008a). Conceptualized as concentric networks of self, family, community, systems, and ideologies, all aspects of this complex ecology affect outcomes. This perspective is incorporated in law in the recognition that context matters. Of these interlocking systems, the most significant are *microsystems*—those that have a direct impact on children (family, peers, community, schools). Where those systems overlap are *mesosystems*, ideally reinforcing the overlapping microsystems. So, for example, the family and schools mutually support academic achievement, and neighborhoods support both the families within them and the schools located within the neighborhoods that serve children. *Exosystems* more indirectly, but no less significantly, impact children through their effects on the micro- and mesosystems, through institutions and systems (for example, policies and systems of anti-poverty support, child welfare, education, health care, and juvenile justice). Overarching the entire ecology is the *macrosystem* of cultural ideals, biases, and beliefs (for example, beliefs about development, core societal principles, and pervasive stereotypes).

Bronfenbrenner revised his model after his early classic work, adding biology, psychology, and behavior in relation to the nested ecological systems. He named his revised model PPCT, for process, person, context (the ecology), and time:

> The developmental process, involving the fused and dynamic relation of the individual and the context; the person, with his or her individual repertoire of biological, cognitive, emotional, and behavioral characteristics; the context of human development, conceptualized as the nested levels or systems, of the ecology of human development; and time, conceptualized as involving the multiple dimensions of temporality—for example unogenetic [lifespan] time, family time and historical time—constituting the chronosystem that moderates change across the lifecourse. (Bronfenbrenner 2005, foreword by Lerner, xv–xvii)

Bronfenbrenner's revision therefore emphasized more strongly individual agency in development (Tudge et al. 2006). Personal characteristics including race and gender are included but not strongly or separately highlighted (id.).

The value of the ecological approach is in seeing the interlocking nature of the various pieces of the ecology. Instead of isolating the child or narrowly focusing on the family as the sole determinant of the child's well-being, the ecological model recognizes that families are only part of the picture; they do not function independently. Ideally, the interlocking systems are functional for all children, sharing what Woodhouse calls generist values of responsibility for the next generation, creating a healthy, supportive ecology. When systems lack that goal, systems on various levels can be highly dysfunctional and even toxic to children (Woodhouse 2005).

One other valuable insight into development comes from neuroscience, which strongly reinforces the importance of the layers of the ecology identified by Bronfenbrenner and the impact of the ecology on the developing brain. The groundbreaking work "From Neurons to Neighborhoods" details the research that demonstrates the importance of family, neighborhood, and community factors, and the policies and systems that impact on those levels, as critical to the healthy development of children (National Research Council and Institute of Medicine 2000). Ongoing research has confirmed those core findings to the extent that the clear implications for children are well established. This work has particularly emphasized the critical period of early childhood, variously framed as birth to three, birth to five, or birth to eight. In this period of rapid neurological growth the foundation of cognitive, psychological, and socioemotional functioning is laid. While a child's brain is not cemented and unchangeable after this stage, this early foundation facilitates all that follows. A further finding of the neuroscience research is that differences in neurological development can emerge early, by eighteen months, reflecting variances in the ecologies within which children grow.

The very plasticity and growth of children's brains also makes them vulnerable to stress (American Academy of Pediatrics 2014). So in addition to differential development reflecting ecological inequalities, stresses in children's ecologies, if they reach toxic levels, can be especially harmful to neurological development in this foundational early childhood period (Center on the Developing Child 2014). Neuroscience tells us both of the impact of negative ecological factors and of the brain's resiliency.

Adverse Childhood Experiences (ACEs) research focuses on the impact of trauma, including complex trauma, and resiliency (ACEs Too High 2016; CDC 2016b; Center on the Developing Child 2016b). The ACEs concept is helpful in describing the consequences of developmental inequality and dealing with those consequences. There is robust neuroscience research on the impact of trauma (Peters and Massey 1983; Graff 2011; Grant, Katz, et al. 2004; Gump 2010; Hood et al. 2013; Hunt, Martens, and Belcher 2011; Mitchell et al. 2014; Triffleman and Pole 2010; Stopford 2015; Hill et al. 1996; Hill and Madhere 1996).

Focusing on neurological development and capability, neuroscience is a more narrow perspective than the ecological model or the linear progression model, both of which include multiple systems as part of development. Neuroscience nevertheless can be particularly helpful in understanding the physical developmental foundation of complex behavior. For example, neuroscience explains why adolescents are both capable and immature, by reminding us that this is linked to the lack of full development of the frontal lobe (Scott and Steinberg 2008). The outsized risk-taking propensity of teens is because their neurological skill at making judgments is not yet fully developed (Fondacaro 2015). Indeed, neuroscience would suggest that from a brain architecture perspective, legal adulthood might arguably be delayed to age twenty-five (Kroger 2004). At the same time, increasing maturity and capacity for judgment may be the basis to encourage independent judgment making as part of the very process of development of judgment and maturity (Rebouché 2011).

Neuroscience allows us to measure scientifically the toll taken on normal brain development by being confronted with severe stressors (CDC 2016b). Just as abuse and domestic violence have an impact on the developing brain, so too do factors like racism, linked particularly to stress (Grant, Katz, et al. 2004; Gump 2010; Hill and Madhere 1996; Hunt, Martens, and Belcher 2011; Mitchell et al. 2014; Peters and Massey 1983; Triffleman and Pole 2010). At the same time, neuroscience reminds us of the brain's resiliency and what factors contribute to that resiliency. Nothing in the neuroscience literature suggests an individual's future is etched in stone early. It does however strongly reinforce the impact of the ecology, or to put it in the terms of the debate of nature versus nurture, neuroscience tells us *both* matter. And the single most critical resilience factor is relationships, and therefore family. Neuroscientists capture this in the acronym SSNR: safe, stable, and nurturing relationships (Mercy and Saul 2009). This leads then to the importance to children of family or functional family support from their surrounding ecologies, which through them impact the child.

Neuroscience research findings thus confirm Bronfenbrenner's insight about the importance of the ecology of development, and the interconnectedness of the most direct microsystems for the individual child, through the nested ecologies of systems that intersect to support or hinder development. At the same time, neuroscience enhances the linear model of developmental progression with concrete links to brain architecture that can explain children's behavior.

When we compare this developmental view combining the linear, ecological, and neuroscience research to what we know of the life course of Black boys outlined in Part I, this developmental perspective minimizes, even submerges, the role of race, gender, and class. For all children who come out at the bottom of unequal hierarchies among children, where inequalities can be connected to group identity characteristics, it hides those critical identity factors behind a model of a developmentally "neutral" child. For example, in recent U.S. Supreme Court cases where the Court has strongly embraced a developmental perspective, the Court has particularly relied on the markers of linear, normative development, and neuroscience scholarship on the progression of brain development in the teenage years. The Court has given some attention to contextual factors, but tends to keep the focus narrower than that suggested by the ecological model. So, for example, in *Miller v. Alabama*, where two cases were consolidated to consider whether juveniles who committed homicide could be sentenced to life without parole, the Court critiqued the practice of mandatory sentences of life without parole because the practice "precludes consideration of . . . chronological age and its hallmark features—among them, immaturity, impetuosity, and failure to appreciate risks and consequences" (2468). In addition, the Court stated that the rule also precluded taking into account the circumstances of the offense as well as of the home and family environment (id.). The Court noted that one of the two defendants, who was an accessory to robbery and murder of a store clerk but did not shoot the clerk, had a family background that the Court characterized as "immersion in violence" because his mother and grandmother had shot other individuals (id.). That defendant was fourteen when charged as an adult, and was African American (id., 2455). The Court described the second defendant's home life in considerable detail as "pathological," including a drug-addicted mother, a life in and out of foster care, and a physically abusive stepfather (id., 2469). This second defendant had tried to kill himself four times, beginning in kindergarten (id.). Also fourteen when he committed his crime, he beat his victim, then set a fire to cover his crime (id., 2462). This defendant was white. In the analysis of the white defendant, the Court seemed to be sympathetic to the difficulties he experienced in his life; in the analysis of the Black defendant, the Court appeared to lay blame on the family for encouraging the use of violence, although the defendant did not commit the acts of violence but rather was charged as an accessory.

The Court did not explicitly take race into account in evaluating the maturity, competence, and responsibility of the *Miller* defendants for their crimes, nor was race explicitly considered in the context relevant to their sentencing. Even if race were not the explanation for the Court's differential evaluation of the two defendants, the absence of consideration of race to assess the life course and developmental pathway of the defendants obscures the challenges specific to race and gender in development.

Racialized Developmental Research and Norms

The absence of attention to race is not surprising given the "neutral" child of mainstream developmental analysis. But it obscures the limits of that model, which is hardly neutral. The developmental research base is not diverse. Much of the psychological research on children that is the basis for understanding and constructing developmental norms has been critiqued as racially biased (Scott 1997). The children initially researched were exclusively white, and research continues to be dominated by the study of white children by white researchers. "[M]iddle class White behaviors, norms and values are used as the standard of normality and psychosocial adjustment against which non-White youth are evaluated" (Gibbs 1998, 70). In addition, white and African American youths are "assumed to have similar experiences and equal access to participation in American social institutions" (id., 70; see also McLoyd and Randolph 1984, 1985; McLoyd 2006a, 2006b).

The research patterns have persisted despite this critique (Quintana et al. 2006). In other words, as with many "sciences," in psychological research on children the assumptions or questions generating research claim universality without examining that assumption or what subjects are studied. Norms reflect who is in the field and what children they study. This suggests the dominant developmental lens is deficient because it is racialized but presented as universal and neutral. So, for example, the application of norms has been completely one way:

> Although it is relatively common to apply models of parenting from Whites of European descent to other ethnic or racial groups, it seems unthinkable to test models of normative development derived from minority ethnic groups on White children of European descent. This double standard illustrates the culturally parochial approach to understanding normative development in much of the extant research. (id., 1134)

If developmental norms are not "neutral," that raises profound issues about what is normative (Parham, Ajamu, and White 2011).

When minority children are studied, historically and currently, the dominant perspective is deviancy (Quintana et al. 2006). As Daryl Scott has noted, "damage imagery" is what has predominated (Scott 1997). "Again and again, contempt has proven to be the flip side of pity" (id., xviii). Most famously, in *Brown v. Board of Education* (1954), intangible harm from segregation and the infamous doll studies read as self-hate were used to justify the necessity and benefit of integration to remedy this harm to Black children (Scott 1997). The research question commonly posed when children of color are the focus is some variant of "what is going on that causes children of color to behave badly?" Connected to this research pattern focused on deviancy is limitation of research subjects to kids characterized as "high risk," "urban," or "urban low income," all of which begin to sound like euphemisms or code words for children and youth of color, ignoring differences among their circumstances (Gibbs 1998). This is not to say urban settings or geography in general are not relevant but rather that the label "urban youth" frequently is code for youth of color. There has been little study of successful youth of color, varying ecologies, or positive models of resilience (Bush and Bush 2013). Much remains unknown about positive developmental pathways for minority children because those questions continue to be so minimally studied (Cabrera, Beeghly, and Eisenberg 2012). One scholar suggests three areas have not been significantly researched for children of color: normative development in context, intergroup relations and attitudes, and identity development (Quintana et al. 2006). Moreover, the evidence from children of color reminds us that all children's development is racialized, although the process of racialization differs for minority versus majority children (id.).

The evolution and development of Black psychology challenges the typical (white) norms of development and normative behavior (Jones 2004). Joseph White argues this is essential because the lives of Black people do not match white psychological theories that explain the lives of whites (White 2004). For example, he imagines the visit of a white researcher into a Black home, where young children have had to master the presence of pain and struggle, and a hostile external world (id., 6). He describes Black psychology, by contrast, in these terms: "improvisation, resilience, transcendence of tragedy, connectedness to others, spirituality, valuing of direct experience, and emotional vitality" (id., 13). The work of William Cross analyzes Black identity research that critically evaluates early work from the deficit perspective and then offers what he calls a "nigrescence" model of Black identity development in the post–civil rights era (Cross 1991). Cross identifies five stages: pre-encounter (non-Afrocentric) (although he sees it as possible to be socialized in an Afrocentric way); encounter (challenge to this initial identity); immersion/emersion (commitment to change); internalization (reconstitution); and internalization/commitment (id., 190). This is not a singular Black identity, but an engagement with Blackness as a challenge to Eurocentric perspectives and learned perspectives on Black identity.

Thomas Parham centers his psychology in African consciousness and principles of personhood (Parham, Ajamu, and White 2011). Building on the work of Asa Hilliard, Parham cites as his conceptual anchors "strong belief in the possibility of human transformation; strong foundation and belief in theoretical and conceptual models of helping; and knowledge of culture at the deep structure level" (id., 7–13). He identifies eight variables distinctive from European worldviews of human characteristics:

the self as interconnected domains, not separable ones; expression of feeling, rather than suppression; collective survival, not individual survival; oral traditions over written traditions; a present focus in time versus future orientation; harmony and balance with the universe, rather than control of the universe; death as transition versus death as the end; and age as honored instead of fighting aging (id.). His model, then, suggests a different focus of values, skills, and competencies; it reminds us that developmental models are not created by science, but are constructed by values that reward behaviors and definitions of knowledge according to a value structure. The orientation defines normalcy; the control of the norm defines deviance (Akbar 2004).

Psychoanalytic theory as well has been criticized as normatively white. For example, one scholar notes Freudian theory centers on white, Eurocentric perspectives drawn from Freud's experiences, particularly his Jewish heritage (Curtis-Boles 2002). Freud's view of family relationships, she notes, has a tendency to over-pathologize, minimize strengths, and misinterpret the behavior and motivations of African American families and individuals (id.). Similarly, Curtis-Boles notes that modern theory on relationships, especially the role of parents, tends to focus on mothers and their responsibility for raising well-adjusted children, but ignores the social context of racism for Black parents (id., 200–204).

The exposure of this bias brings the core assumptions of psychoanalytic theory into question, and it raises questions about whether kids and adults of color are unnecessarily pathologized while also ignoring the basis for their state of being, their strengths, and the cognitive and emotional skills forged in this toxic emotional/psychological environment:

> [W]ritings of minority psychologists and social scientists have appreciated for many years the limitations of traditional psychological theories when applied to people of color. From the early 1900s, pioneers in this field emphasized the importance of cultural values, socioeconomic factors and the realities of discrimination and racism in understanding the psychology and life experience of minority group peoples. (id., 193)

One critique of the existing developmental model in law, therefore, is that mainstream models are based on the experiences and assumptions of middle-class white males (and only more recently have included females). So norms are hardly universal, neutral, or dispassionate. As one researcher put it, "Even the rat was white" (Guthrie 1998). Second, race, gender, and other factors that critically impact development are missing or, at best, marginalized from the mainstream model as a developmental factor. This second critique suggests an essential revision to our current legal developmental model.

6

Developmental Equality

Developmental models generally presume a child unraced and ungen-
dered. That approach misses the role of race and gender in development
and the ways in which race and gender render children unequal, and
subordinate them, because of ways in which their normative development is made more difficult due to the hurdles those identities trigger.
Two scholars whose work describes this dynamic are Margaret Beale
Spencer and Cynthia García Coll. Their work suggests the necessity of
reframing the developmental model to one of developmental equality.
Such a model would be the basis to challenge state policies and institutions, provide a metric for equality, and be the basis for support of racial/
ethnic identity. Such a model might also have the potential to uncover
the replication of privilege.

1. Margaret Beale Spencer

Spencer's phenomenological variant of ecological systems theory
(PVEST) model combines Bronfenbrenner's ecological approach with
phenomenological perspective (the study of the development of human
consciousness and awareness) (Spencer, Fegley, and Harpalani 2003;
Spencer et al. 2004; Spencer, Dobbs, and Swanson 1988; Spencer and
Markstrom-Adams 1990). Spencer sees development as framed by the
interaction of identity, context, and experience. The model considers
the impact of critical identity factors on individual perceptions of self
and opportunities, imposed expectations or stereotypes, and the interaction of these processes with the normal maturational processes such as
puberty and identity exploration in adolescence. According to Spencer,
in this model "risk is best viewed as an *exacerbation of normative challenges and competencies due to larger sociopolitical processes . . . and/
or lack of resources* and resilience as successful coping with these exacerbated challenges" (Spencer et al. 2004, 230). This is a critical part of

Spencer's theory: the normative—meaning normative developmental stages and growth to meet developmental benchmarks—is exacerbated by identity (id.; Spencer 1994).

Spencer's model focuses on five basic components that contribute to identity: risk, stress, coping, identity, and life outcomes (Spencer et al. 2004, 233). The interaction of these components translates into net vulnerability, net stress management, reactive coping mechanisms, emergent identities, and adverse or productive life-stage-specific coping mechanisms (id., 232–33). As youth develop, they are creating an identity that is either reinforced and supported, or not: "Identity lays the foundation for future perception, self-appraisal, and behavior, yielding adverse or productive life-stage-specific coping outcomes" (id., 233).

Spencer's model is specifically designed to take into account the development of youth of color. In this model, both risk and stress are strongly affected by systemic and institutional factors. Systemic factors also come into play when youth adopt a coping mechanism viewed as maladaptive, which can have serious consequences for their emerging identity. As Spencer points out, all children develop in the context of culture, but do so differently: "Some children develop in a cultural context in which their culture, race or ethnicity are considered privileged over other cultural and racial groups. This privilege is, unfortunately, neither recognized as such nor acknowledged as a significant life-course asset" (Spencer 2006, 1149). Neither privilege nor subordination has been explored in most mainstream development scholarship (id., 1151). The dominant questions have been geared to "what" is happening in development, not "how" (id.; Luthar and Latendresse 2002; Steele 1988; Steele, Spencer, and Aronson 2002).

The exacerbation of risk is identified in the early part of Spencer's model and has an impact throughout the individual's process of constructing identity. Risk contributors are factors that are part of self-appraisal and depend on the individual's interaction with society (Spencer et al. 2004). This includes the individual's response to stereotypes and biases. Here Spencer includes race, sex, SES factors, physical characteristics of the individual, and biological/temperament characteristics as factors that contribute to risk (Spencer, Fegley, and Harpalani 2003; Spencer et al. 2004). These are potential risk factors, to be distinguished from the second set of factors, stress engagement, which represents actual stresses in their lives (Spencer et al. 2004). Stress is subdivided into neighborhood dangers, social supports, and daily hassles (id., 232–33, 242). In sum, this part of Spencer's model identifies the interaction of identities, structures, culture, and social factors. Identity factors by their terms generate risk; structural factors trigger stress dynamics.

It is this exacerbation of the normative that should, I would argue, trigger mandatory affirmative action by the state because the exacerbation *flows* from state action. Spencer's model exposes at a very individual level the costs and challenges facing children of color, and their source. Their very identifiable characteristics, by race and gender, are characterized as risks because they are linked to the structural interactions that incorporate stereotypes and cognitive bias, as well as actors within those structures (Spencer, Fegley, and Harpalani 2003; Spencer et al. 2004). In addition, those potential triggers are exacerbated by actual encounters: neighborhood conditions and daily microaggressions and prejudices that are race- and gender-linked to the families and communities within which children of color function, as well as to children's identities. Rather than providing support, that context is itself poorly supported and undermined. The source of those familial and community developmental challenges is state structures and policies.

The remaining factors in Spencer's model continue to expose how individual responses to exacerbated risk are linked to structural factors. Coping with exacerbated risk (the risk triggered by identity factors, located in structures that disproportionately hamper or block development) can be adaptive or maladaptive. Individuals engage in strategies that can help or hurt in relation to structural responses to their behavior (Swanson, Cunningham, and Spencer 2003). Maladaptive actions identified by Spencer include hypermasculinity, reactive ethnocentrism, or personal orientation (Spencer et al. 2004; Swanson, Cunningham, and Spencer 2003). It is important to note, however, that these responses are "maladaptive" to the extent that they are likely to lead to further structural responses that create even more difficult developmental challenges—such as interaction with the juvenile justice system, which can result in direct and collateral roadblocks to development and opportunity. Maladaptive responses are *rational* responses that are treated and responded to as "maladaptive," meaning that they are likely to be met with negative responses by authority figures. Each of the (rational but) maladaptive responses can be further exacerbated by ongoing stress, generating more negative interaction. The lethal interactions between police and young Black men are extreme examples of this interaction, so commonplace that they must be deemed a systemic response, not rogue action (Black Lives Matter 2016; Fatal Force 2015, 2016, 2017). Adaptive solutions on the other hand reinforce positive identities. "Adaptive" represents responses more likely to receive positive systemic reactions, but as with "maladaptive" responses Spencer is describing a reality laced with stereotypes, bias, and danger, not a judgment that these responses can be neutrally framed as "adaptive." This parallels the resistant identities as well as the positive consequences of racial identity as a strength and resilience factor. How this developmental dynamic ultimately affects life stages is Spencer's final factor, with adverse outcomes including juvenile or adult justice systems, mental illness, poor health, and lack of intimacy (Swanson et al. 2003). Surviving this series of challenges is tricky but also generates real strengths:

> Structural racism in American society stems from systematic, institutionalized practices resulting in the subordination and devaluation of minority groups and the setting up of life course barriers for all of its members' life course experiences. The consequences of structural racism for minority youth are twofold. First, minority youth in America often live and mature in high-risk environments characterized by systemic, structural barriers to individual success. . . . Second, instances of resilience . . . often go unrecognized, thus, denying individuals a sense of success and accomplishment. (Spencer 2001b, 53; see also Spencer, Dobbs, and Swanson 1988; see also Spencer and Markstrom-Adams 1990)

A specific example that Spencer discusses in her work is the adoption of hypermasculinity as a coping mechanism, frequently triggering very negative systemic results (Spencer et al. 2004). Fear of violence and insecurity trigger this coping mechanism. Thus, hypermasculinity is an expression of vulnerability (id., 235–41). As Spencer explains, "In addition to the normative maturational challenges, Black boys must also deal with prejudice and the negative, stereotypic connotations associated with Black masculinity, which is often inherently viewed as hyper-masculinity. These stereotypes are pervasive, as they cut across multiple ecological settings" (id., 236). Her model exposes this ultimate "catch-22" of risk and stress that is reinforced and generated from systems that generate highly negative images and assumptions that lead to predictable coping mechanisms that then trigger further negative response (id., 239; see also Seaton 2007). The social and systemic response to white boys acting out as teenagers is frequently that "boys will be boys," that they will outgrow this behavior (which, in fact, most teenagers do); the response to Black boys and other boys of color engaging in the same behavior is to view them as serious threats. What is often lost is the strength and positive aspects of Black masculinities (Neal 2005).

The interaction of race and gender is a particularly strong component of Spencer's model (Swanson et al. 2003). As Spencer points out, adolescent identity development "involves coming to understand one's self as a member of a society within a particular ethnic, cultural, religious, or political tradition; . . . it is a process of defining oneself [by] becoming part of a normative cultural tradition" (Spencer 2001a, 102). For African American males:

> The task of managing an ego-supporting identity while coping with generalized negative imagery is, at best, daunting. . . . [They] are expected to shoulder the traditional negative stereotypes associated with male adolescence in general, along with the added burden of enhanced and often unacknowledged negative imagery linked with minority status. (id., 103)

So the normal maelstrom of adolescent development, characterized by confusion and vulnerability, is exacerbated for Black adolescents by "[n]egative stereotypes, scarcity of positive role models, lack of culturally competent instruction and direction, and problems associated with low socioeconomic status and high-risk neighborhoods" (Swanson, Cunningham, and Spencer 2003, 618). They are aware of the culture's stereotypes and expectations of them as they are at a key developmental stage for identity formation (id.). Two critical settings are school and community environments. Spencer also identifies coping strategies, such as religion, spirituality, and cultural pride, for a positive sense of self (Spencer, Fegley, and Harpalani 2003).

The PVEST analysis exposes how development is impacted in negative ways, and the kinds of interventions needed to build social capital. But Spencer cautions that we not overlook the resilience and strength of Black boys. Most importantly, her model exposes structural and cultural factors that are within the power and control of the state that generate developmental challenges. The identification of the state as the source of developmental barriers should trigger the necessity of state action to correct not only the state's own discrimination in failing to support developmental equality but also its role in actively subordinating the development of children of color. Her model suggests this requires attention to stereotypes and bias, structural locations of developmental barriers, and positive support for constructing identity that includes families and communities.

2. Cynthia García Coll

Cynthia García Coll's child development model focuses on social stratification and its impact on child development—separating stratification into social position, racism, and segregation (García Coll and Magnuson 2000; García Coll et al. 1996; García Coll 1990; García Coll and Szalacha (2004). As with Spencer, her model is a further development of Bronfenbrenner's ecological model (García Coll et al. 1996). Spencer shifts our lens to that of the individual moving through the layers of ecological context, and does so through the lived-out contexts of children of color. Although Bronfenbrenner acknowledged the role of the person in his revised model, he remains best known for his elaboration of the ecological developmental context. Spencer shifts the perspective so we can imagine how this functions for the individual, and she redresses the white tilt of prior "neutral" models by infusing her model with the realities of race, gender, and class. García Coll returns us to context, but like Spencer, she corrects the neutral/white model to incorporate the context in which children of color live. She articulates the impact of culture in the life of every child, but also the uniquely dualistic nature of culture for outsider children: external or mainstream culture and its shaping of institutions has a powerful impact on children individually and on their families, as well as infusing the structures within which they function, including schools, housing, and community resources (García Coll and Szalacha

2004). Families construct as well as live within culture, responding to racial and ethnic subordination by majority white culture, parenting their children to live and survive in two worlds. Families embody both resistance and identity (id.; García Coll et al. 1996; García Coll 1990). García Coll's model "incorporates the contextual, racial, and cultural factors that play critical roles for children who are not part of mainstream society" (García Coll and Szalacha 2004; García Coll et al. 1996).

Three key conclusions flow from her model:

> It is the interplay of . . . *social position, racism, and segregation*—that creates the unique conditions and pathways for children of color. . . . [Second, a] segregated school or neighborhood environment that is inhibiting due to limited resources may, at the same time, be promoting if it is supportive of the child's emotional and academic adjustment, helping the child to manage societal demands imposed by discrimination. [Third, the] behavioral, cognitive, linguistic, and motivational deficits of minority . . . children are more appropriately recognized as manifestations of adaptive cultures, as families develop goals, values, attitudes, and behaviors that set them apart from the dominant culture. (García Coll and Szalacha 2004, 81, emphasis added)

Context thus powerfully impacts development. As García Coll states, "Cognitive, emotional, and behavioral development is profoundly affected by the child's social position within a socially-stratified society replete with racism and discrimination, and by the promoting or inhibiting nature of the child's school and neighborhood" (id., 82). The three aspects of social stratification—social position, racism, and segregation—collectively create the distinctive conditions faced by these children, and "it is these 'non-shared' experiences with mainstream populations that define the unique pathways of development for children of color" (id., 83). These unique experiences can be harshly subordinating and challenging:

> What is the cost to the development of the child who is teased or even hit or kicked by other children in school because he or she has darker skin, slanted eyes, or an accent? What is the cost of coming to know that people of your cultural background are considered dumb, no good, ugly, or lazy?

What is the cost of growing up in a neighborhood that is predominantly non-Anglo and poor? What is the cost of thinking that your teachers do not care if you learn and do not expect you to succeed because of your cultural background? What is the cost of consistently fighting stereotypes and prejudices that are saturated with negative images and demeaning conceptualizations of the culturally different? What are the costs associated with these experiences to an individual's health, well-being, and developmental outcome? What are the benefits, if any? (García Coll and Magnuson 2000, 105)

In her model García Coll identifies eight constructs that affect cognitive, emotional, and behavioral development based on the child's social position within a society characterized by racism and discrimination, plus the supporting or inhibiting nature of the child's school and neighborhood. The eight constructs are social position, racism, segregation, promoting/inhibiting environments, adaptive culture, child characteristics, family, and developmental competencies (García Coll and Szalacha 2004). She maintains that what are labeled as deficits of minority children—behavioral, cognitive, and motivational—are more accurately seen as coping mechanisms and adaptive cultures (García Coll et al. 1996). Diversity is a protective factor, a resource for children (García Coll and Szalacha 2004).

How this context plays out varies by the age and stage of children. García Coll argues the most relevant factors to the child's development from birth to age three are cultural beliefs, caregiving practices, health care practices, family structure and characteristics, socioeconomic factors, and biological factors (García Coll 1990). At middle childhood, defined as ages six to twelve, when children have their first experience of interaction with institutions beyond their families and neighborhoods, the implications are different:

It is during this period that children develop a sense of competence, forming ideas about their abilities, the domains of accomplishment they value, and the likelihood that they will do well in these domains. . . . [D]evelopment of positive attitudes toward school, academic achievement, and aspirations for the future can have major implications for children's success as adults. (García Coll and Szalacha 2004, 82)

Middle childhood is also a time when children experience the direct impact of majority culture: children for the first time may "experience exclusion, devaluation, invisibility, discrimination, and racism, and these may become important potential sources of influence on their interactions and reactions to 'mainstream' society" (id.). Majority culture impacts schools, neighborhood, media, and other institutions that affect the family (id., 84).

One extremely important factor in the developmental context for children of color is segregation, which García Coll defines as not only housing segregation but also economic and social/cultural segregation. She points out that segregation may generate support for children as compared to an integrated setting where children are treated as outsiders (id.). Segregation's effects include what is available in the neighborhood for kids to do, and the level of safety, which can influence parents to isolate their children in order to keep them safe (id., 86).

García Coll also focuses on families' interactions with media/culture, which can embrace or isolate their culture, as well as deliver messages about their culture/identity (García Coll and Magnuson 2000). She argues for rethinking the role of families, neighborhood, and culture: "Most developmental research, clinical interventions, and social policies have regarded the child-rearing values, attitudes, practices, and norms of the dominant culture (that is, white, Anglo-Saxon, middle class) to be optimal for child development" (García Coll and Szalacha 2004, 88). This translates into difference as deviance or deficit, and directing interventions to compensate or correct the deficits. To the contrary, "[f]amilies and children of color develop goals, values, attitudes, and behaviors that set them apart from the dominant culture because of social stratification deriving from prejudice, discrimination, racism, or segregation, and the differential access to critical resources" (id., 88).

> Racism, discrimination, and diminished life opportunities related to segregation constitute the critical, underlying source of risk for children of color. . . . Experiences of exclusion at various societal levels constitute, at a minimum, insults to children's healthy social and cognitive development. Segregation, in its many forms—including residential, economic, linguistic, social and psychological—not only places the child at risk, but also

contributes to significant mistrust among populations of diverse cultural backgrounds. (id., 88)

García Coll's model exposes the presence of racism, and the subsets of prejudice, discrimination, and oppression, as normative for outsider children; identifies segregation as normative, evidenced by the resegregation of American society; and points to schools, media, and health care as critical environments that either promote or inhibit the child. Just as Spencer's model identifies exacerbated risk triggered by identities as normative, García Coll's model identifies subordination in children's context as normative. Equally critical are García Coll's insights about culture. The goal of equality is not to dismantle cultural identity, but to dismantle subordination.

3. A Developmental Equality Model

Both Spencer's and García Coll's models reflect the realities of the developmental arc of the lives of Black boys detailed in Part I. The individual risk factors and the intersectional impact of race and gender, further exacerbated by the high rate of poverty among Black children, are magnified by the absence of family and neighborhood supports as well as at school and, increasingly, on the streets. These stresses trigger responses frequently framed as "maladaptive," deficient, and problematic, and are reflected in negative academic and disciplinary outcomes. Adaptive patterns exist tied to strong racial socialization and racial identity, but even those adaptive outcomes carry risks during adolescence. The risks from policing and potential juvenile justice system involvement are commonplace, and in some cases deadly.

The interlocking systems that create the social position of Black boys, as noted by García Coll, include heath care (or the lack of it, especially mental health care); poor-quality schools; and limited family and neighborhood supports. Families and communities must socialize children, particularly boys, to deal with the real dangers they face, while strengthening their identity of pride and resistance. The developmental tasks are significantly greater; the accomplishments more dear; and the process of development fraught with barriers, ironic and contradictory paths, and pressure to fail rather than support to succeed.

The work of Spencer and García Coll not only provides a framework to analyze the child development life course of Black boys, but also suggests a powerful way to utilize the developmental lens that has emerged in law to achieve equality. Using Spencer and García Coll's work to reframe the developmental model in law generates a developmental perspective that can serve not just to describe *what* happens, but to expose *how* it happens. Development is affected by systems and state-supported culture that marginalize and subordinate some children. A model focused on these dynamics and committed to children's equality can serve as a metric to trigger state responsibility to dismantle state structures and policies that undermine children's development. It may also serve to generate positive state responsibility to support children's developmental equality.

In tandem, these scholars expose the developmental burden placed on children of color. The source of much of that burden is the state. Their stark illustrations of the developmental costs and challenges together with the principles of equality should generate a more nuanced and realistic developmental perspective that might meaningfully be used as a theoretical and practical tool to challenge inequality sustained and supported by the state. Because developmental insights have already made inroads into legal analysis, reframing the developmental model so that it supports all children does not require persuading courts or legislatures to adopt an entirely new analytical tool, but rather to refine and adjust their analysis. Developmental equality, however, mandates far more. It requires analyzing which children are at the bottom of hierarchies among children, and why they are there. When their ecologies are dysfunctional, the analysis begins with questions about the efficacy, fairness, and equity of the structures, policies, and systems that should serve *all* children in order to ensure their equality of development and thus their equality of opportunity. Fused with legal principles of equality, this model exposes the location and sources of inequality that negatively impact the developmental trajectory of children by their identities (singly or in combination). If it tells us the playing field for a child at birth is determined and predictable, and the end result is hierarchy and inequality, not opportunity and support to become the best each child can be, then those systems in place must be reformed to ensure equality, and new systems needed to ensure equality must be constructed. As long as children's starting point is unequal, the means to equality require *equity* along with universality to ensure real equality of development, and thus of opportunity, for all. Unequal outcomes, exposed by fusing developmental knowledge with equality principles, reveal the critical role of state actions and structures in creating developmental hurdles and roadblocks. Together, the powerful critiques of Spencer and García Coll reinforce the importance of intersectional analysis to understand how identity, as currently experienced by children of color, triggers an exacerbated set of developmental challenges that operates to expose children to risk, harm, and failure. Infusing law with this knowledge adds to our existing use of developmental analysis to understand children better, to assess their needs, and to recognize their competency and voice.

By using a developmental equality lens, the source of exacerbated risks is exposed: as long as identity alone, or in combination, triggers heightened developmental challenges or differential developmental support, this analysis exposes continuing inequalities for identifiable groups of children. Spencer and García Coll identify the impact of structural and cultural factors. As long as those factors persist and continue to be supported by the state, the state is complicit in generating children's inequalities. Fundamental equality, long since recognized, should make this pattern, once clear, unlawful as well as morally unacceptable. As the Supreme Court said over a quarter century ago, "A core purpose of the Fourteenth Amendment was to do away with all governmentally imposed discrimination based on race" (*Palmore v. Sidoti* 1984, 432). Making children unequal, supporting them not only differentially but in a way that subordinates some, contradicts our most fundamental idea of equality. The developmental equality lens is then essential to achieving the long-delayed goal of equality. It must include not only dismantling systems but also a substantive standard of maximizing developmental potential for every child.

The power of the developmental equality lens, and its potential, explains the developmental arc of Black boys and vice versa: the pattern of Black boys exposes the barriers and added challenges for children at the bottom. This is a synergistic analysis: the model explains the pattern of their development, by telling us where to focus; and their life course substantiates the model, validating the focus on state-created structures and policies. Developmental equality is essential and critical to legal analysis focused on moving the developmental context of Black boys from a toxic ecology of predictable harm and hopelessness, or even death, to a supportive path valuing their identities, individuality, and opportunities. A 2015 study measured whether adolescents and young adults twelve through twenty-five thought it was likely that they would reach age thirty-five; only half of Blacks thought they would reach age thirty-five, compared to 66 percent of whites (Warner and Swisher 2015). The expectations were even lower for second-generation Mexican Americans (46 percent) and for foreign-born Mexicans (38 percent) (id.). The sharp differential between whites as compared to teenagers and young adults of color illustrates their differential read of the developmental context and what awaits them as adults (id.).

The example of Black boys illuminates, through the developmental equality model, all children who are currently tracked for a life of inequality. Using the developmental equality model in legal analysis is critical to expose structural and cultural factors that underlie the persistence of those inequalities, as a foundation for attacking those sources of inequity via litigation or public policy strategies. It is essential in using this model to draw upon theoretical perspectives and insights that ensure its radical potential. In the following chapter I draw upon critical theory, vulnerabilities theory, economic inequalities analysis, and children's rights to strengthen the developmental equality model before embarking on an exploration of strategies for change in Part III.

7

Theory

The life course of Black boys from birth to eighteen outlined in Part I exposes how the deck is stacked developmentally, as if we marked cribs by race and gender at birth to create hierarchies among children. Such hierarchies, not limited to the example of Black boys, are untenable because they are unfair, immoral, and a waste of talent and human capacity. The case of Black boys reminds us to pay attention to the patterns of inequalities among children, which track historic and present bases of discrimination: race, gender, and class. Our goal as a nation should not be to change the distribution but to eliminate the hierarchies among children and replace them with an equal start for all children and youth.

Developmental equality requires that the trajectory for every child's development no longer be affected, undermined, or challenged by the actions or inactions of the state. Instead, the state would support the ability of all children to reach their developmental potential. We will know we have reached developmental equality when the data about Black boys tell us that they are supported as children and can be successful as adults and citizens. We will know we have reached developmental equality when the other children at the bottom of the hierarchies among children reach their developmental potential and have the tools to exercise their right to equality of opportunity, and realize that opportunity in fact. Until the hierarchies among children disappear, we must ask and continue to ask whether children are unequal by race, gender, class, or those identities in combination. We must ask if other identity factors continue to trigger differential developmental outcomes. Given the deeply entrenched, embedded nature of children's inequalities, it will be necessary to monitor ongoing developmental equality, and be responsive to signs of any return to policies or practices that render children unequal.

Developmental equality asserts the right of all children to claim positive support and assistance from the state to achieve their full developmental potential. This positive support is grounded in their dependency on others to achieve their developmental potential and their right that such support be provided to all children to ensure their equal opportunity to develop to their full potential. It necessarily implicates a broad context because children's development is affected by multiple layers of the ecology. This assumes a standard of developmental support that is robust and meaningful in relation to the equal opportunity of every child. Developmental support would be grounded in empirical evidence of what is necessary for children to grow and thrive. Such data must be critically analyzed to ensure that purportedly "neutral" developmental markers are not culturally biased. Finally, this is not a minimum standard of bare adequacy. Such a standard would merely reinscribe inequalities with a kinder, gentler reality for the children whom we typically find at the bottom of the hierarchy of children. Equality demands a standard that would eliminate entirely developmental hierarchies among children. Developmental differences might remain linked to personal characteristics, but not to hierarchies expressed in structural or cultural barriers.

An equality framework, as a starting point, would include positive rights that generate state obligations; social equality and justice rights responsive to the needs of the most marginalized; and children's rights grounded in children's dependency on adults for developmental growth and success, as the basis for the responsibility of the state to address their developmental needs and unequal starting points.

Achieving developmental equality would require reform and dismantling of existing structures. So, for example, those aspects of the existing educational structure that create differential achievement outcomes would be addressed. Similarly, those aspects of the juvenile justice system that do not foster child well-being and community safety would be dismantled as ineffective and counterproductive. Beyond reform and recasting of existing structures is the necessity of constructing new policies and practices to ensure children's equality. Child poverty is a problem that requires a comprehensive solution. Early childhood, where support of families as well as provision of high-quality child care, health care, and early childhood education are essential, is another critical area requiring new policies to achieve developmental equality. Supporting families means providing a linked set of policies in relation to income, employment, housing, neighborhood programs, and supports so that the immediate ecology of all children supports their maximum development. Critical to this process is structural support but also cultural validation and respect.

The process of dismantling and reform, as well as construction and support, necessitates the use of theoretical tools to enrich the developmental equality model and inform strategies. Theory helps to construct the arguments to establish state responsibility, to frame reform or create new policies, and to monitor for equality in children's outcomes. Theory helps us to see more clearly what is, and to construct change more likely to achieve equality, being aware of the tendency of hierarchy to reconstitute itself. It helps us to define what equality is, from this context of dramatic inequalities, and to be cautious in constructing ways to achieve equality. Theory helps to keep the lens true. The developmental side of the model provides us with the ultimate goal for all children and the insights into how inequalities impact the developmental dynamic and developmental norms. The equality side helps us to understand the dynamic that constructs hierarchies among children and what is needed strategically to move toward equality. Core theoretical pieces for developmental equality are identities theory, vulnerabilities theory, poverty/income inequality analysis, and children's rights.

Identities Theory

It is clear from the example of Black boys that we can only reach developmental equality by taking identities into account, and by being consciously intersectional, paying attention to how critical identities function interactively, not simply in isolation. Identities tell us which children are rendered unequal, what structures/institutions fail them, as well as what supports are needed. When you take identities into account, it exposes the sources of inequalities as structural and cultural mechanisms *that are connected to the state.* Just as significantly, identity has a positive role that is developmentally critical, essential to the strength of subordinated children. This also exposes the different construction of identity for privileged children, and its role in their lives and opportunities, which must be addressed. So to reach developmental equality, we must be race-, gender-, and class-conscious, not neutral, while universal in our dedication to maximizing children's development.

Critical race theory (CRT) and gender theory provide core insights. Central tenets of critical race theory include a rejection of the simple narrative of historical racial progress by focusing on patterns of retrenchment that reconstitute inequality (Carbado 2011, 1607). The deeply embedded nature of racism means the location is structural and comprehensive; as Culp puts it, "race is only skin deep but white supremacy runs to the bone" (Culp 1999, 1638). It is multisystemic, sophisticated, and reactive to change in a way that sustains racial power (Guinier and Torres 2003). Formal equality doctrines fail to address this deep systemic location of subordination, while also defending hierarchy through the principle of color blindness, even treating whites as a racial group in need of protection. Critical race theory identifies the coexistence of subordination with white privilege, sustaining and conferring power on whites, affirmatively protecting them and elevating their position (Harris 1995). CRT calls for color consciousness, remaining focused on structural sources of subordination, and the necessity of cultural transformation (Lawrence 1995; Eisenberg and Johnson 2008; Blasi 2002; Kang 2005; Cook and Weiss 2016). Part of unpeeling deeper racial dynamics is incorporating interdisciplinary research, such as social science data on implicit bias and stereotypes, reminding us of what happens "automatically" but which is nevertheless constructed, and so capable of change.

Although originating in race analysis, CRT embraces intersectionality and multidimensional analysis (Crenshaw et al. 1995; Culp, Harris, and Valdes 2003; Hutchinson 2002). Black feminists challenged feminist analysis to reflect the differential experiences and needs of women, instead of an implicit white women's model (Collins 1998). At the same time, they were critical of CRT for failing to incorporate gender analysis, thus privileging the experience of men of color (and dominantly Black men). Intersectionality is important for reinforcing that the argument for developmental equality, and the use of the data about Black boys, is meant not to elevate or prioritize Black boys but to present them as an example, one of many. As Paul Butler eloquently argues, Black boys and men are an example of intersectionality but should not claim to be exceptional or of higher priority: "the unique raced and gendered discrimination that they face [should be recognized], but that does not position them as the racial standard bearers, obscure the problems of Black women, or advance patriarchal values" (Butler 2013a, 486).

In addition, the example of Black boys and men must recognize their gender privilege in relation to Black girls and women, in addition to their subordination in the hierarchies of masculinities (Dowd 2010). Masculinities theories urge us to pay attention to hierarchies among men as well as men's subordination of women and how intersections with race, class, and sexual orientation are critical to the interplay of privilege and disadvantage for men and among men, and to those conditions under which male privilege is entirely trumped (Dowd 2010). For Black boys this means their involvement with structures that project masculine norms but are hierarchical by race and class. Indeed, class is an equally critical characteristic that dramatically affects how systems operate and for whose benefit or detriment (Forman 2012).

Patricia Hill Collins demonstrates the way intersectionality reveals a more intricate series of patterns of discrimination: "In a fundamental way, African American women are caught in the crossfire of two different ways of organizing groups. Race, class, nation and ethnicity all rely heavily on segregation and other *exclusionary* practices to maintain hierarchy. In contrast . . . gender relies more heavily on surveillance and other *inclusionary* strategies of control targeted toward the proximate other" (Collins 1998, 223, emphasis added). Prioritizing or defining the content of racial solidarity to exclude gender, or gender solidarity to exclude race, uses one form of resistance to subordination to reinforce another hierarchy of subordination (id.). Differences within intersectional groups are also important to recognize, to not essentialize those groups: all Black girls or all Black women are not the same. At the same time, although particularity is essential, it does not erase commonality: "when it comes to oppression, there are essentials" (id., 224). The commonality is in subordination, not in its effects (id.).

Complexity analysis, another variant of intersectionality analysis, reminds us that an identified gender system is likely not acting solely on one axis (Dowd, Levit, and McGinley 2012). Thus, every time a system might appear to be gendered in a particular way, it is critical to "ask the other question(s)" (Matsuda 1991): If we think the problem is linked to how we see boys, how does this construct girls? How does it construct race? Does it reflect class hierarchies? Are there other identities, such as sexual orientation or disability that generate subordinating or unequal outcomes? The goal is to identify interconnections and aggregation of systems and types of bias and subordination, and how they operate at different levels and in different ways. This generates knowledge to root out subordination, not exceptionalism or hierarchy.

Identities analysis, in sum, provides tools that keep us focused on individual aspects of identity as well as intersectional or multiple identity interactions; identifies structural sources, and the interaction of structures, as critical sites of subordination; and identifies the functioning of culture, in addition to status, as a critical mechanism justifying and rationalizing inequality. For developmental equality, identities theories suggest that it is essential to identify structures that fail to serve all children, by serving children hierarchically; pay attention to the interaction of structures; interrogate and rework developmental norms; and recognize that when you take identities into account, it reframes analysis of what is going on, the sources of inequalities. It also reinforces how essential it is to monitor systems given the historical reconfiguration of hierarchies and the ability of the dominant group to domesticate even the most radical reforms, or reverse them.

Vulnerabilities Theory and the Responsive State

The focus on the structural, so critical to identities theory, is also central to vulnerabilities theory. Vulnerabilities theory conceptualizes the role of the state as a responsive state (Fineman 2008, 2010). This obligation is triggered by the universal human condition of vulnerability, or vulnerabilities, and the role of the state in responding to vulnerabilities, and doing so fairly and justly. Critical to the use of this analysis is how a standard beneficial to all can also benefit the principle of equality. One key proposition should be that the state should not create vulnerabilities, or exacerbate them. And if the state is committed to providing support, it should be bound to do so for all who are vulnerable in that respect (id.). Vulnerability is not the same as weakness or incapacity; it is important to note that vulnerability is also a positive characteristic, critical to healthy relationships, and characteristic of openness and receptiveness to learning (Brown 2010).

Vulnerabilities theory centers around our common humanity: we are all vulnerable in some respects, and that links us to dependency on each other and/or on the state (Fineman and Grear 2013; Turner 2006).

Children, then, are inherently vulnerable, although this changes as they reach adulthood. Conceptualizing the "person" or "human" as inevitably and essentially vulnerable is starkly different from the autonomous subject of the liberal state. If the state is organized around human vulnerabilities, then its role is to be a responsible and responsive state, and to respond equally (id.). The goal is to foster resilience, through shared responsibility between state, society, and the individual. This is a focus on the universal and emphasizes commonness rather than differences. The rights of individuals are rights claimed because of their humanity, not because of socially created entitlements (id.). It articulates a theory of the state and the subject that translates into affirmative duties and positive rights. It was conceived as a way to transcend the limitations of existing equality jurisprudence while remaining responsive to inequalities along identity lines (Fineman and Grear 2013). It also draws upon universal concepts and arguments of human rights discourse (id.). At the same time, it incorporates the particular because no individual should be favored or disfavored, and each person is individually situated. "The nature of human vulnerability and the process of building resilience through institutions mandate the state to be active, involved, and responsive to vulnerability—monitoring institutions and better ensuring that the promise of equality of access and opportunity is realized" (id., 2–3).

Fineman would reject using identities theories because of the limited scope of current equality doctrines, and because she argues that they feed into a dialectic of individual responsibility and deviance rather than the universality of dependency and vulnerability (id.). Her focus is structural, on the assumed and actual role of the state, and interrogating that role to require benefit as needed and to benefit all equally. The benefit of vulnerability as the focus is facilitating interconnected, interdependent, collective approaches (id., 26). Vulnerabilities theory shares and derives from a human rights focus; seeing humans in terms of "vulnerability, dependency, reciprocity and precariousness" from which rights are derived and obligations of the state (Turner 2006). Within this framework, multiculturalism requires, according to one scholar, "sustained economic growth and opportunities for social mobility, especially for minority groups; a national, secular education system that contributes to social mobility and integrates children of different ethnic and religious traditions; freedom to choose marriage partners, high rates of intermarriage, and liberal divorce laws; and finally, the rule of law and a government that is overtly committed to policies supporting multiculturalism" (id., 140).

Frank Rudy Cooper has pointed to the valuable intersection between identities theory and vulnerabilities theory, but is skeptical about using vulnerabilities theory alone (Cooper 2015). I remain convinced as well that paying attention to identities is central to inequalities and to achieving equality. Cooper is concerned that vulnerabilities analysis alone, without the insights of identities theory, could sustain subordination rather than dismantle it. As Cooper succinctly states, "Identities, while socially constructed, are materially crucial" (id., 1347). Consistent with scholars who have identified white favoritism as co-constitutive with anti Black bias, Cooper suggests that the conferral of privilege along identity lines should be incorporated with vulnerability analysis. Will Kymlicka similarly argues that "it is legitimate, and indeed unavoidable, to supplement traditional human rights with minority rights. A comprehensive theory of justice in a multicultural state will include both universal rights, assigned to individuals regardless of group membership, and certain group-differentiated rights or 'special status' for minority cultures [that are both protective of culture and to ensure equality]" (Kymlicka 1995, 6).

Vulnerabilities theory adds to what identities theories have to offer by reinforcing the focus on the structural; articulating a theory of a responsive state that justifies positive rights; and encouraging strategic choices that link to universal human rights. Children because of their dependency easily fit the theory as vulnerable subjects. They are dependent on others but also represent the positive definition of vulnerability as essential to maximum human development. Differential support of children and the creation of negative barriers to their development violate the state's responsibilities by imposing negative vulnerabilities and doing so differentially, while also shutting down positive vulnerability critical to healthy adult relationships. The insight from the analysis of the life course of Black boys is that Black children and youth, and others at the bottom of children's hierarchies, suffer intensified negative vulnerabilities due to state structures that harm them or fail them because of their identities.

Economic Inequality

Analysis of poverty and income inequality, and its intersection with racial inequality, provides additional perspective critical to strategic thinking. Children at the bottom of hierarchies among children are frequently linked by economic factors. The work of several scholars particularly reinforces the structural focus from both identities and vulnerabilities analysis, as well as suggesting particular strategic policies. They also underscore the intersection of multiple systems in the creation and sustaining of poverty, economic inequality, and its profoundly racial pattern.

Barbara Reskin masterfully summarizes the disparities in interlocking systems of what she terms the "race discrimination system," using a systems theory approach, and argues it is critical to simultaneously address the interlocking systems (Reskin 2012). She identifies housing, employment, health, education, credit, and justice as critical systems. She emphasizes structure plus the interacting nature of separate structures (such as, in my description of Black boys, the poverty system, educational system, and juvenile justice system). "These domains are reciprocally related and comprise an integrated system. A system of race-linked disparities . . . is a meta-level phenomenon that shapes our culture, cognitions, and institutions, thereby distorting whether and how we perceive and make sense of racial disparities" (id., 17). Thus she connects structures to culture, our understanding and rationalization of the inequalities we see and experience. Interventions to deal with this interlocking system must operate simultaneously on the interacting systemic pieces. She calls the systemic interaction a discrimination system writ large and identifies three aspects of the system: "(a) disparities *systematically favor certain groups*, (b) disparities across subsystems are *mutually reinforcing*, and (c) one source of within-subsystem disparities is *discrimination*" (id., 19). The discrimination is tied to a comprehensive belief system that is reinforced by observed disparities. She argues the focus of change should be *leverage points* in the systems, and *simultaneous action* on an entire system that must be robust and comprehensive.

Douglas Massey and Nancy Denton similarly focus on the intersection of systems, particularly those that rely on geographic segregation to sustain poverty. They would argue the leverage point is housing (Massey and Denton 1993). "Residential segregation is the principal structural feature of American society responsible for the perpetuation of urban poverty. . . . Deleterious neighborhood conditions are built into the structure of the [B]lack community. They occur because segregation concentrates poverty to build a set of mutually reinforcing and self-feeding spirals of decline into [B]lack neighborhoods" (id., viii). Segregation builds an intersecting set of systems that perpetuates poverty for Black neighborhoods (id.). Massey and Denton underscore the role of government in creating and sustaining housing segregation, and the weakness of the Fair Housing Act as a vehicle to reverse this discriminatory pattern (id.). Ian Haney-Lopez, using Massey and Denton, calls this the *racial stratification system*, that is, the unequal system created as a result of structural racism. As he points out, "racial categories arise and persist in conjunction with efforts to exploit and exclude" (Haney-Lopez 2010b, 1027).

William Darity describes this process as *stratification economics*: "[t]he 'positional arrangements of the racial groups.' . . . Race prejudice or racism is functional. . . . It promotes a set of structured, cumulative advantages for certain socially marked groups and structured, cumulative disadvantages for others. It is a cornerstone of group-based inequality" (Darity 2009, 804). Rather than a focus on slavery exclusively, Darity's analysis includes legal segregation under Jim Crow and ongoing discrimination in the post–Jim Crow era (id.). This yields persistent poverty. Moreover, the benefit to those at the top from cumulative advantage is justified by racial ideology that justifies the position of those at the top. It is functional and beneficial for those at the top, linked to their material well-being. Darity argues the remedy is restitution: to put the victims of stratification economics in the position that they would have been in had discrimination not occurred, meaning "the adoption of a national program that would eliminate racial disparities in wealth, income, education, health, political participation, and future opportunity to engage in American social life" (id., 795).

Or as Charles Tilly puts it, exploitation and opportunity hoarding are exercised to the benefit of privileged groups over subordinated groups (Tilly 1998, 9). *Durable inequality*, as he calls it, rests in institutions that affect opportunity and mobility (id., 21). Economic advantage is hard-wired; as one group of scholars points out, the historical example of the New Deal, constructed to deal with widespread economic harm, was to construct support systems that systematically excluded by race (Brown, Barbarin, and Scott 2013). These institutions function using allegedly neutral principles that effectively exclude such that dominant whites never notice their race privilege: "the last thing a fish notices is the water," and the last thing white people notice is their race (Tilly 1998, 34).

William Julius Wilson, the renowned poverty scholar who has tracked the class transformation of urban neighborhoods, similarly identifies the construction of poverty and its concentration in racially segregated neighborhoods based on federal policies in housing, roads, and postwar benefits (Wilson 2009, 38). His work confirms the responsibility of the state, the hand of the state, in creating poverty and its racial identification. He emphasizes not only the role of structures, but the interaction of structures and culture in resolving the issues created by poverty, although he identifies structures as primary (id.). He calls for race- and class-based solutions to effect change (Wilson 2011a, 2011b) and particularly highlights the essential problem of joblessness (Wilson 2011a).

A recent study exposing this comprehensive system from the perspective of teenagers is Carla Shedd's work detailing the very different worlds of low-income kids of color in Chicago depending on whether they remain in their largely segregated neighborhood or migrate into the world outside their neighborhood and experience a differential structure of opportunity (Shedd 2015). Shedd's ten-year study of Chicago teenage kids of color found that kids who transcended the boundaries of their segregated, low-income neighborhood to attend schools with greater opportunities were exposed to worlds beyond their neighborhood, but that opportunity also communicated stigma, as students most often felt subordinated, not equal, to their peers (id., 58). Shedd's work begs the question of whether the solutions lie in destroying concentrated poverty, a model of integration in some form, or transforming those neighborhoods.

Patrick Sharkey's compelling analysis and solutions to issues of poverty combine research about families, neighborhoods/communities, and intergenerational patterns (Sharkey 2013). He reinforces the interconnected systems in geographic space that constitute poverty. He concludes that poverty persists because of community subordination that links to generational replication of lack of opportunity. This multisystemic locus of poverty reinforces its continuance; solving poverty similarly must be multisystemic but also locally oriented. His solutions, highlighted in the final chapter, provide a concrete way to address poverty.

The work of scholars who have focused on economic factors, income inequality, and race underscores the interconnectedness of structural inequality and its geography. It also reminds us that developmental equality cannot be achieved without a comprehensive attack on poverty. Sharkey's argument for neighborhood and transgenerational change is persuasive in particular from the ecology of Black boys because their families and neighborhoods provide such developmental strengths critical to their positive identity. This positive factor is retained and sustained by Sharkey's solution, providing a way to developmental equality that values the strengths of communities of color.

Children's Rights

A final set of tools critical to developmental equality comes from children's rights. As with the prior theoretical perspectives, children's rights keeps us focused on the structural and interconnected systems, but it also returns us to identifying and defining what children need and are entitled to because of their status. Children are distinctive. Developmental theory and evidence is a strong argument for the necessity of support for children to achieve their developmental potential. The argument is grounded in needs, dependency, and vulnerabilities, as well as evolving capacity and agency. Just as important, it is grounded in their equality, an equality of opportunity measured by developmental outcomes. Their claim is one of equality, justice, and human rights.

The United Nations Convention on the Rights of the Child (CRC), although not adopted by the United States, is nevertheless a critical starting point to think broadly about children's rights. The four key principles of the CRC are the best interests of the child (Art. 3); the right to life, survival, and development (Art. 6, Art. 5, evolving capacities); the right to equality or nondiscrimination (Art. 2); and respect for the voice of children/their empowerment (Art. 5). These principles encompass the notion of the state's positive obligations to children, and where those obligations lie. Developmental equality draws on the intersection between developmental rights, equality rights, and the best interests of children (Dowd 2016b). The CRC is a comprehensive framework that has enjoyed worldwide acceptance in principle even if it is differentiated and uneven in application (Gal 2011).

At the outset, it should be noted that the CRC has its limitations. For one, there is no implementation mechanism or litigation mechanism (Fottrell 2000; Todres, Wojcik, and Revaz 2006). Second, as Michael Freeman, among others, points out, this universalist frame can mask differences among children in social contexts where class, gender, ethnicity, race, and culture matter (Freeman 2012). So childhood cannot be understood without those variables; it cannot be universalist without rendering children's inequalities invisible. Others go further, critiquing the framework and conception of the CRC as Westernized, essentialist, and less relevant to the Global South (Hanson and Nieuwenhuys 2013). Even with these critiques and cautions, children's rights has a rich body of knowledge because of the widespread adoption of the CRC and nearly universal (the United States being the exception) adoption of this macro-level set of values and dialogue. It therefore provides the potential for a starting framework of both universal entitlement and attention to equality that is responsive to the existing unequal hierarchies among children, and draws upon the metrics, experiences, and policies of other countries confronting hierarchies among their children. Its shortcomings can be guideposts to a refinement, not a basis for rejection of the value of the CRC.

Some scholars would ground a reframed analysis for children in the more clearly established realm of family rights. Maxine Eichner, for example, makes a strong case for support of *families*, in order to ensure children's positive rights to care (Eichner 2010). She would articulate this claim within the well-established recognition of the importance of family autonomy and privacy from intervention by the state, but expand this to include stronger family support. Children's needs would remain primarily served by their families. Eichner agrees on the identification of needs, but argues her approach is more likely to persuade policy makers and other decision makers by expanding the scope of children's support from within existing legal frameworks rather than displacing them, or adding an express children's rights regime.

On the other hand, Anne Dailey would argue for less of a focus on the hierarchical model of family law that so strongly supports parents, and instead would orient from the perspective of children (Dailey 2011, 2016). Dailey argues for children's right to care as essential to develop cognitive abilities necessary to achieve autonomy. She looks to developmental theory to determine what children need to attain independence, and argues that leads to the critical role of family, particularly in children's early development, and therefore children's "fundamental rights in the caregiving relationship," including "a minimum level of caregiving services from the state" (Dailey 2011, 2103–4). Dailey characterizes children's rights as "transitional rights," their rights as they shift from complete dependency to independence (Dailey 2016). She articulates their rights to include relational rights not solely with respect to their parents but with respect to all relationships in their lives, defined from the child's perspective.

Barbara Bennett Woodhouse, probably the best known and leading advocate for children's rights, offers the most powerful model for children's rights, grounded in their needs and capacities within an ecological perspective inspired by the work of Bronfenbrenner. If the ecology is not supportive, children will not do well; and their dependency gives them nowhere else to turn and insufficient agency to chart their course individually. The interlocking systems of the ecology—health, education, housing, relief from poverty and food scarcity—must work synergistically for children's positive support, through the support of families, neighborhoods, and communities in all systems, as well as at the macro level of culture and ideas. Instead of the individualistic tradition that ignores the needs of children, children's rights would support their positive claim, and their equal claims (Woodhouse 2008b; Freeman 2011b).

Woodhouse's model is worth considering in detail; her framework provides a critical vision that identifies some of the macro-level challenges to implementation of a vision for developmental equality. In *Hidden in Plain Sight*, she argues that core principles of children's rights are embedded in American history and law, paralleling the provisions of human rights and specifically of the CRC (Woodhouse 2008a). Not only does this mean that the United States' failure to adopt the CRC does not make sense, but her analysis suggests CRC principles in fact are already embedded in our law. She identifies five core human rights values in U.S. culture: privacy, equality, protection, dignity, and autonomy. She links those to a fundamental conception of children's rights that captures the fluidity and evolving nature of children: rights that are *needs-based* and *capacity-based*. Her framework for thinking about children's rights is grounded in developmental and ecological concepts, or *ecogenerism*. The "eco" part links to the developmental principles of Bronfenbrenner and others and focuses on structural and cultural components to children's well-being through the layers of the ecology. The "generism" side is her articulation of the core value of society's responsibility to children: "that quality of commitment to the flourishing of the next generation that exemplifies human maturity" (id., 30). The ultimate claim of rights, she argues, is a moral one.

Of particular importance to developmental equality is her articulation of the equality principle, and the responsibilities it generates. She points out how important equality of opportunity is for children: "This principle seems especially important in the lives of children, who inherit at birth the inequalities that shaped their parents' lives. Applying the twin measures of children's needs and their capacities for autonomy to equality rights for children would refocus our sights on creating an environment for children that supports their capacities for growth and achievement of their natural potential" (id., 39). But that focus on opportunity cannot ignore the unequal position from which children begin: "[N]o scheme of rights for children can ignore the fact that children do not begin life on an even playing field. A society committed to the values of equality will strive to give all children a fair start on their developmental journey and a fair chance at arriving safely at their destination" (id., 40).

What most gets in the way of implementing this kind of world for children is the American commitment to individualism and seeing children as a private responsibility: "It will not be possible to accomplish [early childhood] reforms as long as Americans view care and education during early childhood as an individual responsibility of persons who choose to have children rather than as a shared investment in our human capital infrastructure that benefits society as a whole" (id., 160). In her current work, she reemphasizes the further deterioration of children's ecologies in the United States and elsewhere as the result of the Great Recession of 2008 as well as more generally the forces of globalism, capitalism, technology, and inequality (Woodhouse, forthcoming). One might argue that for those intergenerationally trapped at the bottom, it has been toxic for a long time. Woodhouse reiterates the importance of significant investment in children for their benefit and society's benefit that rests in large part on the embrace of a principle of solidarity. She powerfully articulates the importance of equality of resources in addition to equality of opportunity for children:

> Is poverty something to be cured or something to be escaped? This question exposes the different roles of mobility and solidarity. Solidarity is that sense of relationship to others that makes us want to help our neighbor in distress instead of turning away or blaming him for his condition of dependency. How we define our family and our neighborhood and how we draw boundaries of solidarity has profound effects on the ecology of childhood. (id., 22)

The core framework distilled from Woodhouse includes the following elements: that we (1) approach developmental equality ecologically (interconnected systems, structure, and culture); (2) define equality as meaning a fair start and fair chance with resources provided in light of where children start, which is not equally; (3) conceptualize children's rights as a combination of needs-based rights and capacity-based rights; (4) recognize that this will require redistribution of resources based on principles of solidarity and precautionary/prevention of risk; and (5) remain vigilant against the threats to children's ecology not only from inequality but also from globalism, unrestrained capitalism, and technology.

Children's rights therefore provides an expanded mechanism to confront the inequalities that plague children and families, and offers a powerful strategy to confront equality as a whole. Supporting, even mandating, action by the state is essential to provide real opportunities to the children of today who face daunting intersectional structural inequalities that may further rigidify our persisting race and class inequalities. Through the eyes of children, it might be clearer to see our way forward.

And where does theory lead? Where can keeping these elements in mind take us? Borrowing from Patricia Hill Collins, my goal is "visionary pragmatism," a clear view of equality and concrete ways to take steps to move in that direction (Collins 1998, 228). In Part III, I consider statutory and constitutional litigation strategies, as well as what I conclude is the more likely path to achieve developmental equality, a set of public policies to establish a New Deal for Children.

PART III

Strategies

8

ACEs and Compton

A Strategy for Change?

The developmental equality model points to the necessity of systemic change as well as a more nuanced application of developmental principles throughout legal regimes affecting children in order to achieve the equality of all children. Are there existing statutory frameworks to achieve those ends? If so, then developmental equality can utilize those frameworks as a starting point. Antidiscrimination statutes such as Title VI (Glennon 2011) or other regulatory models requiring attention to and solutions for racial disproportionality (Johnson 2007) would seem to provide a possible avenue to reach race discrimination. But neither of those approaches has an intersectional approach nor a foundation to incorporate a developmental norm. A recent California case is closer to combining a developmental norm with an equality norm, using disability and education laws (*P.P. v. Compton Unified School District* 2015). This innovative lawsuit against the Compton school district uses developmental research and the cutting-edge tool of ACEs (Adverse Childhood Experiences) to craft a system-wide claim for meaningful, developmentally sound education for the children of Compton. Because this might serve as a step toward developmental equality, this chapter takes a close look at the case and, in particular, at ACEs as a tool for change.

Compton, located in Los Angeles County, south of Los Angeles, is a predominantly working-class city of roughly a hundred thousand (City-Data.com 2016). The racial makeup of the city is 56.7 percent Latino, 39.8 percent Black, 1.4 percent Asian, 1.3 percent other, and 0.8 percent white. Median income is approximately $43,000; 22.4 percent of households are headed by single parents. The city has a higher rate of violent crime and property crime than the average U.S. city. Infamous for danger and crime, Compton is also famous as the birthplace of rap musicians and was popularized in the movie *Straight Outta Compton*. The city is served by a single school district, the Compton Unified School District (Compton Unified School District 2016).

P. P. v. Compton Unified School District, filed May 18, 2015, in the District Court for the Central District of California, was brought by the Public Counsel Law Center and Irell & Manella, LLP (id.). The lawsuit asserts that the district, with knowledge of the circumstances of the community that it serves, and the experiences confronted by many of its students, has a duty to take those ecological factors into account system-wide to fulfill its duty to provide an adequate public education to the students. Federal disability statutes are the primary basis for the claims, as those statutes require that students with disabilities be accommodated and provided services so that they can be educated (*P.P. v. Compton Unified School District Complaint* 2015). The student plaintiffs stand for all students in the district for whom the district has failed to provide an education; the teachers stand for all teachers who have been secondarily affected by working with students within a system that ignores student needs.

The *Compton* claims rest on a foundation of developmental science as applied to the particular circumstances of the named plaintiffs, as well as the pervasiveness of such experiences given the ecology of the community. Developmental research, including the ACEs framework, as well as work detailing the impact of poverty, racism, and community violence, is the basis for asserting that the experience of trauma due to individual and community-wide factors affects children as they develop, and therefore their ability to learn, because of its impact on their cognitive, socioemotional, and physical development. For the children in Compton, trauma is linked not only to unique, singular, traumatic events but also to persistent, daily trauma, creating conditions of complex trauma. Exposure to complex trauma affects learning abilities and behavior in ways that conflict with achievement goals and expectations about discipline; it can also generate mental health issues that create needs for therapy and particular mental health interventions to support individual children.

According to the complaint, the knowledge that these conditions exist in Compton is a given, and so is the knowledge of their impact. In order to educate children in such a community, what is required is a holistic, whole-school approach that is trauma-sensitive. This would include three key components: training all staff, establishing supportive practices

framed around building resilience for all students, and providing specifically focused mental health services as needed to individual students
(*P.P. v. Compton Unified School District Complaint* 2015). The obligation
to engage in such an approach, the complaint alleges, is linked to the
school district's obligation to provide an appropriate education to the
students of its community under the conditions in the community and
to inform parents of their children's right to support in order to learn.
Failure to provide such support is analogized to the segregated school
systems struck down in *Brown v. Board of Education*. Failure to support students who experience complex trauma translates into a denial
of education because the district fails to deal with the known disabilities
of a disproportionate number of students. Just as a student with a hear-
ing or sight disability would be denied an education without support,
or a student with a physical disability who is excluded from buildings
and classrooms would be denied an education, so too the students who
come to school affected by complex trauma that goes unaddressed are
effectively excluded from an education. Moreover, they are also subject
to harsh disciplinary policies, suspension, and expulsion. In "alternative"
schools they are treated harshly and often excluded again. Such policies
and practices exacerbate and retraumatize students.

The demographic and community data about Compton is irrefutable
information about poverty, violence, and the rate of other traumatic
events. The linchpin of the lawsuit, however, is the impact of those conditions on students. For it is the theory of this lawsuit that because these
toxic factors are known and widespread, and their impact on students
is known, the school is obligated to approach the education of their students differently. Otherwise students are functionally excluded from
an education, and thus excluded from an opportunity critical to their
life chances that is guaranteed by the state. Because the conditions in
the community are so pervasive, the school's response must not be particular and individual, but system-wide. In essence, the suit is aiming
at structural change, one as massive as *Brown v. Board of Education*.
Its potential is therefore enormous. But the lawsuit also has its limits
and potential downsides. Viewed from the perspective of the goal of
developmental equality, these negatives argue not for pulling back from
Compton, but rather for considering it as only a first step, using a very
blunt but available instrument to begin to address a much broader set

of problems. Treating this as the primary strategy, however, would only reinforce the very problems it tries to address.

The Science: The Foundation for *Compton*

A critical foundation for the *Compton* case is the use and application of ACEs research. Developmental research and the developmental equality model expose the developmental hurdles typically faced by Black boys in general terms. ACEs focus on specific traumas identified as having particularly negative long-term effects. According to the linear developmental perspective described in Chapter 5, early childhood is one of the most critical developmental periods. As Bronfenbrenner points out, ecologies of development, his nested layers, either can positively support development if they are healthy and mutually supportive, or can have negative consequences if levels or interconnections are dysfunctional or in conflict with each other. Neuroscience confirms Bronfenbrenner's ecological model, demonstrating the critical role of environment and experience in childhood development, especially in early childhood. Developmental equality reminds us that identity characteristics like race, gender, and class alone and in combination can trigger developmental risks and experiences and define context in ways that undermine families, neighborhoods, and communities. Both Spencer and García Coll emphasize how this plays out structurally in health care, education, juvenile justice, and other systems.

Compton attempts to incorporate this broad developmental knowledge, and in addition adds the ACEs framework. Research using ACEs connects childhood adversity to long-term outcomes, first in connection to health, and more broadly to developmental impacts that affect learning, achievement, and educational opportunity (Felitti et al. 1998). The original ACEs study published in 1998 was a collaboration between the Centers for Disease Control and Prevention (CDC) and Kaiser Permanente, the large health maintenance organization (HMO) centered in California. The study was designed to explore the possible links between childhood experiences and adult health outcomes and behaviors (id.). The original study was exploratory, asking a series of questions to the HMO's clients about their childhood (Anda 2009). The mean age of study participants was fifty-six; they were dominantly white (75 percent) and middle class (39 percent were college graduates), and were divided roughly equally between women and men (9,367 women, 7,970 men) (CDC 2016a). The questions participants were asked focused on households and families, particularly whether individuals had been victims of maltreatment (American Academy of Pediatrics 2014). These categories were chosen because of past evidence connecting maltreatment to health outcomes (Anda 2009).

The study found a dramatic and remarkable connection between adverse child experiences in the first eighteen years of life and negative physical and mental health outcomes in adulthood. Those findings have been replicated by many other subsequent studies. The ACE factors that emerged from this initial study continue to be used, and are grouped under categories of abuse (emotional, physical, and sexual abuse factors); neglect (emotional and physical neglect factors); and household dysfunction (mother treated violently, household substance abuse, household mental illness, parental separation or divorce, and incarcerated household member as factors) (CDC 2016a).

An individual's ACEs score is the total number of ACEs present in childhood. In the original ACEs study, two-thirds of the participants had at least one ACE; one out of five reported three or more ACEs (id.). In the original and subsequent studies, as the number of ACEs increases, the risk increases for negative health outcomes, including alcoholism and alcohol abuse, chronic obstructive pulmonary disease, depression, fetal death, low health-related quality of life, illicit drug use, ischemic heart disease, liver disease, intimate partner violence, multiple sexual partners, sexually transmitted diseases, smoking, suicide attempts, unintended pregnancy, early smoking, early sexual activity, and adolescent pregnancy. It is important to remember that one's score is based on the number of experiences one has had with a factor, from one to ten, but there is no further range in scoring based on frequency once one meets the threshold.

One of the most important consequences of the ACEs study was to change the thinking of health care professionals about how individuals are viewed when they present with health problems or when their adherence to good health practices stalls. By extension, other individuals, like teachers or day care providers, similarly might think differently and approach things differently when a child presents with problems or poor school achievement. Instead of asking, "What's wrong with you?" the ACEs framework encourages us to ask, "What happened to you?" This refocuses the evaluation to their environment and experiences, and changes our understanding from individual bad choices to the impact of context on a reasonable child or adult's behavior.

In addition, the ACEs framework focuses attention on the difference between experiencing some trauma (a relatively common experience) and experiencing toxic trauma or complex trauma. It differentiates between some stress, which can be positive, and stress that can be negative and/or toxic. Toxic stress is due to "strong, frequent or prolonged activation of the body's stress response systems in the absence of the buffering protection of a supportive, adult relationship" (American Academy of Pediatrics 2014, 2). When toxic stress is prolonged and involves multiple factors, it is termed "complex trauma." The National Child Traumatic Stress Network differentiates between episode-specific reaction to threatening circumstances (simple trauma) and complex trauma, where the stresses continue, generating an adaptive response that becomes maladaptive as the stressors persist (National Child Traumatic Stress Network 2016).

The worst outcomes can come from "strong" stress (such as the loss of a parent); frequent stress (as from a pattern of intimate partner violence); or prolonged adversity (such as physical neglect that might arise from circumstances of persistent poverty, or the disruptive circumstances of homelessness). The ability of the individual to be resilient in the face of stress is affected most critically by the immediate family structure, as well as the potentially mediating effect of other immediate adults, such as other family members, neighbors, community members, or teachers.

Most importantly for children, a higher ACEs score also has an impact on the likelihood of "learning and behavioral issues" (American Academy of Pediatrics 2014, 2). The negative outcomes are linked to development, especially brain development. As one of the principal investigators on the original ACEs study, Dr. Robert Anda, has noted, "ACEs disrupt neurodevelopment and can have lasting effects on brain structure and function—the biologic pathways that likely explain the strength of the finding from the ACE Study" (Anda 2009, 2). Anda summarizes the key findings of the ACEs research as follows: ACEs are common; multiple ACEs have a very detrimental impact, or can have that

impact in the absence of resilience, due to neurodevelopmental consequences; and the problems that are linked to high ACEs are themselves
also linked (id., 4; Perry 1999, 2007).

The ACEs framework is intimately intertwined with increasing
understanding, largely based in neuroscience and epigenetics, of the
development of the brain, particularly early development. Neuroscience research explains the link between ACEs and the higher risk of
adult negative outcomes for health and overall development (American
Academy of Pediatrics 2014). This does not mean that ACEs are determinative and irreversible. To the contrary, as the American Association
of Pediatrics notes, early experiences have an impact on multiple systems: social/behavioral, neuroendocrine, and genetic. But they are not
determinative: "The ability of an individual to successfully overcome
negative experiences from trauma depends on many factors related to
the complex interaction between these systems" (id., 3). Importantly,
"[c]hildren survive and even thrive despite the trauma in their lives" (id.,
4). Resilience factors include "cognitive capacity, healthy attachment relationships (especially with parents and caregivers), the motivation and
ability to learn and engage with the environment, the ability to regulate
emotions and behavior, and supportive environmental systems, including education, cultural beliefs, and faith-based communities" (id., 4–
5). In addition, programs designed for children who have experienced
ACEs are emerging that focus on building resilience through working
with parents and children.

The interaction of ACEs and development reinforces the important
conclusion not only that ACEs matter but that environmental ecologies matter *even if ACEs are not present*. First, the brain is not complete
at birth, but rather is developing rapidly particularly from birth to age
three (Center on the Developing Child 2007). Second, how the brain
architecture continues to develop is strongly affected by the child's environment (a nurturing, loving, and stimulating environment is key).
Third, caregivers are critical. Fourth, early life experience with trauma
affects the response system to stress and can cause epigenetic modification, so the person's genetic blueprint is modified with respect to stress.
Fifth, there is interaction and reinforcement of these realms that can
produce negative outcomes. So, the social and physical environments
have an impact on biology and development; and changes in the neuro-

endocrine system can affect brain architecture, what pediatrics calls the ecobiodevelopmental model (American Academy of Pediatrics 2014, 4).

Given the critical importance of the early years of development, then, adverse experiences (which ACEs measure) translate into excessive stress that interferes with development (Center on the Developing Child 2014). Overly engaging the stress mechanisms of the brain makes one more vulnerable to mental or physical negative outcomes (for example, depression or anxiety, or diabetes and stroke), producing higher amounts of adrenaline and cortisol, and this affects brain structure. Sustained stress affects learning, memory, and regulation of stress responses. The importance of the neuroscience goes beyond providing an explanatory link for the correlation between ACEs and adverse outcomes. The strong bottom line of the neuroscience literature is that the years from birth to three, or even further, birth to five, are critical to development and to equality in development (Center on the Developing Child 2007, 6–7).

A differential in development might arise not because of a concentration of ACEs with negative implications for development, but rather due to the lack of resources or more limited resources that impact a child's development (Center on the Developing Child 2014, 7). For example, the vocabulary differences that have been measured at eighteen months related to parental education and class are linked to a startling differential in the number of words that children have experienced: higher income children have experienced on average thirty million more words by age three than have low-income children (Hart and Risley 2003). This research identifies the factors that affect development along with programs or interventions that can close the gap, equalizing developmental support and therefore developmental opportunity (Center on the Developing Child 2007).

What is most promising about the neuroscience research is that its bottom line is clear: "Four decades of data from a small number of intensive programs demonstrate that it is possible to improve a wide range of outcomes for vulnerable children well into the adult years, as well as generate benefits to society that far exceed program cost" (Center on the Developing Child 2007, 2; Huebner et al. 2016). A strong surrounding environment provides the basis for the best development of brain architecture: because the brain is developing at a fast rate, the rate of development and the nature of development depend on experiences, and on interaction and relationships with others. The research identifies "effectiveness factors" in the first five years of life as well as specific successful programs in some areas: (1) medical care during pregnancy and proactive care for children; (2) early and strong support for vulnerable families, particularly home visiting programs that benefit both the parents and the child (like the Nurse Family Partnership); (3) high-quality child care and preschool programs (like the Abecedarian Program); (4) support programs for families with significant adversity that target both the child and the parent, with full services organized around the provision of child care and early education (like the Perry Preschool and Head Start programs); (5) intensive services for children who have experienced toxic stress from abuse, neglect, parental depression, domestic violence; (6) income supplements for families below the poverty line, linked to parental employment; (7) reducing environmental neurotoxins; and (8) delivering supports that are responsive to the child and to the community (Center on the Developing Child 2007, 3–5).

This work emphasizes that development from birth to three is intensive in multiple domains: cognitive, linguistic, social, emotional, and motor (id.). The environment of development is critical: "When inadequate stimulation is provided or barriers to opportunities for productive learning exist, these can lead to early disparities in capability that generally persist in the absence of effective intervention" (id., 7). These differences appear by eighteen months, and the gap widens if the environmental differential goes unaddressed. Between three and five, "increasingly complex social behaviors, emotional capacities, problem-solving abilities, and pre-literacy skills [are developed]. . . . In the absence of intervention, early social class disparities in language and social-emotional development can become increasingly apparent during this period and grow with age" (id., 7). Translated for *Compton*, this means a great deal happens for Compton's children before they enter school. The same is true for Black boys, and all other children who are at the bottom of children's hierarchies.

Neuroscience research thus emphasizes that the process of development makes one's caregivers and community critical. Inequality starts here and is replicated here. Even in the absence of any ACEs, this plays a huge role. Investing in changing this sharp inequality reaps astounding returns. The policy implications of this research are suggested in the landmark study "From Neurons to Neighborhoods" as two paths: first, using this knowledge to maximize the development of human capital; and second, focusing immediately to do something for kids as we find them (National Research Council and Institute of Medicine 2000). As the study points out, the policy agenda and rationale are economic but also moral and human.

Critiquing *Compton* and ACEs

The *Compton* lawsuit is an attempt to apply this developmental research to ensure educational access and opportunity, and developmental equality. Imagine for a moment that the lawsuit successfully established its claims, that the injunctive relief requested was ordered, and that other school districts adopted proactive policies to prevent being sued. Recall the relief being sought: training all school staff, targeted mental health services, and schoolwide resiliency training for all students.

From that perspective I suggest several critiques of the case. First, the use of a disability framework as the basis for the *Compton* claims is troubling. It has the potential to feed into persistent racial and ethnic stereotypes of incapability, lack of intellectual capacity, and dangerousness. In many respects responses to trauma are reasonable and rational; they are simply adaptations. But more importantly, the disability framework may render invisible the causes of incapability, difficulty, delay, or behavior. Or it may tend toward identifying causes in the individual or the individual's family, rather than in structural harm.

Second, the lawsuit treats outcomes long after harm, unnecessary harm, has occurred. In other words, it focuses on resilience without reaching systemic origins and discrimination. It might be argued that it does have the potential to change systems, as a means to avoid legal liability. That indeed would be a much more powerful outcome. But by necessarily focusing on schools and education, it would be limited to education. This would only modify but not disassemble the system, nor would it lead further back to early childhood and circumstances during pregnancy and at birth.

Third, the ACEs framework utilized in the case is a model that merits very careful use, critique, and conceptualization for several reasons.

The origin of the model and its uses began far from the environment of districts like Compton. In addition, the factors that are part of the ACEs framework focus strongly on the family. They therefore ignore the impact of structural factors like poverty, community violence, and racism that powerfully affect families. The ACEs framework ignores and excludes other potential ACEs factors as well as non-ACEs independent reasons for adverse developmental outcomes. Not only should the factors be reconsidered, but we should also ask whether an adjusted ACEs framework or ACEs in conjunction with race would ensure that the powerful potential of ACEs would be used in a different way. Rather than being used to build resilience to trauma, ACEs might be used proactively and structurally to prevent trauma.

ACEs Factors: Expand the Factors?

The promise and the limits of ACEs are well worth examining carefully. The ACEs framework is incredibly powerful and can make a remarkable difference for developmental equality. Its positive contribution is making the developmental process and the consequences of negative factors or challenges in that process visible, understandable, and transparent. The logic is apparent for all, because all or many of us have ACEs. For example, I have two ACEs: my parents divorced when I was in fifth grade, and my mother suffered from mental illness. Virtually every time I present the ACEs factors to an audience, everyone in the room can identify an ACE in their childhood. ACEs link us, rather than identify "us" and "them."

The research also demonstrates the impact of cumulative, complex, and sustained ACEs. ACEs therefore have the potential not only to be used to trigger essential resiliency programs to counter adverse effects but might also be used to identify systemic factors that *cause* ACEs that are *caused by, or should be solved, minimized, or diminished by, the state.*

So what counts as ACEs factors is critical. As ACEs are configured in the original ACE model, still used by many advocates, the framework is limited: the focus is on families, and the consequences are particularly linked to child maltreatment. Additional adverse experiences, based on subsequent research, may make the model more useful as a tool for developmental equality. Finkelhor, Shattuck, Turner, and Hamby explored

ACE limitations in their 2013 article (Finkelhor et al. 2013). As they note, the original ACEs study asked adults retrospectively what they had experienced, with respondents ranging in age from fifty-five to fifty-seven. This raised the issues of bias in recollection. Second, based on developmental scholarship, more factors might have been included: "peer rejection, exposure to violence outside the family, low socioeconomic status, and poor academic performance" (id., 70). Combining these insights, they suggest adversity should be measured in childhood to improve the use of ACEs and to better explore the interaction of ACEs. In addition, doing so would expose short-term effects and perhaps better expose the pathways that generate the long-term effects. "Childhood behavioral and emotional symptoms very likely represent crucial mediators linking adverse childhood experiences and the longer term health-related problems found in the ACE sub-studies" (id., 71). These researchers replicated the ACEs study in a group of youth to see if they could refine the factors, using psychological distress as an outcome measure. They measured the significance of both old and new ACEs factors, and found some factors in the original scale dropped out and some new factors achieved significance, resulting in a revised scale of factors: emotional abuse, physical abuse, sexual abuse, physical neglect, emotional neglect, household mental illness, property victimization, peer victimization, exposure to community violence, socioeconomic status, someone close experiencing a bad accident or illness, below-average grades, parents always arguing, and no good friends. One of the most notable aspects of this revision is its expansion away from an exclusive household/family focus to a broader relational focus (friends, neighbors, community), as well as including school and socioeconomic factors.

What is the value of adding factors? Doing so incorporates developmental knowledge of what has an effect on children's development, and the authors suggest additional factors that might be considered, including low IQ, parental death, and food scarcity. Some of the additional factors that were significant were a variety of forms of victimization or interpersonal violence that better capture cumulative effects. The authors also caution about the use of ACEs as a risk assessment tool, versus as a tool for prevention. The latter use would require evidence of causation rather than simply correlation. They also caution that there are reasons to intervene and prevent harms even if they do not have the long-term effects that are captured by ACEs. In other words, the harm itself is inherently a reason for action, rather than limiting action only to mitigating long-term effects. Finally, they point out that there is already consensus on the harms; the ACEs framework is simply a new tool, but does not necessarily expose new knowledge of what harms children.

A second study, by Peter Cronholm and colleagues, focuses on not only expanding or changing the ACEs categories but also changing the demographics of the group studied, shifting from white middle-class adults and home-based experiences to a more economically and racially diverse urban population in Philadelphia (Cronholm et al. 2015). This study had 1,784 respondents, all eighteen or older. Demographically, the study participants were 45.2 percent white, 43.6 percent Black, 3.6 percent Latino, 3.7 percent Asian, and 3.9 percent other, a composition significantly different from the Kaiser Permanente study and representative of Philadelphia census categories. The Philadelphia group was younger as well, almost a reverse of the age percentages in the Kaiser Permanente study.

The participants were asked about ACEs using both the conventional and an expanded ACEs framework. The expanded framework included the following additional factors: witnessed violence, felt discrimination, lived in an unsafe neighborhood, experienced bullying, and lived in foster care. The data collected were used both to compare the existence of ACEs in the original Kaiser ACEs study and to determine if the added factors were relevant. The factors and demographics of participants go beyond those studied by the Finkelhor study, based on known health disparities by race and ethnicity as well as SES, in addition to known impacts of community factors for Black and Latino youth. The added domains and factors were generated by a review of the literature as well as community-specific information, with questions adapted from other existing surveys.

The conventional ACEs scores for the Philadelphia respondents were higher than those for the Kaiser Permanente group for every ACEs factor other than those for sexual abuse, emotional neglect, and physical neglect. For the expanded ACEs categories, the participants' experience was quite high for witnessing community violence (40.5 percent), racial discrimination (34.5 percent), and living in an unsafe neighborhood (27.3 percent). Higher expanded ACEs were more prevalent for certain groups, particularly males and persons of color. "Together these findings support the long-standing notion that higher levels of adversity exist in minority and lower-income populations" (id., 359).

Gender, race, and poverty are associated with the expanded ACEs but not with conventional ACEs. So using only conventional ACEs will underreport adversity, and that underreporting is specific to certain groups: men, people of color, divorcees, and those below 150 percent of the poverty level (id.). As the researchers remind us, the pathways and links between experiences and outcomes are still being sorted out, as well as how they lead to impairments and negative behaviors. But what is critical is understanding how they function in different populations. "Large, enduring, macrosocial factors such as poverty, racism and classism have been associated with poorer health and health disparities but have proven resistant to mitigation as economic gaps widen in the U.S." (id., 359). This study, and its expanded ACEs framework, is the first to incorporate community-level adversity.

One final example of modification of the original ACEs factors is contained in the 2013 data report from Child Trends on adverse indicators, which uses nine adverse indicators developed for the 2011–12 National Survey of Children's Health (Child Trends 2013). They include economic hardship, divorce or separation, death of a parent, parental incarceration, witnessing intimate partner violence, neighborhood violence, mental illness, substance abuse, and being treated unfairly due to race/ethnicity. This set of ACEs includes both household and community factors, by incorporating poverty, racism, and community violence.

These examples of critiques of the ACEs model point to the importance of refining it. One underrepresented trauma in the model is racism. Even to the extent that it is (sometimes) included, it is not representative or inclusive. Other possible factors for inclusion might include juvenile justice system involvement, encounters with police in school or on the street, and school discipline, including school exclusion.

Using ACEs: Proactive Policy and Structural Change?

A second improvement to the ACEs framework is not the metric itself but rather its use. The primary focus of ACEs research and scholarship is its usefulness to identify populations with high ACEs and then link them to programs that build resilience and healing. But ACEs might be used *proactively* in communities to prevent or ameliorate risk factors and build resilience. Even more radically, ACEs could be useful *structurally*, to demonstrate flaws, lack of performance, or the need for reform in particular systems.

An example of the proactive use of the ACEs framework is a Washington State initiative that uses ACEs to map out the prevalence of adversity for both children and their communities, to understand the ecological context in which the child is functioning, and to determine the resources that they might draw upon (Blodgett 2015). The state of Washington is involved in a broad, groundbreaking strategy to achieve developmental success for all the children in the state based on legislation enacted in 2014 (Blodgett 2014, 2015). It is statewide but community-centered. The policy uses ACEs in a more expanded way, by gathering data not only on children but also on adults, thereby examining the range and intensity of ACEs in youth but also in the adults of the surrounding community (Blodgett 2015). In addition, poverty is treated as an interrelated but independent source of adversity; and race/ethnicity is tracked as another source of adversity. The use of ACEs scores, poverty measures (e.g., free school lunch data), and demographic data regarding ethnicity (here, Hispanic children, as they are the largest non-white group and outcomes are racialized) represents a more sophisticated and expansive approach to supporting kids and their families. The factors are mapped by school district, and the policy focus is on community building and engagement that go beyond building resilience to poverty interventions.

Three factors stood out to the Washington State researchers: the severity of adult ACEs, the level of poverty, and school size and ethnic diversity (id.). These translated into ten findings. Adult ACEs are common, but not evenly distributed among adults or among communities. High-ACEs adults range from 11 to 51 percent of the communities. As the number of adults with high ACEs rises, the outcomes for kids get worse. While "poverty and ACEs are only modestly related" (id., 4), poverty is an independent factor in outcomes. "Poverty is a powerful independent influence on academic, youth and community success distinct from the impact of ACEs which occur across all income levels" (id.). The impact of ACEs shows up in elementary school, and is highly correlated to suspension. Poverty is strongly linked to unexcused absences, failure to graduate from high school, and failure to pursue postsecondary education.

Finally, the research found that ethnicity functioned like poverty, as an independent factor related to outcomes. In Washington, both ACEs scores and the rate of poverty are highest among Hispanics, and schools with high Hispanic enrollment are high on both factors. "Hispanic school enrollment represents a third factor that has its own distinct set of influences on community and school risk and protective factors, which at the same time is associated directly with our measures of both poverty and adversity in communities" (id., 37). "The impact of ethnicity and poverty on academic success is systemic and significant. Race and ethnicity define the character of communities and are important to understand as characteristics that mediate academic success" (id., 40).

The Washington State initiative suggests the potential for a broader use of ACEs in conjunction with ethnicity and poverty to evaluate community resources and needs. To that extent it represents a more ecological approach to identify what creates the barriers to developmental equality. It remains to be seen whether structural change, as opposed to resilience building alone, will be a focus of the Washington State findings.

ACEs and neuroscience might be used to focus on systemic pieces that determine developmental outcomes for groups of children. If so, this effort must begin at birth, and even prior to birth. A significant downside to the *Compton* litigation is that it starts too late, when kids begin school. This is not to say that kids from kindergarten onward do not merit support but that the early impact of ACEs, as well as the early impact of inequalities apart from ACEs, if unaddressed, can have a significant impact on children's education, even assuming their school is adequately resourced.

By eighteen months, if not sooner, the separation, segregation, and hierarchy that create children's inequalities have already begun. The lesson from neuroscience and early childhood researchers is that zero to three is critical because of the developmental significance of this time frame. If ACEs could be minimized, however, inequality would still remain. The early childhood literature identifies the differences in inputs linked especially to poverty, education, and neighborhood that differentiate children as a group so that gaps present at eighteen months begin to widen by three and are even greater by the start of school. Inequality among children is a predictable developmental outcome if this pattern remains unaddressed. Inequality will exist even if ACEs are low or irrelevant to developmental outcomes.

ACEs then might be used in conjunction with developmental neuroscience to construct systems of support. In early childhood, what is distinctive is the remarkable lack of policy rather than its presence. Interventions could aim to prepare children for school as well as prevent or intervene and provide resilience support regarding ACEs. This would mean children arriving as equals at the kindergarten door (Duncan and Magnuson 2014). Comparative data provides some context on what might be considered to build an egalitarian start as suggested by the developmental equality model (Tanner, Candland, and Odden 2015). The United States has a high rate of child poverty, a low rate of spending and money transfers, and a limited safety net (Gould and Wething 2012). OECD countries, by contrast, adhere to the concept of "social protection," providing policies addressing risk, chronic poverty, and vulnerability. The World Bank identifies the OECD safety net as including minimum income, housing benefits, family benefits, lone parent benefits enabling work, and child care benefits (Tesliuc 2006). Additional programs suggested in a recent White House report on early childhood include home visitation programs to help parents, early childhood education, and high-quality child care (Executive Office of the President 2015).

What are the chances for dramatic reform to achieve developmental equality using existing statutes and ACEs? Paul Butler writes about the limits of criminal justice reform amidst a time of seemingly intense pressure for change (Butler 2016). Butler begins with this proposition: the system is working the way it's supposed to. He argues law can be a "ratchet" for changing racial injustice, but he urges us to focus on effects and unintended consequences because of the pervasiveness of racism. In other words, we should continue to press for legal reforms, but realize that such reforms may be inherently or unintentionally limited. Legal reform, Butler argues, can be a ratchet: it may help some people, even if it will not resolve systemic problems. Such ratchets are essential, but stopgaps. They will not achieve transformation. For developmental equality, we need both: ratchets and transformation.

Giving kids resilience tools is a good thing. It would help Black boys; it would help Compton and Washington State. But it would not remove the barriers; it would only provide a partial way around them. Hierarchies among children would remain, and at worst, ACEs counts could become another stigma or reinforce old tropes of deficiency. An adaptive tool would be given while social position remains unchanged, to use the insights of Spencer and García Coll.

Every theoretical insight reminds us to pay attention to structures and outcomes based on identities. Using developmental research and ACEs to build resilience leaves structures intact. Indeed it strengthens them by telling us the harms can be addressed; a simpler, less expensive, less radical option is enough, rather than structural change. The state remains hierarchical and inegalitarian rather than responsive. Children are not deemed our responsibility and they gain no rights.

The potential and limitations of the *Compton* case, the ACEs framework, and neuroscience research can move us in the direction of change, but underscore the importance of systemic change. Otherwise we risk reinscribing inequality by rendering it invisible or focusing too narrowly. A broader focus and vision is essential. ACEs and neuroscience, while important, must be challenged themselves lest they re-create more structural problems. In addition, they must be used to identify and dismantle structural barriers.

The Flint water crisis triggered visceral and strong responses to officials' deliberate indifference, permitting a daily necessity, water, to be a source of harm and lifelong loss for the children of Flint ("Flint Water Crisis" 2017). The barriers that we place in the way of allowing all children to develop to their utmost potential, targeted to their identities and the circumstances of their families, divide and separate children just as much as the toxic water of Flint. Resilience approaches treat only the symptoms, not the illness or the source of the illness. Inequality can and should be eradicated.

One way to change the macrosystem of ideas and concrete structures is through constitutional dialogue. A constitutional challenge to systems suggests a potential framework for broader, macrosystemic change grounded not in disability but in equality, by expanding the developmental perspective present in some constitutional doctrines relating to children and youth, and linking that to robust equality arguments. I turn to this possibility in the next chapter.

9

Constitutional Strategy

A more challenging litigation strategy than using existing statutory structures might consider constitutional litigation. Constitutional analysis not only has the potential to effect national-level structural change but also is a key component of the macrosystem of values and principles that define the beliefs and commitments that determine our definition of the state and our responsibilities to each other. The blatant and radically negative role of the state (federal, state, and local governments) with respect to Black boys, and other groups of children, is so profound that it suggests an argument that the state violates basic constitutional rights by placing developmental hurdles in the way of identifiable groups of children and supporting them unequally. It is an argument for fundamental fairness, justice, and equality, along with social responsibility for all of the next generation.

Dismantling barriers to developmental equality might be articulated under a theory of children's rights under equal protection, substantive due process, or both. Dismantling existing developmental barriers within the educational system, for example, would depend upon an argument that leaving them in place violates the core principles of *Palmore* (1984) and *Brown* (1954) that equality requires that the state not reinforce or produce inequality. Challenging the juvenile justice system and policing practices might use a developmental equality argument to expand developmental principles that have emerged in juvenile justice cases. The potential for a robust children's rights analysis exists without the necessity of challenging entrenched doctrine, although the recognition of children's rights would doubtless generate resistance similar to that faced by any reframing or changed understanding of constitutional interpretation. Children's rights is uncharted and undeveloped territory in constitutional law, but that very nebulousness, combined with threads of recognition of a doctrine of children's rights, may suggest room for doctrinal development. The recognition of developmental principles in a range of cases is one of those threads.

To the extent this suggests positive rights, beyond dismantling barriers and challenges, this is likely to generate resistance, given the view of many that our Constitution is only one of negative rights (*DeShaney v. Winnebago County Department of Social Services* 1989). Yet the meaning of equality for children, and their special dependency on the systems of society to achieve their developmental potential, arguably generates such obligations, parallel to those recognized internationally by other countries under the CRC (Dowd 2016b). Also essential to children's rights would be overruling *San Antonio Independent School District v. Rodriguez* (1973). Education as a fundamental right is clearly suggested by the language in *Brown v. Board of Education* (1954) and *Plyler v. Doe* (1982). This approach might open the door to establishing other foundational affirmative rights in the poverty, child welfare, and juvenile justice systems.

It might be argued that the *Obergefell v. Hodges* (2015) decision suggests the possibility of a doctrinal opening to positive rights. Reframed constitutional analysis could bring a vast range of law and policy under scrutiny. As noted in *Washington v. Davis* (1976),

> A rule that a statute designed to serve neutral ends is nevertheless invalid, absent compelling justification, if in practice it benefits or burdens one race more than another would be far reaching and would raise serious questions about, and perhaps invalidate, a whole range of tax, welfare, public service, regulatory, and licensing statutes that may be more burdensome to the poor and to the average black than to the more affluent white. (id., 248)

Although in *Washington v. Davis* this very prospect was cause for the Court to adopt a limited view of what constitutes discrimination by the state, it might be argued that structural discrimination analysis dictates reassessing the Court's conclusion, that to the contrary, such structural scrutiny is consistent with a deeper understanding of how discrimination functions and replicates inequality.

To achieve developmental equality might then require a challenge to the inadequacies of constitutional equality doctrine under equal protection. Such a challenge might be based on incorporating the robust scholarship on implicit cognitive bias and stereotyping to reframe the definition of intent; recognizing discrimination based on patterns of disparate impact as essential to achieve the constitutional design and meaning of equality; and disavowing the principle of color blindness, which so often has only reinforced white privilege, in favor of embracing color consciousness and the value of racial diversity as the hallmarks of equality.

One path of constitutional argument, then, is to raise the question of whether it is time to challenge the doctrine that we have. Alternatively, an opening may exist to bypass that difficult path through a children's rights argument that incorporates equality, along with specific substantive rights connected to development. With any strategy, it is important to recognize that what is needed for developmental equality is both (1) *dismantling* developmental barriers, and reforming systems that negatively impact children, and (2) *creating* policies and structures to support all children under positive rights to developmental support that ensure the equality of all children to reach their developmental capacity.

In this chapter I sketch potential arguments by revisiting one of the classic family law cases, *Moore v. City of East Cleveland* (1977), from the perspective of John Moore Jr., the child at the center of that case. John Jr.'s life circumstances parallel those of many contemporary Black boys and youth, but his perspective is missing from that case. I explore what his claims might have been within a developmental equality framework. I then consider the challenges within equal protection and substantive due process analysis. Finally, I argue that the constitutional vision embedded in my arguments is not simply a forward-looking argument for reinterpretation, but rather is an argument embedded in our constitutional history, by looking at critical dissenting opinions in several close cases. Nevertheless, the constitutional road is difficult and steep. In recognition of that, I suggest an alternative strategy, a New Deal for Children, in Chapter 10.

Reimagining *Moore v. City of East Cleveland*

In order to imagine the potential constitutional arguments for developmental equality, we might reconsider a case that is broadly understood as a high-water mark in constitutional law as applied to children and families, *Moore v. City of East Cleveland* (1977). Indeed, *Moore* might be used in a constitutional strategy to argue for equal support of all children, just as *Moore* stands for equal respect of many family forms. But I want to suggest we use *Moore* differently: to consider how the case might have been litigated if brought to claim the child's rights to developmental equality, rather than the parent's (here grandparent's) familial rights. In *Moore*, the U.S. Supreme Court found that a Cleveland single-family housing ordinance, which defined "family" in such a way that the city had ordered Inez Moore to remove her seven-year-old grandson John Jr. from her household or face a criminal punishment of a fine or jail time, violated her constitutionally protected family rights.

How would we tell the story of *Moore* from John Jr.'s perspective?

The ordinary act of registering John Jr. for school was the apparent trigger for efforts to exclude him from school (Lenhardt 2016; Dowd 2017a). The order mandating his removal from his grandmother's house (and so removing him from the school district) came after an earlier effort by the city to deny his entry into school had failed. In the late 1960s, John came to live with his grandmother, Inez Moore, in East Cleveland after his mother died, when he was less than one year old (Davis 2008; Abrams 2013). Details about John's mother are limited, but it does not seem unusual that John's father would have turned to *his* own mother for help. Indeed, in the gendered norms of the day (and even today) this might be expected: the death of John's mother left a vacuum of maternal care, a gap filled by John's grandmother. Between the death of John's mother and his entry into school, John's father lived in his grandmother's household some of the time. Eventually, however, his father remarried and made a home with his new wife. It is unclear why John remained with his grandmother, but this might have been based on the stability and continuity that arrangement provided, and/or the desire to solidify John Sr.'s new marriage. It also might have reflected the strength of John's other family ties in his grandmother's house. John's cousin, Dale Jr., who was four years younger than John, was raised with him as if they were brothers, and Dale's father, Dale Sr., lived in the household. John also had the benefit of a large group of cousins, twenty in all, some of whom lived next door, in the other half of his grandmother's two-family house. Thus, John had a stable, embedded set of family ties in a robust extended family. This family was a critical resource for him to counter the adverse effects of losing his mother at such a young age.

John's life, however, intersected with legal structures intended to manage and control East Cleveland by race and class (Lenhardt 2016). Those structures would converge on this seven-year-old because of his identity as a Black boy in a low-income family when he began school. Although the Black populace of the Cleveland area, including the suburb of East Cleveland, was no longer subject to express Jim Crow segregation, there were efforts to "manage" integration in the 1960s to prevent white flight, through the use of zoning and housing codes (id.).

Schools were a primary structure for managing the process of racial change (id.). When Inez Moore tried to register her grandson for school in 1972, she was told she could not do so because she lacked formal legal guardianship of John Moore Jr. This must have seemed ridiculous to the person who had parented John since he was an infant, and was his primary caretaker. The guardianship requirement may have been an effort to stem the number of Black children entering the school system, particularly low-income Black children, who would be disproportionately more likely to be in a household other than that of their parents (Dowd 2017a). Inez Moore decided to fight this policy. Legal Aid brought a class action on her behalf and families similarly affected. The school board settled by eliminating the guardianship requirement (Lenhardt 2016).

But this victory appeared to have triggered a retaliatory effort now that Inez Moore was on the city's radar. Shortly after the settlement on the guardianship issue, on January 13, 1973, housing code inspectors appeared at Inez Moore's door (*Moore v. City of East Cleveland* 1977). John, it was claimed, was "illegally" in her home and would have to be removed, which would also mean he could not be registered for school. A year after the initiation of the investigation, in January 1974, Inez Moore was cited in a criminal complaint, and ordered to remove John from her home within ten days or face jail time and a fine. Now the city was asking her to expel her grandson from her house, which seems absurd and outrageous. It seems entirely too coincidental to think this investigation was accidental. Legal Aid again represented Inez, beginning the lawsuit that would take over three years to reach final resolution. On May 31, 1977, which would have been near the end of the school year, when John was eleven, the U.S. Supreme Court in *Moore* declared the housing code provision unconstitutional (id.). John was allowed to remain in his home, with his family, and stay in school. One can speculate that he was old enough during much of this period to understand what was going on and the possibilities of what might happen to him if the negative decisions of the Ohio courts were not overruled. One can only speculate what further impact this had on his life, and whether he continued to be a target for state intervention. We do know that when Legal Aid attempted to locate him as an adult, he was incarcerated (Lenhardt 2017).

John Jr.'s Constitutional Claims

Moore was brought and won by John Jr.'s grandmother Inez Moore, and the primary challenge in the case was getting the Court to recognize that her extended family deserved the same constitutional protection as a marital nuclear family. The court decided that it did, and the case is widely viewed as a victory for a broad definition of family forms as deserving of constitutional protection against undue state intrusion. "Ours is by no means a tradition limited to respect for the bonds uniting the members of the nuclear family. . . . [T]he Constitution prevents East Cleveland from standardizing its children—and its adults—by forcing all to live in certain narrowly defined family patterns" (*Moore v. City of East Cleveland* 1977, 504, 506).

What if the lawsuit had been brought on behalf of John Jr., as a violation of his rights? How would we define and construct his interests, and the harms he would suffer, if he was forced out of his grandmother's house and then forced to change schools? In addition to the impact on his functional parent-child relationship with his grandmother, could a claim be brought based on the harm of losing his functional sibling relationship with his cousin Dale Jr., and his relationship with his uncle? What impact would his removal have on his cousins or other members of his extended family or, for that matter, on children in the neighborhood and the community who would witness the power of the state being used to remove a seven-year-old from his home? What claims might he make about the further consequences of the city's order, including his removal from school, midyear if immediately carried out, and forced enrollment in another, unknown school?

In addition to these relational and individual harms, John Jr.'s story suggests structural claims involving the systemic links between housing regulation and school. If those policies disrupted children's development, could they be challenged on that basis? Was there a disproportionate impact of these policies? Did the brunt of those efforts fall on Black children who, like John, might be not only forced to move, but also forced to change schools? Is there a class component to these policies and their effect as well, where they are more likely to impact a low-income child? Is there a systemic claim that ought to be brought on his behalf focusing on the framework of housing regulation as it intersects with public education?

There is also a structural link in John's situation to income inequality, wealth inequality, and employment discrimination. The fathers of both John and Dale were present and engaged in the lives of their sons, but both appear to have struggled financially, and hence were dependent on their mother to house themselves and their sons. What dynamics or systems might be implicated in their economic difficulties that intersect with housing and education? In other words, do we need to ask other questions linked to gender as well as race and class, and their intersections, to determine if John was being targeted because of the "sins" of his father? These are not the sins of illegitimacy (which would entitle John Jr.'s claim to heightened judicial scrutiny) but rather the sins of poverty or near poverty (viewed as individual "fault" or shortcomings rather than the product of discrimination). Patterns then and now of persisting employment discrimination lead to income inequality that limits housing choices (Massey and Denton 1993; Sharkey 2013). The intersection with race limits housing still further, for John Jr. and today's children, even in the absence of low income. The connections between parental housing and income with differential schools generate inequality in developmental supports for the children of low-income parents. Thus, in addition to challenging the immediate system causing harm, we might also look at the degree of support of John Jr., his father, and his extended family; and the quality of the support for his family, neighborhood, and community. In addition to challenging school policies, we might also look to the structures in place (or not) during John's early childhood, and therefore his school readiness as he entered school. Finally, we might explore the extent of the support provided to him connected to the loss of his mother.

John Jr.'s potential claims are powerful and fundamental ones about inequality. The state's differentiation among children based on family form, race, and class, causing harm to his fundamental rights to familial relationships, to his necessary caregiving, and therefore to his primary developmental support, as well as disrupting his education, translates into the creation of developmental barriers and differentiation. The potential claims that John Jr. might raise are not simply a matter of historical curiosity. Inequalities among children today mirror those faced by John Jr. and similarly involve intersections of education, housing, and other state policies and structures. Evidence of historic employment, housing, and opportunity discrimination indicates that families currently are undermined in their ability to provide developmental support due to the intergenerational impact of state policies that continue to impoverish certain citizens and communities, and thus affect their children (Roithmayr 2014; Sharkey 2013). Even the Black middle class is not similarly situated or advantaged as compared to the white middle class: they "still live in poorer neighborhoods than the majority of whites on all measures" (Pattillo 2005, 305). This differential is most strongly linked to persisting resistance of white neighborhoods to integration. "It is almost sociological common knowledge that African Americans have been and remain the most residentially segregated group in the United States" (id., 312). This reflects a vast difference in racial preferences: Blacks prefer a neighborhood 50 percent Black, 50 percent white; whites prefer a neighborhood 80 percent white, 20 percent Black (id., 318). While integration can be challenged as the goal, as long as resources are tied to racial configuration, segregation, whether imposed or voluntary, is meaningful for opportunity.

Equal Protection

Making claims for developmental equality grounded in differential state support of children and the construction of barriers for some children, whether on behalf of John Jr. or of others, is difficult based on current constitutional doctrine. The substantial doctrinal hurdles include the stringent intent requirements of Equal Protection; the inability to bring a disparate impact claim save under very limited circumstances; the narrow view of permissible affirmative action; the doctrine of color blindness; the limited use of diversity as a justification for race- and gender-conscious action; the separation of race and gender, rather than intersectionality analysis of multidimensional discrimination; denial of education as a fundamental right; refusal to recognize class- or poverty-based claims as entitled to greater scrutiny; and interpretation of the Constitution as a guarantor of negative rights, not as a basis for positive/ affirmative rights.

Several strategies might improve the possibility of contemporary claims, but they all require changes to equal protection doctrine. First, the concept of intent might incorporate the robust scholarship on implicit cognitive bias and stereotyping to reframe the definition of intent, or to add a concept of reckless discrimination (similar to tort standards that treat recklessness as equivalent to intent) (Kang 2005; Kang and Banaji 2006; Girvan 2015). So, for example, Stephanie Bornstein has suggested the use of a recklessness standard in the context of Title VII claims: " [T]he burden to prove intentional disparate treatment under Title VII should be met by an employer's knowing and reckless disregard for the operation of implicit bias and stereotyping in its workplace" (Bornstein 2017, 1103). Translated to John's claim, this would be a basis to argue that if a state actor chooses policies that have foreseeable consequences or harmful developmental impacts when there are other choices that would be developmentally supportive, this knowing disregard or recklessness is the legal equivalent to discriminatory intent. This would not eliminate the intent standard, but expand the circumstances under which the intent standard would be satisfied.

Second, rather than stretching constitutional analysis of intent, disparate impact analysis could be embraced as reflecting contemporary understanding of how discrimination functions, and as essential to achieve the constitutional design and meaning of equality. Ironically, the very rationale for rejecting disproportionate impact now makes it essential to recognize this principle. As noted earlier, in *Washington v. Davis* (1976), the case rejecting the use of disparate impact theory, Justice White rejected that theory in part out of fear for its consequences: "[A disparate impact rule] would be far reaching and would raise serious questions about, and perhaps invalidate, a whole range of tax, welfare, public service, regulatory, and licensing statutes that may be more burdensome to the poor and to the average black than to the more affluent white" (id., 248). Exactly. Structural, embedded, interrelated systems perpetuate hierarchy. Embracing disparate impact doctrine is justified based on a range of arguments grounded in history, current context, and the nature of the workings of racism. As Darren Hutchinson has so eloquently argued, to do otherwise turns the Equal Protection Clause on its head, protecting the privileged, rather than seeing equal protection as an antisubordination tool (Hutchinson 2003). Embracing disproportionate impact would refocus equality on the very patterns that bespeak ongoing, interconnected inequality, like those evident in the context of John Jr.'s life, and that remain in the lives of Black boys and other children at the bottom of children's hierarchies.

Finally, in terms of our vision of equality, and the necessity of positive rights and remedies, we would disavow or reframe the principle of color blindness, which has only reinforced white privilege, in favor of embracing color consciousness and the value of racial diversity as the hallmarks of equality. The oft-cited quote of Justice Harlan endorsing color blindness, in dissent in *Plessy v. Ferguson* (1896), when read in full context makes clear this connection between color blindness and white privilege:

> The white race deems itself to be the dominant race in this country. And so it is in prestige, in achievements, in education, in wealth and power. So, I doubt not, it will continue to be for all time if it remains true to its great heritage and holds fast to the principles of constitutional liberty. But in view of the Constitution, in the eye of the law, there is in this country no superior, dominant, ruling class of citizens. There is no caste here. Our Constitution is color-blind, and neither knows nor tolerates classes among citizens. (id., 559)

Race consciousness, not color blindness, is essential to confronting embedded privilege that sustains white dominance, and in order to achieve equality.

Reframed equality analysis could bring a vast range of law and policy under scrutiny. While it is beyond the scope of this volume to make those arguments in detail, this brief framework suggests the outlines. It might be argued that, indeed, it is time for exactly a reframed equality analysis to happen, and to start with children and youth.

Fundamental Rights

Framing John Moore Jr.'s claims as fundamental rights claims under substantive due process offers more potential, but confronts the antipathy and mixed reaction toward expansion of fundamental rights claims. On the other hand, to the extent his claims fit within the familiar, accepted substantive due process categories, they are more likely to be successful. These would include claims of intrusion into his family rights and relationships (*Troxel v. Granville* 2000; *Obergefell v. Hodges* 2015). If children in essence have the mirror image of their parents' and families' constitutional protection, as well as derivative protection for the impact on them of any negative view of their parents or family (such as the inability until recently for same-sex couples to marry), then such a claim would be fairly unremarkable. To the extent that John's claims are distinctive, it would expand and make more robust the scope of familial constitutional rights as not simply parent-centered. Other potential relationship claims (e.g., sibling rights and functional relationships) would face a steeper uphill climb to recognition, given the persistent resistance to expanding the scope of fundamental rights to nontraditional or atypical family relationships (*Michael H. v. Gerald D.* 1989).

Beyond claims relating to familial relationships, the claims would be more difficult. No fundamental rights claim would exist for disruption of John's education, for example, without revisiting the Court's position that education is not a fundamental right (*San Antonio Independent School District v. Rodriguez* 1973). There might be some ability to claim infringement of a state constitutional right to education, but systemic change even under those claims has been elusive (Rebell 2009). A string of legal victories challenging state funding schemes brought under more robust state constitutional provisions guaranteeing education rights has been difficult to translate into concrete funding and policy changes. Most recently in the long-running Connecticut school litigation a trial court found statewide constitutional violations for the failure to remedy inequalities that result in differential education for the state's children, a landmark ruling nevertheless now tied up in appeals (*Connecticut Coali-*

tion for Justice in Education Funding v. Rell 2016; Harris 2016a). Given the centrality of education to children's development, a federal constitutional reversal indeed might be feasible and timely.

Similarly, under existing fundamental rights doctrine there is no fundamental right even to a basic survival level of economic support (Black 1986; Chemerinsky 1993; Rose 2010). Thus claims linked to poverty and economic rights are likely to have limited success as fundamental rights claims. Under current fundamental rights doctrine, then, only some of John's claims might be actionable, particularly those relating to family relationships, but not including structural claims or rights to education that would maximize his development and growth. A shift in doctrine to support developmental equality might best be accomplished under a children's rights theory.

Children's Rights

Children's rights and needs necessitate asking the question, "What about the child's perspective?" rather than subsuming their interests in concepts of "family" or "parent." Children's rights necessarily involve the intersection of children's fundamental or substantive rights and their equality rights. Because of the unique claims that children can make upon the state, constitutional arguments for children's rights might include claims of positive rights to the necessary supports to achieve their developmental potential and maximize their opportunity. The argument for children's positive rights is that they are inescapably linked to children's equality: all children must have developmental support to achieve their developmental capacity and become productive, participatory citizens. Because children are embedded in families, neighborhoods, and communities, the developmental support of children means essential attention to the policies, institutions, and structures that support the elements of their ecology, in order to ensure the individual life course of every child and equality among all children (Woodhouse 2008a). This would mean not only protection for children from the inadequacies and inequalities of state policies and institutions but also a claim for positive rights. Equality for children, and their special dependency on the systems of society to achieve their developmental potential, arguably generates such obligations.

A robust children's rights doctrine is most strongly found in acceptance of developmental arguments in the Court's juvenile justice cases, and the recognition of the rights of minors as constitutional persons (*Roper v. Simmons* 2005; *Graham v. Florida* 2010; *Miller v. Alabama* 2012; *Bellotti v. Baird* 1979; *Hodgson v. Minnesota* 1990). In the juvenile justice cases, the Court recognized that because adolescents are still neurologically developing, judgments of their culpability and consequences must take that into account. The vulnerability of youth in school discipline (*Safford Unified School District No. 1 v. Redding* 2009; Nance 2016) and juvenile justice situations requires recognition and constitutional protection. At the same time, youth can be sufficiently mature to make considered decisions about contraception and abortion (*Planned Parenthood of Central Missouri v. Danforth* 1976; *Planned Parenthood of Kansas City v. Ashcroft* 1983; *Bellotti v. Baird* 1979). The reproductive rights decisions may be especially relevant to the developmental course, ensuring that youth will "stay on track" regardless of the decision that they make.

The broadest read of the cases that embrace the importance of developmental research and its value in constructing legal standards would suggest that entire systems (for example juvenile justice) should be developmentally informed, and thus could be challenged if they functioned in a way contrary to our knowledge of development. So, for example, much of the structure of juvenile justice arguably ignores adolescent development, confounds rehabilitation, and promotes recidivism (Dowd 2011a). Thus it is a developmentally negative system with no benefit to public safety. One might also argue that the racial and ethnic disparities that continue to characterize the juvenile justice system mean that the bad developmental outcomes generated by the flaws of the juvenile justice system are suffered disproportionately by boys of color (Nunn 2002; Bell 2015). Similarly, the educational disciplinary systems in many school districts could be challenged as contrary to developmental knowledge of why kids behave the way that they do, and as contrary to sound developmental principles in the structure of the school's response (Glennon 2011). Glaring inequities among schools further exacerbate the problem by generating hierarchies among children. Moreover, as with the juvenile justice system, school disciplinary policies typically function disproportionately by race and gender, exacerbating the developmental harm for particular kids (Nance 2016). Schools' role in transmitting youth into the juvenile justice system through the school-to-prison pipeline also is developmentally unsound (Nance 2015).

Expanding the reach of the developmental perspective to a constitutional standard for evaluating systems that focus on children would have significant impact. In addition, a claim for children's rights would be enormously bolstered by understanding children as having a claim to positive constitutional rights including a system not simply developmentally informed, but designed to foster the maximum developmental capacity of all children. In *Moore*, it would mean not only challenging and dismantling the immediate systems causing harm, that is, the housing/zoning policies in combination with the school policies, but also providing John Jr. with an education that would foster his positive development, not simply a minimally functional education. It might also cause us to examine more broadly developmental supports outside of school available to his family, neighborhood, and community.

A claim of positive rights for children and youth would track arguments similar to those made by a number of scholars in relation to poverty, for a positive right of minimum economic support sufficient to avoid poverty (Chemerinsky 1993; Black 1986; Edelman 1987; Michelman 1968). Erwin Chemerinsky suggests positive rights are grounded in multiple places in the Constitution: the Equal Protection Clause, the Ninth Amendment, the Declaration of Independence, a corrected interpretation of the Privileges and Immunities Clause, and "life" as protected in the Due Process Clause (Chemerinsky 1993). Charles Black argues that a right of livelihood is essential to the general welfare (Black 1986). The words of the Declaration of Independence, he argues, are critical to why we are here: "rights to life, to liberty, and to the pursuit of happiness." Together with the Thirteenth and Fourteenth Amendments, they reflect a right to "a constitutional justice of livelihood" (id., 1104). This serves not only individual liberty but also the general welfare articulated in the preamble to the Constitution (id., 1106). Indeed it is essential: "If we fail in this cutting and joining, all our brave words about human rights will slowly or soon come to be seen as fatally flawed, it will grow too late to transmute hypocrisy into commitment, and such part of the hope of earth as we still guard and cherish will be found one marooning to have flickered out in the night" (id., 1117). Children cannot achieve readiness for this right of livelihood without developmental support.

Peter Edelman argues for a right of subsistence based on substantive due process and equal protection. No inequality is more critical to address, he argues, than poverty; this requires a "survival" or "subsistence" income (Edelman 1987, 3). "The government has acted impermissibly in the degree to which it has created and perpetuated severe poverty" (id., 4). Edelman argues two lines of analysis: one, that there has always been this right in our constitutional structure, or two, that it is a right triggered by the consequences of government actions "in economic arrangements that foreseeably resulted in the current maldistribution" (id., 4). The implicit right is a fundamental rights argument; the maldistribution due to government actions is an equal protection argument. He particularly focuses on the evolution of the Constitution during the Depression, and the proactive role of government in the economy dating from that time. "Our entire system of legal rules shapes wealth and poverty in the United States. . . . Moreover, a whole series of specific governmental policies have contributed to the intensification of poverty" (id., 43).

An argument for children's developmental rights would closely parallel the argument for economic rights sufficient to exercise personhood and citizenship, but would differ because in order to have *equal* developmental opportunities, a robust (as opposed to a minimal) support of development is necessary. A children's rights argument to developmental equality would enable reaching the intersecting systems that affect children in their ability to reach their developmental potential. Just as material sufficiency is essential, so too is developmental support for children. For that support to be meaningful, it cannot be minimal, but must instead be a right to development to the extent of each child's potential. Particularly important for John Moore Jr., and all children, is his right to develop to his potential, a right equal to that of other children without respect to identity, race, gender, or class.

Children's rights provides an expanded mechanism to confront the inequalities that plague children and families, and offers a powerful strategy to confront equality as a whole. Supporting, even mandating, action by the state is essential to provide real opportunities to contemporary children who face daunting intersectional structural inequalities that may further rigidify our persisting race and class inequalities. Through the eyes of children, it might be clearer to see our way forward.

Constitutional Possibilities: A Dissenting Vision

Evaluating the arguments for John Moore Jr. and the children at the bottom of children's hierarchies suggests the necessity of reclaiming a different vision and understanding of the Constitution. Alternative constitutional interpretations that recognize precisely such interpretations exist in robust constitutional dissents that outline a very different constitutional conception of equality and liberty, and might further advance the conception of children's rights (*Shelby County v. Holder* 2013, 2632–52; *Parents Involved in Community Schools v. Seattle School District No 1* 2007, 803–76; *City of Richmond v. J.A. Croson Co.* 1989, 528–62; *McCleskey v. Kemp* 1987, 320–45; *Regents of University of California v. Bakke* 1978, 388–402; *Personnel Administrator v. Feeney* 1979, 281–88; *Washington v. Davis* 1976, 256–71, *Palmer v. Thompson* 1971, *United States v. Guest* 1966, 761–62, 774–86; *Korematsu v. United States* 1944, 233–42, 256–71; *Civil Rights Cases* 1883, 26–62; *Slaughter-House Cases* 1872, 83–111). So in addition to a children's rights argument based on (1) extending the family fundamental rights cases, (2) articulating the unique position of children (children's exceptionalism), and (3) making a positive rights claim to developmental equality, a final argument might be to recall a different vision of equality and liberty. The dissents in early Thirteenth and Fourteenth Amendment cases as well as several dissents in modern affirmative action cases reflect that different vision.

The decision in the *Slaughter-House Cases* (1872) was the first critical case to narrowly construe the Thirteenth and Fourteenth Amendments only a short time after their enactment. While much of the decision has subsequently been reversed, its narrow interpretation of the Privileges and Immunities Clause remains (*McDonald v. Chicago* 2010). Under that view, federally protected rights under the clause are quite minimal; federal citizenship in essence is treated as subordinate to much more important state citizenship. The dissenters in *Slaughter-House*, on the other hand, understood the clause in a far more robust way, as protecting the fundamental rights of all citizens, a constitutional interpretation that in contemporary application would arguably include the special rights and privileges of children and youth to have the equal opportunity to develop into citizens.

As Justice Field puts it, the clause "was intended to make of every one born in this country a *freeman*" (*Slaughter-House Cases* 1872, 90, emphasis added), a term of art that would confer "natural and inalienable rights which belong to all citizens" (id., 96). As he reads it, this clause is the basis for those broad fundamental rights: "The privileges and immunities designated are those *which of right belong to the citizens of all free governments*" (id., 96, emphasis original). Justice Bradley as well interprets the clause as establishing fundamental, universal, and natural rights in a democracy (id., 14), which include not only political rights but also personal rights, mirroring the three claims of the Declaration of Independence: to life, liberty, and the pursuit of happiness (id., 116). "But even if the Constitution were silent, the fundamental privileges and immunities of citizens, as such, would be no less real and no less inviolable than they now are. It was not necessary to say in words what the citizens of the United States should have and exercise all the privileges of citizens. . . . Their very citizenship conferred these privileges" (id., 119). This argument bases the broad claim of rights on the status of being a citizen; it is what citizenship is. It is a grand and powerful conception: Justice Swayne characterized the amendments as "fairly construed . . . to rise to the dignity of a new Magna Carta" (id., 125).

The second critical case with a powerful dissenting vision is the *Civil Rights Cases* (1883). This case also limited the reach of the Fourteenth Amendment, holding that the protections provided by the amendment reach only state action, not private action. The decision recognized that the Thirteenth Amendment abolishing slavery applied to both private and public action, but then defined what was abolished in a narrow way. Justice Harlan in dissent finds it ironic and contradictory that the very Court that upheld slavery and imposed its laws on unwilling states now construes, through the state action requirement, a limit on enforcing citizens' fundamental civil rights and equality (id., 1). To do so ignores what was known to be the source of challenges to equality, which were not solely public authorities but also private individuals and entities who acted with state sanction or impunity (id., 52). Justice Harlan grounds his interpretation in part on *Dred Scott*, the infamous opinion denying the recognition of any Black man as a constitutional "person" (id., 36). The role of the Thirteenth Amendment, Harlan points out, was to reverse *Dred Scott* unequivocally (id., 38). "[T]heir freedom necessarily involved immunity from, and protection against, all discrimination against them, because of their race, in respect of such civil rights as belong to freemen of other races" (id., 40). Congress's power to legislate therefore extended to that full scope, to public and private action. With respect to the Fourteenth Amendment, "*[P]ositive rights and privileges were intended to be secured, and are in fact secured, by the fourteenth amendment*" (id., 45, emphasis added). Those positive rights are "those which are fundamental to citizenship in a free government" (id., 47).

Three years later Justice Harlan dissented again, in *Plessy v. Ferguson* (1896), which upheld the constitutionality of separate but equal facilities. Harlan's dissent is powerful and consistent with his *Civil Rights Cases* dissent, arguing for the importance of strong protection of legal, civil, and political rights. Again, he talks in terms of the positive rights created by the Thirteenth and Fourteenth Amendments. "These two amendments, if enforced according to their true intent and meaning, will protect all the civil rights that pertain to freedom and citizenship" (id., 555). Citing earlier opinions by the Court, he noted,

> The words of the amendment, it is true, are prohibitory, but they contain a necessary implication of a *positive immunity or right*, most valuable to the colored race—the right to exemption from unfriendly legislation against them distinctively as colored; exemption from legal discriminations, implying inferiority in civil society, lessening the security of their enjoyment of the rights which others enjoy; and discriminations which are steps towards reducing them to the condition of a subject race. (id., 556, citing *Strauder v. West Virginia* 1880, 306–7, emphasis added)

Harlan argues it is clear that the purpose of segregated cars at issue in *Plessy* was to convey inferiority and subjugation. One could make the same argument about current state policies that perpetuate differentials among children that undermine their equal development and yield predictable results in terms of their opportunities and life course as adults. As Charles Lawrence has argued, establishing the meaning and outcome of state policies need not be limited to the facial discrimination of Justice Harlan's day; rather, it must reflect our understanding of what it means within the realities of ongoing discrimination and how it functions today (Lawrence 2001).

Justice Harlan nevertheless is no radical. "The white race deems itself to be the dominant race in this country. *And so it is in prestige, in achievements, in education, in wealth, and in power. So, I doubt not, it will continue to be for all time* if it remains true to its great heritage and holds fast to the principles of constitutional liberty" (*Plessy v. Ferguson* 1896, 559, emphasis added). His confidence in white racial superiority is grounded, it appears, in his recognition that the benefits that whites have enjoyed will remain as an intergenerational transfer of the value of whiteness (Harris 1993). So while Justice Harlan strongly defends "every right that inheres in civil freedom, and of the equality before the law of all citizens" (*Plessy v. Ferguson* 1896, 1147), he does not imagine this to include social equality, or he anticipates the powerful continuance of discrimination by the use of "neutral" government structures overlaid on inequalities. Harlan's dissent has to be used, then, with great care. His view of positive rights is critical. His statements supporting white superiority are a reminder that positive rights must pierce the social realm as well, and that even powerful positive rights can, if not carefully protected, devolve into the re-creation of hierarchy.

Indeed, it is that broad and deep understanding of the scope of inequality, and the importance of positive, proactive steps to achieve equality, that emerges from a second set of dissents, those in the modern affirmative action cases. Beginning with the key case of *Bakke* (1978), and most recently in *Parents Involved in Community Schools v. Seattle School District No. 1* (2007), the Court majority has narrowed the potential for the state to accomplish equality by the use of affirmative action, while strong dissents articulate the necessity of a different scope of action to achieve real equality.

In *Bakke* the Court refused to permit the state to remedy "societal discrimination" because it is "an amorphous concept of injury that may be ageless in its reach into the past" (id., 2757). In dissent Justice Brennan points out that as long as we ignore our history we will repeat it. He situates the analysis in the constitutional history of support of slavery and Jim Crow, making color-blind policies ineffective in achieving equality (id., 2767). Justice Marshall's dissent similarly tracks the history of constitutionally supported discrimination and state actions to discriminate, subordinate, and segregate. He concludes that equality is far from a reality (id., 2801). "At every point from birth to death the impact of the past is reflected in the still disfavored position of the Negro" (id., 2802). Contemporary research on economic inequality (Chapter 6) brings this analysis forward along with the continuing role of the state.

More recently, Justice Breyer has taken up the role of articulating the consequences of this narrow view, in the equally if not more segregated contemporary housing and school patterns that the Court refuses to permit to be the basis for broader affirmative action in public education (*Parents Involved in Community Schools v. Seattle School District No. 1*, 2007, 2802). Justice Ginsberg also powerfully writes of the continuing need for the extraordinary remedies of the Voting Rights Act in light of the record of how discrimination evolved, and how a second generation of discrimination continues to seek to limit voting rights and voting power of Black voters (*Shelby County v. Holder* 2013).

One final case that offers a powerful dissenting vision that is especially critical for children's positive rights is *DeShaney v. Winnebago County Department of Social Services* (1989). In that case, the majority held that a child who had come to the attention of the state due to allegations of abuse nevertheless had no constitutional claim based on the inadequacy of the state's protection, which ultimately led to horrific, permanently disabling injury. The dissents in that case argued that once a state creates a system, it owes a duty to those intended to benefit from the system. With respect to schools in particular the claim is even stronger, since by definition all minor children are expected to benefit, versus the child welfare system at issue in *DeShaney*, designed to benefit all but triggered only with respect to specific children brought to that system's notice. The issue of positive rights in the absence rather than the presence of action (for example, the lack of universal child care or early childhood education) might trigger this barrier. "[I]naction can be every bit as abusive of power as action, that oppression can result when a State undertakes a vital duty and then ignores it" (id., 1012). Justice Blackmun condemns the "formalistic reasoning" attempting to draw a line between action and inaction (id.).

These dissents provide a vision of a Constitution that is strongly committed to the equality of all its citizens, and requires affirmative steps to accomplish equality and dismantle state barriers. It links in particular to the grand vision of the Declaration of Independence, separated from its assumed exclusions when drafted as to who was included in "We the People." It adheres to the racial vision of the Reconstruction Amendments (Tsesis 2016; Black 1960). That vision would clearly support a vision of children's rights that includes developmental equality.

A final caution or reminder about constitutional arguments for developmental equality is to be mindful of remedy restrictions, and therefore the ultimate limitation of constitutional arguments even if they were successful. *Brown* and the decades of school litigation are testimony to that, as is the reality of an even more segregated and unequal public education system than was present when *Brown* was decided in 1954 (Orfield and Lee 2004). While constitutional litigation assuredly has spending implications, just as clearly, the judicial branch is limited in its ability to order spending or to order reorientation of spending priorities at any governmental level. Thus even if John Jr. or contemporary children were successful, limits on judicial power might affect the reach of even the most successful constitutional argument.

Developmental equality should be a part of children's rights, included in our constitutional jurisprudence of the meaning of liberty, justice, and equality. While constitutional litigation may be important to changing the macrosystem of ideas, it is neither essential nor sole. The clearer and more pragmatic path to developmental equality is affirmative public policy, to which I now turn.

10

A New Deal for Children

Equality for all children is fundamental. All children should be supported to achieve their maximum positive development because of the inherent value of children and their dependence on adults. Well-functioning individuals confer social and economic benefits for everyone, and the equality of all is inextricably linked to the equality of each one. The developmental equality model is foundational to achieving racial and gender equality that is our unrealized promise to all.

A litigation strategy is inherently limited. The framework of existing statutes, not designed for dramatic reform, and the uphill battle to establish constitutional children's rights to positive state action might well sharply confine or domesticate the full nature of developmental equality. Incremental strategies can easily become boundaries. Children's positive rights and their entitlement to robust support to achieve their developmental potential would best be achieved by new legislation as affirmative policy. This would require a radical break, a broad vision: a New Deal for Children. In the current political climate a New Deal for Children might seem impractical and unimaginable. But I would argue this is precisely the time to articulate what is needed, and then face issues of political strategies. "What we can't imagine, can't come to be" (hooks 1989, 176).

A New Deal for Children would be a proactive, affirmative approach to establish the structures, policies, and funding necessary to ensure the maximum development of every child. It would be constructed on the scaffold of three primary principles: equality, development, and the best interests of children. It would reflect equality, equity, and universalism. The underlying vision of the New Deal would be affirmative, egalitarian support for all children to achieve their full developmental potential.

This would be a radical break from the current deal for children. Despite protestations of how we love and value our children, our actions suggest the contrary. We do not ensure that their mothers have guaranteed, high-quality prenatal care, nor that they can count on healthy environments to support their pregnancies. We do not ensure that their parents will have some time off for critical initial bonding and care when children are born or adopted, or that they will be paid during leave so that all parents of whatever family form or income level can afford to take leave. We do not ensure that their parents can take time off to care for them when they are sick, even though we know that on average children will be ill from typical childhood ailments at a minimum multiple times a year. We do not provide high-quality health care once children are born, nor do we address or ameliorate the social determinants of health. We do not ensure that all children are economically secure or even have enough to eat each day. We do not guarantee that children are safe and secure, but tolerate neighborhoods of violence, including violence from police sometimes directed at children and youth. We do not ensure all parents are supported as caregivers. Some parents, disproportionately fathers, are incarcerated and therefore unavailable to their children if they do not pay child support, even if they are unable to do so. All parents are challenged to balance work and family, and may suffer workplace discrimination because of their care of children. We permit implicit bias and stereotypes to continue to pervade the systems that affect children most directly, most notably schools, from preschool through high school. We fail to provide all children with high-quality child care, preschool, or public education; to the contrary we openly sustain unequal public care and education systems. We treat children who make bad decisions or behave badly like criminals in our juvenile justice system rather than rehabilitating and restoring them to success.

Our children, under the current deal, face a reality of unfairness, inequality, differential valuing, and potential risk and harm from the state. A child of color, a child born into a poor or working-class family, will get less support and, at the same time, will be targeted for more negative consequences than a white child of middle-class or greater means. And the inadequacies and risks are gendered as well. Under the current deal, our children, all of our children, are given the message that only some kids matter. The future is not wide open for all. For some, there is likely no future at all.

A New Deal for Children envisions equality for all children to reach their developmental potential, to have a fair chance, an equally supported chance, when by definition they are dependent on others for their growth and success. A New Deal for Children imagines an affirmative, positive set of coordinated reforms to replace the hierarchies among children, and supporting all children to their developmental potential. It is consistent with entrenched U.S. legal principles of equality, as well as internationally recognized children's rights. A New Deal would include reform of existing systems; the creation of new systems necessary for children's developmental success from birth to young adulthood; a broad attack on children's poverty; and a comprehensive attack on racism and embrace of an inclusive, multicultural society. The construction of the New Deal would be consistent with principles that derive from the theoretical lens of critical identities theory, vulnerabilities theory, economic equality, and children's rights. This means attentiveness to identities and intersectionality; a structural focus that links vulnerabilities, whether identity-based or otherwise, place-based and structurally focused economic policies; and operating from the perspective of the child, for the equality of all children.

A New Deal for Children would potentially include policies, programs, and entitlements that are beyond the scope of this volume. I focus on developmental equality here, but the New Deal might in addition comprehensively address other needs of children. For example, it might also include the empowerment of youth as an essential recognition of their evolving capacity and as a precursor to their full "voice" as adults. The New Deal might include reorientation of policies intended to protect children from violence in its many forms, from both familial and nonfamilial sources. It might include specific policies for refugee children and unaccompanied migrant minors. By calling for a New Deal for Children I hope to encourage other advocates to add to what I begin here. My focus is what a New Deal would need to include for developmental equality amidst a current reality of developmental hierarchies, differences, and inequalities among American children.

My call for a New Deal for Children expressly draws upon the broad and dramatic scope of the New Deal of the 1930s. Just as the deep poverty and unemployment of the Depression generated radical change focused on workers, so too the harsh inequalities among children and their implications for our society require a comprehensive New Deal for Children. The New Deal of the 1930s was intended to rescue unemployed, desperate workers whose massive unemployment and its effects on families threatened the very fabric of society. The combination of the first and second phases of the New Deal generated a plethora of policies and agencies to address the immediate economic crisis but also fundamentally reshaped the relationship of citizens to their government. Although not all legislation and agencies were sustained over time, the changed role of government remained. Landmark policies continue to provide critical supports and benefits, most notably Social Security (providing pension, disability, and death benefits), unemployment benefits, as well as regulatory regimes in labor, housing, banking, and securities law.

President Franklin Roosevelt's call to action, "The only thing we have to fear is fear itself," was a reassurance that the government would provide support and solutions amidst economic catastrophe. The 1930s New Deal focused on men because the dominant social understanding (the macrosystemic view) was that the economic system rested upon men earning a wage sufficient to support a family. The assistance created to restore that version of the social contract in the face of the Depression was not only gendered but raced, targeted to benefit white men and their families. Indeed, the structure of the New Deal reinforced, perpetuated, and strengthened racial hierarchy. In the midst of this dramatic effort to provide economic support, hierarchy was embedded and sustained long after the Depression ended (Katznelson 2006; Wilson 2009). That hierarchy continues: "[T]he persistence of racial inequality stems from the long-term effects of labor market discrimination and institutional practices that have created cumulative inequalities by race. The result is a durable pattern of racial stratification. Whites have gained or accumulated opportunities, while African Americans and other racial groups have lost opportunities—they suffer from disaccumulation of the accoutrements of economic opportunity" (Brown et al. 2005, 22).

A New Deal for Children should draw upon the broad comprehensive model of the 1930s, but its goal of developmental equality requires that it must address hierarchies rather than re-create them. I borrow the New Deal name as an example of what is possible, of what has been done, to counter the critique that broad legislative or policy initiatives are impossible to imagine or achieve on this scale. Indeed, the claims of new policies identified in the early Trump administration, as I complete this volume, are no less potentially comprehensive but rely on a radically different construction of macrosystemic ideas that arguably reinforce and deepen the inequalities I focus on here. The reminder of the subordinating aspect of the 1930s New Deal captures the critical insight of the developmental equality model: that in order for children to be equal, we must operate from the realities of their inequalities based on race, class, and gender in order for all children to reach their full potential. A New Deal for Children is an example of a broad, radical response to the need for essential change, as well as a reminder that unless coupled with a powerful commitment to equality, such radical change can become another means to reinforce hierarchies rather than destroy them.

The 1930s New Deal example also is not unique. This was not the only time that the state responded comprehensively to a broad problem or set of issues, reframing its responsibilities and structure based on shared critical values. The G.I. Bill, enacted in the 1940s after World War II and still ongoing, provides military veterans with affirmative support to achieve educational and economic capabilities (Katznelson 2006; Wilson 2009). As with the New Deal, the G.I. Bill originally included explicit limitations on support that disproportionately affected African American veterans and their families, who disproportionately failed to benefit from the intended outcomes of those policies, were actively blocked from opportunities by government-sanctioned redlining policies, and were stymied by local authorities charged with implementing the program. "The federal government, though seemingly race-neutral, functioned as a commanding instrument of white privilege" (Katznelson 2006, 18).

Another example of comprehensive reform and support is President Lyndon Johnson's Great Society, an array of programs enacted in the 1960s designed to confront issues of poverty and race discrimination. The legacy of that effort remains in the lasting structure of Medicare and Medicaid, fundamentally reshaping health care, and the Civil Rights Act of 1964, a powerful tool to combat discrimination. So a New Deal for Children is not unimaginable or impossibly visionary. To the contrary, it links to these prior efforts at comprehensive change and reminds us how important it is that the goal of equality be zealously guarded and carefully, comprehensively defined.

With these examples in mind, a New Deal for Children proceeds from the assumption that two commitments have been made that are essential to developmental equality: (1) to maximize the developmental potential of all children from birth to adulthood and (2) to achieve equality among children, defined as the equal ability to maximize their developmental capacity and opportunity. A New Deal for Children would require not only these commitments but symbolic and actual leadership, resources, and policies. This would include a dedicated, federal, cabinet-level effort to prioritize children in federal spending; support of federal, state, and local efforts to maximize children's development; and shared knowledge and models of programs and systems that work, measured by the delivery of supports to all children for their optimal developmental achievement. Borrowing from structures in place elsewhere in the world, a cabinet-level department, the Department of Children and Youth, with a cabinet-level secretary, would most strongly communicate this vision and commitment.

What would be included? In the balance of this chapter I articulate components of the New Deal, and suggest their implications.

Components of the New Deal for Children

1. Developmentally informed
2. Structural change: system reform and system creation
3. Poverty elimination and income inequality reduction
4. Cultural change: confronting racism
5. National standards and local empowerment: universalism, equality, and equity
6. Metrics

Developmentally Informed

The heart of the New Deal is that policy, practices, and outcomes reflect the developmental equality model and its goal of maximizing developmental opportunity and outcomes for every child. In order to be developmentally informed, policies, practices, systems, and outcomes must reflect (1) linear developmental knowledge, (2) equality of outcomes linked to both individual and intersectional identities, and (3) a comprehensive ecological perspective. Family must be prioritized because families are developmentally critical; and their ecologies are also critical, particularly their neighborhoods and communities.

Developmental equality requires a fundamental equation that combines scientific knowledge with attention to hierarchies among children that signal subordination, in order to yield the result of ensuring support of all children to their developmental capacity. The goal is not resilience from hierarchies but reduction and elimination of hierarchies.

Consistent with the developmental equality model, policy must be sensitive to, and differentiated by, the *linear progression* of children, meaning their developmental stages and ages, and to the range of developmental aspects (physical, mental, cognitive, emotional) of each stage. What is essential in early childhood development is not the same, for example, as needs in adolescence. Increasingly, as children develop, the world outside the family and neighborhood becomes critical in terms of how children will be treated and accepted as children and as adults. In addition, the developmental perspective requires attention to the individual characteristics of the individual child. The linear perspective is a range, not an absolute. It also is premised upon a child without disabilities in terms of setting norms. It is essential that all children be evaluated according to their individual characteristics, and that disabilities are included within the framework and robustly supported.

Children's developmental equality irrespective of stage cannot be separated from their families, and therefore policies cannot separate supporting children from supporting their families, however structured or constructed. This *family-first focus* is especially important in the critical developmental period of birth to three or birth to five. At all developmental stages and ages, however, it could be argued that the family's role and support are critical from birth to young adulthood, so potentially extending the age range of the New Deal to twenty-five. A corollary to the primacy of families is to recognize the importance of families' ecologies, centered in neighborhood, community, and wage work. The developmental equality model emphasizes this focus, based particularly on the work of Spencer and García Coll. Developmental science, neuroscience, medicine, child development, psychology, economics, sociology, and other fields give us a full, rich picture of what is needed to maximize the developmental potential for every child, and thus the construction of policies. These fields act as guides to illuminate and identify where change and reorientation is needed, as well as what structures need to be dismantled.

Developmentally informed policy also incorporates the *importance of race, gender, and class* as long as those characteristics generate challenges for some children. A critical goal is equality for all children and to confront the negative role of identities in the current deal, as well as to appreciate the positive attributes of identities. This means paying attention to the component pieces of the models of Spencer and García Coll and how they play out individually and ecologically. This aspect of ensuring that the New Deal is developmentally informed is the basis for norms or standards for what might be put into place, as well as the trigger for dismantling challenges and barriers that generate hierarchical, unequal developmental outcomes tied to race, gender, and class.

In addition, this component of being developmentally informed reminds us to remain critical and analytical about developmental norms. Consistent with what we know of scientific knowledge, and the historical presence of bias in the research and models of development, critique and analysis of the scientific base are essential. In addition, enriching that base with enhanced knowledge of the developmental arc of children of color and other subordinated children can contribute to refining knowledge of both the challenges and unique strengths of subordinated children. Data and equality goals must always, and persistently, include ongoing questioning of norms, attention to hierarchies, and attention to outcomes. As Freire reminds us, we are not simply creating a New Deal *for* or *to* children, but must engage them as themselves. This is a set of goals "which must be forged with, not for, the oppressed (whether individuals or peoples) in the incessant struggle to regain their humanity" (Freire 1990, 33). This fits especially strongly with the message from the development of Black boys of the strength of their identity, of their being, amidst developmental challenges. We do not need to fix them; we need to liberate them. And the standard of "optimum development" must be one that we constantly interrogate to ensure it is not a norm of hierarchy and subordination masquerading as science or as being "neutral." So the role of data and metrics should not be passive. Rather, it should remind us, here and elsewhere, to keep questioning norms, how we got them, who did the research, and why—the developmental research clearly tells us that. And if movement toward developmental equality is achieved, in the process norms and goals must be reassessed, both to prevent domestication and to press for full developmental equality, and sustaining that outcome for every child.

Finally, to be developmentally informed also clearly means the New Deal must be *ecological* in its perspective, both horizontally and vertically. Structures interconnect, and those interconnections are critical to the interlocking impact on developmental equality. This is the insight of Bronfenbrenner's ecological model, confirmed by neurological science, as modified by attending to hierarchies in order to ensure that the developmental ecology works equally well for all children. Currently, structures interconnect to reinforce inequality; families interconnect with communities in resistance; individual children face inordinate challenges simply because of who they are and due to systems designed for them to fail rather than to succeed to their fullest potential. Any recasting of systems must include attention to their interconnecting impact, intentional and unintentional, and guard against the replication of inequalities. So linked ecologies and systems must be required to pay attention to whether their overlapping and interacting qualities all serve developmental equality. Exposure of dysfunctional system interaction that undermines children's developmental equality should trigger the necessity of reform and should be monitored to change outcomes.

Models of potential ecological approaches are provided by the countries of the OECD, the group that includes the United States as a member and includes countries that have economies and governments most like ours. One of the major differences from the American context for most other OECD countries is that supporting child development is on the policy agenda, and has been for some time. Consciousness need not be raised; it is already there, in large part due to the embrace of the CRC (OECD 2009a, 28). It is an issue not of *whether* to engage in policy, but of *what* to do. This is a strong reminder of the importance of the macrosystemic level of the ecology.

The OECD's child well-being focus and research are based on an interlocking framework organized on six dimensions: material well-being, housing and environment, education, health, risk behaviors, and quality of school life (OECD 2009a, 2009b; UNICEF 2009). Some but not all are further broken down by sex, age, and migrant status (OECD 2009b, 32). The approach is linked to the development and accumulation of human capital (id., 25). Similar categories are encompassed by the Duke University Child and Youth Well-Being Index, an American index used to compare how well states support children's needs (Land 2017). Indicators are not programs; but indicators link to sectors and structures. The six areas of OECD indicators link developmental outcomes that are related to families, neighborhoods, and communities as they interact with economic, work, educational, health, public safety, and other systems. No one country stands out on all six indicators, a very telling fact; and no aggregation is done of all factors since no research exists to suggest how to weight factors or relevant correlations of aggregation (OECD 2009b).

Indicators link to policy guidance. So, for example, material well-being is linked to policies to reduce poverty including cash assistance, tax benefits, work incentives, and child care, all of which affect parental employment and reduce child poverty (id., 33). Educational factors are linked to public education, including early childhood education, and connect to both achievement and equality, as well as after-school programs and youth employment and postsecondary education. Housing policies and broader environmental factors touch families, neighborhoods, and communities, thus how children function outside their homes. Health and safety link to risk factors but also to the kinds of environments that generate adverse health outcomes. Measures at birth link to the quality and equality of health care prenatally and after birth. The most severe outcome, youth mortality, links to rates of violence and harm from a range of sources, including links to policing.

The 2009 OECD study on child well-being summarizes its findings under the heading "Childhood Decides" (OECD 2009b). This singularly powerful statement underscores the importance of a New Deal for Children. Childhood decides for all children, and for children in relation to each other. Development matters and equity matters. According to the 2009 summary, the data suggests the following policy implications: money matters, but it matters significantly where money is spent, for whom, and how. Money for children in the OECD countries is spent, apart from health, on cash benefits and tax credits, education, child care, and other in-kind services. Education accounts for the greatest amount of spending in most countries, followed by cash benefits and child care. Where there is particular variation among countries is in the amount of education spending in the early years, with the highest rate of spending for ages birth to five equal to one-third of education spending, and the average rate of early education representing about one-quarter of the education budget. The policy recommendations from the full analysis include spending more and concentrating more on the early years; spending more for children at risk of poor well-being throughout the developmental cycle, but especially early; mixing in-kind services with cash; spending more prenatally and during the early years; sustaining statistical visibility of children; and continuing to experiment (OECD 2009b, 8). The OECD data are a rich source for imagining comprehensive, ecological developmental perspectives translated into policy.

One other model of ecological reform is the Harlem Children's Zone (HCZ). The power of the HCZ model is its comprehensive approach to the development of the children and youth who utilize all of its available services, which range from prebirth supports to college completion. It is a strong model for localism, experimentation, and difference. It is distinctive, however, from the OECD model in that its very localism within the American framework is an exception to the structures within which it functions. In some respects this is a Band-Aid or transitional approach because it represents adaptation to or a work-around of existing systems, since its local focus by definition means the inability to effect system change. It responds to the risks created by systems, and to some degree constructs private institutions alongside failed public ones. But it is unable to address the poverty system; or the threat posed by policing and the juvenile justice system. Its response to the educational system is to create a separate, far better system. Nevertheless, it is a model of in-place transformation, local control, and comprehensive strategy.

The HCZ model, the brainchild of Geoffrey Canada, provides the resources equivalent to those typically enjoyed by middle-class children to children in the zone, one hundred blocks in Harlem, New York. Founded in 1994, HCZ has evolved to include a pipeline that supports children and their families from before birth to the completion of college. The pipeline for children infuses the entire community with support. This includes support for parents prior to the birth of their children (Baby College), early childhood education (Harlem Gems), and K–12 education (Promise Academy). It also includes parenting programs, programs for children prior to preschool, after-school programs, fitness programs, guidance programs, college support, community association organizing, health programs, mental health programs, family crisis intervention services, drug and alcohol referrals, and domestic violence prevention (Dunn 2010, 7). The shape of specific programs is research- and data-inspired, monitored and evaluated, and up for constant review and reevaluation (McCarthy and Jean-Louis 2017). The Zone has been primarily funded with private support, at a cost of $100 million. The estimated spending per child is $5,000 annually (often compared to per-child jail costs of $60,000 per year and per-child juvenile detention costs of over $100,000 per year). Roughly 12 percent of its revenue, $9 million in 2009, came from government funding. Promise Neighborhoods, an effort to expand the example of the Zone, was initiated under the Obama administration (Page and Stone 2010). The advocacy and tenacity of Geoffrey Canada is unique, living up to his motto of "Whatever It Takes" (Tough 2008). The benefit of this evolution is its freedom from government bureaucracy, but the story of its growth also is a testament to how government structures were a major headache and continuing challenge for the Zone.

Certainly there have been critics and analysis of the Zone. Most importantly, a study by Dobbs and Fryer concludes that the educational component could be separated from the wraparound community services that are a distinctive part of the model (Dobbs and Fryer 2009; Whitehurst and Croft 2010). If that analysis holds true, it may close the achievement gap but not fully support developmental equality. The wraparound services are designed to reach families and the community, to continue to foster maximum child development. In addition, they promise family and community development, independent of the impact this has on children, and a long-term approach to developmental equality. The idea that children can succeed but their families and communities might be left behind contradicts the importance of those elements in the lives of children and youth, and the impact of community change for the community to reimagine itself.

Ecological approaches, linear developmental stages, and attentiveness to hierarchies are the core aspects of the principle that the New Deal be developmentally informed in order to achieve each child's maximum development and opportunity to achieve. That principle must be used to eliminate challenges and build supportive structures. System change for every child's benefit is the goal: to eliminate barriers created by state structures and to impose a duty to ensure equality.

Structural Change: System Reform and System Creation

The fundamental change necessary to achieve developmental equality is structural, moving from interconnected systems of inequality differentially affecting children to interconnected systems that individually and collectively achieve developmental equality for all children. A key piece of structural change is holding structures accountable to produce equal developmental outcomes for all children, defined as maximizing their developmental potential. Evidence of hierarchical outcomes or failure to achieve developmental milestones should trigger reform of structures affecting children's development, however radical that reform might be, up to and including dismantling harmful, unequal structures. In addition to radical structural reform, a New Deal includes attention to structural needs, such as those in early childhood, where there is largely an absence of support or uneven support for children.

The scope of comprehensive structural change would include, but is not limited to, the following areas:

Health, including prenatal health, children's health, and family health, focusing on health equity and the determinants of health, not simply treatment; including also nutrition support and supportive family visits

Education, beginning with early childhood education, continuing through primary and secondary education, and postsecondary college or other training; including mental health screening and early identification and support for learning disabilities and other disabilities

Parental support, including economic support, education, skills, services, birth and adoption paid leave, leave to care for sick children or to participate in children's educational activities, and other policies to ensure work-family balance

Universal high-quality child care and after-school programs

Adolescent youth services support, including work, skills, enrichment, and well-being; fostering positive identities of race and gender; safety, nonviolence, positive sexuality; and juvenile justice as a system of well-being and rehabilitation with incarceration as a last resort

Child and family well-being and crisis support, prevention to the extent possible of domestic violence and child abuse and neglect by effective inter-

ventions, after minimizing factors that contribute to these behaviors, and
providing effective systems for children who go into foster care

Resilience support for sources of toxic stress or episodic stress to children,
families, and communities

Anti-poverty, economic-stabilization measures including cash transfers, in-
kind transfers, services, and support

Housing, either separately or as part of an overall economic policy, ensuring
neighborhoods without concentrated poverty or concentrated poor housing conditions

Public safety, including positive relationships between police and children,
and peaceful neighborhoods

I suggest this list only as a sense of what might be included in
structural change and construction, not as a roadmap or bureaucratic
diagram. Nor does it address levels and/or interaction of levels of government. This preliminary structural list is not intended to preclude creative thinking about how the primary subdivisions would be organized,
or how one might think about smaller pieces of the interconnected ecologies. The point of my articulation of the structural aspect of the New
Deal for Children is to suggest the broad scope and location of what is
needed to accomplish children's developmental equality. Most important
is to understand the structural focus as mandating a thorough structural
reorientation akin to the radical changes made in the 1930s New Deal,
the 1940s G.I. Bill, and the 1960s Great Society.

Structural change required for the New Deal for Children would include a combination of reforms of existing structures and constructing
new systems. The changes needed in existing structures are radical. So,
for example, with respect to education, in order to achieve egalitarian
schools, the funding and resources available to every child must be equitable (although not necessarily equal). Maximum development does not
vary by zip code; school resources should not as well. The map of opportunity should be the same for every child. This requires the equalization
of resources as well as the upward increase of resources if equalization
yields inadequate resources for optimal development calibrated by community, as well as the upward increase of resources if children have particular needs. This would mean we would no longer characterize schools

as "good" or "bad," based on local knowledge of the school and its district, or grade schools to create an educational hierarchy. While schools should be held accountable, they should not be asked to do the same thing with wildly different resources in terms of money, facilities, and so on. Moreover, if the evaluation of children in the school district indicates widespread common needs or if particular students have distinctive needs, those needs must be addressed.

Another critical educational reform is that school disciplinary systems must be radically reassessed and restructured to serve children's well-being and developmental needs. The school-to-prison pipeline must be dismantled. Any replacement system must be developmentally informed, part of a schoolwide culture of rehabilitation and community involvement, focused on child well-being and school safety. In the vast majority of cases, disciplinary outcomes can be linked to a proactive, rehabilitative, schoolwide restorative justice system that teaches life skills and serves developmental goals while healing and compensating victims.

Similarly, the juvenile justice system is long overdue for a drastic overhaul to construct a system centered on child well-being, child development, and public safety (Bell 2015; Bilchik 2011; Dowd 2015). It must be a fair system, not one mired in racial disproportionality. This requires not just changing the complexion of kids in the system but changing the way the system defines its goal. Incarceration should be limited to only those who cannot be served or helped other than by confinement. The system would be radically redesigned from a system of punishment and collateral consequences to one that focuses on identifying what will return the child to a positive developmental path and be safe for the community. The vast majority of kids would be diverted or reached much earlier to deal with any underlying issues, such as mental health issues that would be dealt with by a comprehensive and well-funded mental health system (which might prevent kids with mental health issues from ever coming into contact with the juvenile justice system). Those kids who had committed nondangerous crimes would be recognized for what they are: teenagers, acting like teenagers. Child well-being would focus on education, skills, a plan for reconciliation and restitution with those they have harmed, and reabsorption into a community built on support of their development and realizing their goals. Such a system would not confuse particular behavior with a potential for a lifetime of antisocial criminal acts. Detention or incarceration would be a last resort invoked only when alternative solutions are not feasible given the high level and seriousness of the harm done.

As Rios and others have argued, this should be a youth development system, not a youth destruction system (Rios 2011; Mincy 1994; Lawrence 2011). And as Geoff Ward reminds us, a reconstructed juvenile justice system should be inextricably intertwined with communities and their role and input, essential to the creation of what he calls "racial democracy" (Ward 2012). A racialized, punitive system must be replaced with an entirely different system that is not a tool of racial subordination nor of the destruction or harm to any child's development.

In addition to system reform, there must be system creation. Early childhood requires the construction of a system to ensure a fair start; it simply does not exist apart from piecemeal programs highly uneven in quality and access. What is needed is a universal system of preschool and high-quality child care prior to the formal beginning of school in kindergarten. The aim of such a system would be to ensure an ongoing high level of care when children are not with their parents, as well as ensuring all children have the same opportunity to be ready for school, and that none can be identified by race or class in terms of an achievement gap on the very first day of kindergarten.

Such a system must be integrated with other forms of early childhood support that feed the development process at that stage. Indeed, a focus on early childhood would begin before children are born, ensuring that to the degree possible their parents have planned their children and are prepared for parenting, and that a robust health care system has supported a healthy pregnancy. In addition, parents' workplaces and public policy would support family and work responsibilities and balance. Systemically, the core principle would be that children should be supported in the families into which they were born.

At birth, families provide the most critical developmental support from birth to age three. In light of that, support of families is critical. This would include income support; employment support if needed; housing support; health care, including parental education and well-child visits through programs like the visiting nurse program, to provide in-home support and education; and any additional support needed to optimize parental and familial care. For most children, their parents will place them in care while they work. The child care system available to all parents must be of uniformly high quality, developmentally informed.

Barbara Bennett Woodhouse captures the care/education interface with the term "educare," a combination of care and developmentally informed education that reaches all developmental realms (Woodhouse 2008b). So, for instance, it would include children's development of emotional intelligence as well as their cognitive growth. In such a system children with disabilities would receive attention to their specific and special needs in order to maximize their development. High-quality early childhood education would be available to all children along with the supports necessary to sustain that education outside the formal educational structure. The goal would be to maximize developmental opportunity and prevent early educational achievement gaps. Ongoing research and follow-up to maximize those goals would be essential, as well as to ensure that equality remains a key goal and actual outcome for all children.

The early development of children is essential to equality, so that children arrive at kindergarten as equal as they were at birth. No gaps should exist; no resilience should be necessary. No longer should the accident of birth, the identity of their parents, or the vagaries of income matter.

Examples of how to approach early childhood policy can be drawn from the OECD, which has focused on this area as a subset of its comprehensive child well-being approach (OECD 2001, 2006, 2012, 2015b). The OECD policy guidance in this areas includes "care" with "education," captured in the acronym ECEC, establishing a continuum of care from birth, intertwined with robust work and family policies as well as policies to address specific needs of immigrant families. This links into the traditional education system, conceptualized as K–12, as a seamless system but adjusted to different developmental stages. The OECD's 2006 report presents five key policy goals for early childhood:

- To attend to the social context of early childhood development
- To place well-being, early development, and learning at the core of ECEC work, while respecting the child's agency and natural learning strategies

- To create the governance structures necessary for system accountability and quality assurance
- To develop with the stakeholders broad guidelines and curricular standards for all ECEC services
- To aspire to ECEC systems that support broad learning, participation, and democracy (OECD 2006, 16–17)

These principles underscore an approach that is universal and equality-focused, ensuring all children have the early childhood context to grow and thrive, but at the same time to devote additional resources to children who are less well developmentally supported (for example, children of recent immigrants) because their families and communities are less well supported, creating developmental challenges not of children's making. Uniformity in the face of inequality reinscribes inequality. Equality requires equity. Mechanisms that re-create challenges that identify children as "at risk" or facing developmental challenges are the structural embodiments of ongoing inequality.

Poverty Elimination and Income Inequality Reduction

Because the correlations between poverty and development are so powerfully negative, a New Deal for Children must end child poverty, and this critical goal deserves a separate focus because of its multisystemic implications. The mechanisms for addressing child poverty would include income supports for families that would bring them not just above the poverty line but to a level where they can provide developmental support for their children or can do so with the provision of supports that they otherwise would be unable to afford. Second, children would have decent housing situated in healthy neighborhoods. Third, their families, of whatever form, would have the employment and care supports necessary for healthy development, along with child health equity. Families, as the first and most critical ecology for children's development, would be supported instead of stressed. Employment opportunities along with high-quality child care, early childhood education, and after-school care would be critical, as would health care for all family members and attentiveness to the social determinants of health. Those might include also screenings beyond those optimally part of regular care in early childhood. So too they might include ACEs screening in early, middle, and adolescent periods, and early detection and responses to learning disabilities or any other disabilities.

Child poverty cannot be ended without focusing on families and neighborhoods, and eliminating communities with a high concentration of low-income households. The scholarship on the intersecting systems of poverty is critical to addressing all the interlocking pieces that impact the most direct part of the ecology for children's developmental equality, the quality of their family relationships. Such an attack on child poverty must critically encompass a range of family forms, including in particular strengthening so-called fragile families (Fragile Families and Child Wellbeing Study 2015). This might include specific support programs for single-parent families, which are disproportionate in low-income families. It also might encompass gender-specific strategies to increase the involvement and positive presence of both fathers and mothers, and support of social parents.

Clearly there are multiple systems that are involved with addressing child poverty. They include the work/employment sector, to provide opportunities and meaningful work for all parents; adult education, to provide training and education for those parents who lack the skills to independently support their children; and training and support in care for those parents who have not been engaged with their children.

The most promising approach to comprehensive, multisystemic solutions to poverty is Patrick Sharkey's pathway to equality centered in neighborhoods (Sharkey 2013). Sharkey focuses on interconnected systems in geographic space that constitute and perpetuate poverty. He concludes that poverty persists because of community subordination that links to generational replication of lack of opportunity. His solution is not to remove some (deserving? however defined?) families from impoverished communities, but to invest and transform whole communities, with an eye to immediate change and creation of a healthy developmental context for kids but also for adults. He insists that the investment and support must be sustained in order to achieve change over generations. "I argue for a policy agenda designed to generate intensive and sustained investments in the nation's most disadvantaged neighborhoods with the dual goals of avoiding areas characterized by high levels of concentrated joblessness and creating areas that feature safe, enriching environments for youth" (id., 11). His two key principles are recognizing poverty as a multigenerational problem, based on his analysis of the lack of significant economic progress for Blacks since the 1970s, and "investing in place" (id., 12).

Sharkey's analysis dovetails with the ecological focus of developmental equality, and the record of the importance of family, neighborhood, and community in the lives of Black boys and youth. His work is reinforced by the research of Alexander, Entwisle, and Olson in Baltimore, *The Long Shadow* (2014), where they identify the barrier to opportunity for low-income children as early cumulative disadvantage within their families because of the lack of resources in their communities. The importance of Sharkey's approach is also echoed in Carla Shedd's *Unequal City* (2015), a study of Chicago's geography of inequality and its reinforcement, however unintended, by enticing youth otherwise insufficiently supported to cross boundaries to obtain opportunities. As Shedd points out, that strategy leaves neighborhood inequality in place while communicating to those who cross boundaries that they do not completely belong.

The movement for child health equity suggests a related strategy, albeit focused on the single system of health care (Goldhagen and Mercer 2011; Goldhagen et al. 2015). Advocates of child health equity argue that medicine needs to reorient the practice paradigm of pediatricians. This perspective sees child well-being as attached to interlocking systems and factors: social, political, economic, cultural, and environmental determinants of health. Health is connected not merely to genetics but to epigenetics; disparities are linked to racism, sexism, and classism (id.). Health care does not have a major impact on health outcomes; rather, these broader determinants do. Health equity is organized around child rights, social justice, and health equity using the CRC as a framework that should lead to a different medical model as well as to different policy ranging from clinical and community practices to national policy. This reorientation is on the agenda of the American Association of Pediatrics as a means to confront the health disparities of children and achieve health equity (American Association of Pediatrics 2017).

Child health equity mirrors the arguments of those who have focused on social investment and social determinants. In health care analysis work by Rachel Rebouché and Scott Burris, social determinants analysis identifies the importance of social conditions and resources to health outcomes—a more powerful factor than genetic makeup or individual choices (Rebouché and Burris 2015). Solutions or policies focus on changing the social determinants in a way that supports health care, and healthy lives, for all. Similarly, such an approach would define different consequences when developmental equality analysis exposes the complicit or primary role of the state in sustaining social determinants that yield inequalities. It would require not only elimination of the barrier where it manifests as state involvement in replicating inequality and creating developmental hurdles but also facilitating positive support. By identifying the social determinants of inequality, it might attend to more effective ways to reverse those outcomes, and sustain the focus on structural change. Monitoring such policies might function much like performance criteria in health care, in addition to providing resources to those who can control and use those resources.

Sharkey's place-based anti-poverty strategy, including health equity in conjunction with the work of other scholars and disciplines, holds the promise that poverty and income inequality will not be determinative of children's developmental opportunities and outcomes.

Cultural Change: Confronting Racism

Just as structural change, including a robust anti-poverty policy, is essential to the New Deal for Children, so too is cultural change. Embracing the principle of developmental equality requires macro-level changes to our culture of who is responsible for children, to what our level of responsibility is, and to our dedication to real, meaningful equality. In the preceding chapters I have made the case for developmental equality from the life course of Black boys, exposing the inequality and trajectory for failure of the current deal for children that replicates their place at the bottom of a hierarchy of children. It cannot be sufficiently emphasized that the embrace of the core value and "rightness" of developmental equality is a precondition to support of a New Deal for Children.

Beyond this macro-level cultural change essential for the New Deal to be embraced, within its framework attention to cultural issues is critical. First, the core principle of cultural change for developmental equality is the valuing of every child, as well as each child's identities and communities. Standing in the way of that principle is the reality of cognitive bias and stereotyping among the human actors in every system, both those who interact directly with children, such as teachers, police officers, health care workers, and day care workers, as well as those with less direct interactions with children, such as employers, community members, and political decision makers and leaders. It is clear from the developmental data on Black boys that human actors within systems that they encounter have generated significant developmental challenges and barriers, particularly in education and juvenile justice.

Second, another cultural issue that needs to be part of the New Deal is recognizing how positive racial identity is critical to the resilience of subordinated racial groups, and the implications of that for developmental norms and identities for all children. How might identities be supported, including positive non-subordinating racial and other identities for historically dominant groups of children?

Finally, affirmative valuing of diverse cultures and identities is integral to the support of every child's developmental potential. Instead of interconnected outcomes of inequality that function on the axes of race, gender, and class, the New Deal would achieve outcomes of equality that when measured and evaluated by race, gender, and class no longer display hierarchies along those identities or their interconnection. In place of purportedly neutral standards that reinforce inequalities and erase multiple identities, there would be affirmative valuing and inclusion that is pluralistic and affirmative. Thus the elimination of hierarchies among children would have an affirmative cultural focus, moving from privilege, discrimination, stereotyping, and segregation to appreciation, valuing, cultural pluralism, diversity, and the dismantling of skin, gender, class, and other privileges. It would take a page from the affirmative racial identities of communities of color, and affirmative and non-hierarchical masculinities.

Combatting the powerful impact of race systemically and culturally is essential to constructing the New Deal. It requires sustained, affirmative engagement and change particularly around racism. As critical race theory reminds us, race is bone-deep in our system, embedded and replicated. The goal of cultural change would be not only to eradicate subordinating policies and effects from supposedly neutral institutions, but to engage, actively, to combat and eliminate racism particularly as it affects children. It would mean support of positive racial identity, including non-subordinating white identity. A New Deal for Children would be committed to changing culture, and committed to paying attention to outcomes to ensure equality.

Jerry Kang has powerfully argued for the necessity and the ability to counter implicit bias through the use of scientific data about bias to frame ways to deal with it, what he calls "fair measures" (Kang and Banaji 2006). The depth and strength of the research on cognitive bias in education and employment provides a tool essential to removing bias from the actors in systems that affect children's development, as well as to confront the learned biases of children (Nance 2013; Project Implicit 2017).

Social dominance theory complements that focus with examination of individual, group, and institutional levels of the phenomenon of social dominance, and the replication of hierarchy, as the consequences of structure and its interaction with culture (Pratto, Sidanius, and Levin 2006). For concrete measures to combat system justification, there is the analysis of Gary Blasi and John Yost on changing system framing or frame shifting (Blasi and Yost 2006). These are some of the many approaches in the rich literature on stereotyping that can be drawn upon to change or eliminate stereotypes and their impact on those who act on them, and those who are the objects of the stereotype.

We must counter stereotypes and bias but also recognize, validate, and value positive identity and recognize it is white identity that needs the most reshaping. One of the strongest aspects of development of children of color is both the necessity and the strength of their racial identity. This is both defensive and offensive, in the sense that it is necessary to survive within a dangerous and skewed structure that creates challenges and harms for them. At the same time, it is a testament to positive racial identity despite adverse systemic and cultural norms. It is also a testament to their families' parenting. It calls attention to the differential construction of racial identity for whites. We might use Carla Shedd's work on boundary crossing to create different, positive experiences of such crossings and ensure that they go in multiple directions. We have campaigns about domestic violence, drinking, smoking, and gender equality to remind us that we have affirmatively engaged in culture change. We engage in cultural programming all the time in the curricula of schools and the adoption of curriculum standards.

Finally, the cultural challenge of race also requires us to ask the other questions and understand and shift the cultural frame for other identities and intersections, of gender, class, religion, immigration status, and others. What are the other cultural justifiers for inequality, and what other supports sustain a "majority" culture?

The model for policy here is not to dictate culture but to imagine and support the proliferation and valuing of culture for the purpose of recognizing the role of culture in development and the importance of valuing a child's culture of origin, as well as the cultures they experience. The best model for this might be the ways in which the arts have embraced (and struggled to practice) cultural diversity.

National Standards and Local Empowerment

The strategic approach of the New Deal, to implement policies that are developmentally informed to reform and create structures to ensure children's developmental equality, requires both national standards and local empowerment. National standards of excellence and support are critical in order for every child to succeed. But supporting local empowerment, leadership, and implementation within local ecologies is also essential. The ecological focus reminds us of this critical balance, as place-based strategies that tell us we must bring the margin to the center, and deal with the most subordinated communities and children, or we will once again re-create hierarchy instead of destroying it. Based on the principles of families as primary, and the importance of families' neighborhood and community, strategies must be local. Neighborhoods are critical to children's development, and thus a sense of how the interconnected pieces operate on the ground locally, where the needs are, is crucial (Woodhouse, forthcoming).

At the same time, it is essential to have vertical implementation through national policy. A national policy guarantees developmental equality for all children and is a universal entitlement that must be implemented in relation to measured inequalities. Universalism captures the essential movement from the current system that permits variations from state to state, locality to locality, school district to school district, to a universal standard of outcome so that geography no longer equates to inequality. At the same time, to account for differences in needs, local flexibility is required not only to equalize the actual operation of systems but also to encourage local buy-in and empowerment. In order to achieve the universal guarantee of developmental equality, for as long as child projections, realities, and outcomes remain differentiated particularly by race, gender, class, or the intersection of those identities, or are identified by any other factor that triggers differentiated outcomes (e.g., refugee status, family disruption, childhood trauma such as loss of a parent), achieving the universal requires attention to the particular in terms of groups, neighborhoods, and communities, and in relation to individual children. The universal standard does not mean "sameness" or "identical," where that standard would in fact create hierarchies because, either in transition or even beyond transition, children come into systems differentiated in their preparation or their challenges.

Universalism is combined with equality and equity. The universal expectation of developmental support to the developmental capacity of each child is the promise to all children. Existing hierarchies require doing equity, that is, responding to differentials and blockages that replicate those hierarchies, with a range of policies and supports designed to promote true equality of opportunity and support to each child's developmental capacity. Differentiated supports are essential to achieve the same equality of developmental support. The successful elimination of challenges and barriers might mean that certain supports would no longer be necessary to compensate for hierarchy-creating hurdles. The hurdles would be gone. Nevertheless, it is likely that even with the success of structural and cultural change, developmentally informed, children born equal will nevertheless not be born in equal developmental circumstances, and therefore equity will demand differential supports for each child to enjoy equal development opportunity and support. In addition, individual children may have different needs that require differentiated support.

One way of capturing the local and the national, and the promise of the universal along with the necessity of equity policies, is the concept of a developmental equality audit. That is, armed with a clear, detailed concept of developmental equality, an audit would take stock of the existing context, and identify what could be done, how it could be done, and strategies for change. At the national level, this might use Ursula Kilkelly's audit concept to rigorously evaluate policies, systems, and practices of the New Deal for Children as well as other, more indirect state action that affects the New Deal. Kilkelly uses the CRC to engage in "rights-proofing" of law, policy, and practice (Kilkelly 2011, 186). This is an audit of existing or proposed policies that could be used as a strategy equivalent to an environmental impact statement, making the impact on children a critical piece of *all* policy analysis. Using the categories of the CRC, especially its four main principles, would generate an impact assessment of proposed or existing government policies, proposals, and budgets; collect comprehensive and disaggregated data on every aspect of children's lives; and make visible the presence or absence of children in budgets with respect to their social and economic rights. Children could be involved in this process as part of their empowerment and "voice" rights under the CRC. The method Kilkelly proposes could be qualitative or quantitative, but what is most critical is matching the audit to the provisions of the CRC, or of developmental equality. This could set benchmarks and standards as more policies and practices are audited.

A different kind of audit could capture local issues, resources, and challenges as a means both to provide supports essential to equality and to ensure community voice and empowerment. This would build on Robin Lenhardt's "race audits" to create a developmental equality audit. Lenhardt proposes race audits as a way, within the existing context, and without new comprehensive policy or litigation-driven mandates or remedies, to take stock of local conditions by focusing on the "mechanisms" of discrimination, rather than the motives (Lenhardt 2011b). I would suggest modifying her approach to incorporate the comprehensive approach of the New Deal for Children, and using its principles for system change. Lenhardt likens her audit strategy to the concept of "opportunity mapping," which identifies resources (or the lack thereof) by zip codes and neighborhoods (Powell, Kearney, and Kay 2001). She grounds her strategy in the scholarship of structuralism, showing cumulative disadvantage across domains. The audit concept captures both the macro and micro levels: how past and present government decisions, systems, or structures categorize or exploit by race; whether all groups have equally benefitted; the impact of spatial arrangements; the pattern of intergenerational wealth, social capital, and participation; and whether stigmatization has been created and fostered. At the micro level, the audit queries what specific agencies have done to include or exclude racial minorities, encourage broad participation, or facilitate initiatives inclusive of the entire community. Her audit concept brilliantly captures both structural and cultural components, while through its choices of macro-level norms it invites envisioning what the role of government should be. Lenhardt sees the audit as a way to engage all stakeholders, understand racial structural dimensions, and identify what needs to change and how (Lenhardt 2011b). This is paired with her intention to encourage and support locally generated change by "equality innovators" (Lenhardt 2011a). My adaptation of her strategy would use the audit as a means to identify local needs, strengths, and potential, consistent with her goal of local empowerment.

Metrics

Finally, metrics and monitoring are critical to the New Deal in order to ensure developmental equality: so that it is race-conscious, sex-differentiated, class-sensitive, and intersectional and remains sensitive to any identifiers of groups or individual children who are at the bottom. This is a bottom-up/outsider-in strategy of inclusion that stays focused on the margin until children at the margin are included at the center.

Collecting data relevant to constructing and sustaining policies and structures that achieve developmental equality is critical. By this I mean using data to concretely achieve goals and enforce change, not collecting data to simply keep identifying and reidentifying the problem, or what has been called, in the juvenile justice context, endless "adoration of the question" (Bell and Ridolfi 2008; Khalifa and Briscoe 2015). Data collection is essential to crafting policy and monitoring outcomes. A model for robust data collection might be found in several instruments developed by UNICEF for its campaign "A Fair Chance for Every Child" (UNICEF 2015). MODA (Multiple Overlapping Deprivation Analysis) is a tool that builds on the UNICEF Global Study on Child Poverty and Disparities and the Oxford Poverty and Human Development Initiative's Multidimensional Poverty Index. It is notable for bringing together comprehensive identity factors, structural impacts, and dynamic impacts. "It (a) selects the child as the unit of analysis; (b) adopts a life-cycle approach; (c) applies a whole-child oriented approach; (d) measures monetary poverty and multidimensional deprivations simultaneously for each child; and (e) enriches knowledge from sector-based approaches" (id., 32). A second UNICEF tool, MoRES (Monitoring Results for Equity System), is designed to identify action that needs to be taken and how well actions work. MoRES analyzes "the key factors or bottlenecks that are constraining results for the most disadvantaged children, finding and implementing solutions, and regularly tracking progress toward results" (id., 32). This puts the most marginalized children, rather than a neutral child, at the center, a key component of the developmental equality model. The UNICEF frameworks are sophisticated, ecologically focused, and inclusive of issues of social exclusion in addition to metrics focused on poverty. Nevertheless it is acknowledged that there is underinclusion of data on identity factors based on race and ethnicity, although some inclusion of gender. These inadequacies must be addressed to use this model. One other model for gauging long-term outcomes that might be useful for ongoing evaluation and analysis is the U.K. Millennium Children studies, which follow children longitudinally and provide valuable data on long-term implications of policies, instead of data snapshots (Dex and Joshi 2005; Hansen, Joshi, and Dex 2010).

The goal of metrics is holding systems accountable, by requiring the dismantling of systems that create barriers to development for some or all children, and evaluating the outcomes of new developmental supports. System outcomes are critical to achieving developmental equality, as well as making the case for system change. Social science data are critical to undermine assumptions that can drive invalid conclusions and assumed responsibilities or outcomes, or to demonstrate how stereotypes or bias functions. Positive legislative change, including dismantling inegalitarian systems or aspects of systems, or affirmative supports for developmental equality, must be grounded in evidence-based solutions that continue to measure outcomes to ensure equality goals. The importance of data does not counsel delay in implementing the developmental equality model but does underscore its significance lest that model be domesticated, ignored, or hijacked.

Conclusion

At least one set of U.S. researchers has suggested that a comprehensive set of policies supportive of children is feasible under a spending proposal called the One Percent Proposal. They suggest that a comprehensive set of policies for kids could be accomplished by spending one percent of the GDP (gross domestic product) of the United States (Sawhill 2003). Inspired by the example of the Blair government, which set out in 1999 to eliminate or significantly reduce U.K. child poverty by 2010, these experts recommend comprehensive programs for children within a one percent budgetary limit. The one percent figure in 2003 translated to spending of $1 billion. In 2016, one percent would translate to roughly $1.8 billion. Comparatively, at the time the One Percent Proposal was published, 7 percent of the federal budget was spent on Social Security and Medicare, 3 percent on defense, and 2.5 percent to service the debt. The One Percent Proposal includes early childhood development including prenatal care, health insurance, early childhood education and mental health services, infant care, a minimum standard of living, early childhood education beginning at three, and allowing mothers of very young children some release from work requirements (id., 17). Also included are policies to increase the earnings of single mothers; prevent early childbearing; strengthen fragile families; accomplish greater academic achievement; provide universal preschool for four-year-olds; and improve neighborhoods for children by relocating children and their families to neighborhoods with a low poverty rate. While this approach is not as comprehensive as the New Deal for Children, it nevertheless suggests that the New Deal is financially feasible. The current cost of ineffective and unequal systems also can be factored in. Finally, the dollar calculus must consider the losses in productivity from the failure to support the human capital of every child. A group of experts recently estimated that lost productivity linked to inadequate early childhood support ranges globally up to 30 percent of adult productivity per country (Huebner et al. 2016).

While it is not perfect, our system for supporting older Americans, the combined consequence of the 1930s New Deal and the 1960s Great Society, is a comprehensive approach that recognizes their needs and the legitimacy of support of elders through Social Security, Medicare, and the broad policies of the Older Americans Act. The guiding principles for elders are recognition of their contributions and responsibility for their care. The prologue to the Older Americans Act states:

> The Congress hereby finds and declares that, in keeping with the traditional American concept of the inherent dignity of the individual in our democratic society, the older people of our Nation are entitled to, and it is the joint and several duty and responsibility of the governments of the United States, of the several States and their political subdivisions, and of Indian tribes to assist our older people to secure equal opportunity to the full and free enjoyment of [income, health, housing, institutional care, employment opportunity, retirement, research benefits, freedom, and independence]. (Older Americans Act 1965)

A New Deal for Children similarly reflects our obligation and responsibility for the well-being and equality of future generations and supports the equality, opportunity, and future contribution of all. A New Deal for Children is essential to the ability of all children to realize their potential and grow into adults who contribute to their family, community, and society. That each child is assured this support, rather than an array of challenges, roadblocks, and setbacks, is a commitment to the value of each child, and principles of fairness, equality, and justice in our society. While such a set of policies might well be justified on economic terms alone, for the social good from this valuable contribution of human capital, it is the moral imperative that is even stronger. No children choose their circumstances; we should no longer choose to identify children's opportunities and trigger their potential failure based on race, ethnicity, gender, class, or any other identity. Instead, we should live up to the promise of justice and equality for all by ensuring opportunity and developmental support for those at the bottom of current hierarchies among children, and ultimately destroy those hierarchies for our own, greater, good. "Let us draw upon . . . love to heighten our awareness, deepen our compassion, intensify our courage, and strengthen our commitment" (hooks 1989, 26–27).

If we return to Black boys, to what they teach us, to the questions they force us to ask about all subordinated children, then ultimately we must measure the value and strength of the New Deal for Children against the arc of their life course under the current deal. The New Deal should change the trajectory and end result of their development and contribute to fulfilling our obligation to them of ensuring their equality.

This should send us to our hospitals, to see the roomful of babies just born. What would a New Deal for Children mean for the babies born today? The current deal means that we could look at the cribs in a hospital nursery and imagine a marker has been placed on each crib. All children could be coded, for developmental support or developmental barriers, for opportunity or failure. If for failure, not just lack of support, but barriers placed in their way. The coding would be patterned by race, gender, and class. While particular babies might transcend their marked code, it would be difficult and exceptional. A New Deal for Children removes those markers. Each child is as well supported as the next. Even the one just rescued from a harrowing refugee trip. Even the one born with physical or other disabilities. Our gaze through the window at those new lives could then rest secure in the knowledge of their equality, of our social integrity, and of the as yet unrealized but supported potential of those lives just begun.

ACKNOWLEDGMENTS

A book is always a process, and this one has been a particularly long process, with much help along the way. The origins include my work on masculinities, *The Man Question* (New York University Press, 2010), which included analysis of Black masculinities; and my work on juvenile justice while Director of the Center on Children and Families, resulting in two edited collections of work, *Justice for Kids: Keeping Kids Out of the Juvenile Justice System* (New York University Press, 2011) and *A New Juvenile Justice System: Total Reform for a Broken System* (New York University Press, 2015), work that continually confronted the racial disproportionality of the juvenile justice system. An invitation to consider the question of unfinished equality from the *Indiana Journal of Law and Social Equality* in 2012 resulted in an article where I focused exclusively on Black boys and youth. I expected that to be it. But I could not let it go, and it did not let me go. The deep injustice and inequality in the lives of Black boys and youth became an inescapable project, carried on in parallel with other commitments, and then a subject that I was finally able to explore exclusively.

I was strongly supported by several deans at the University of Florida Levin College of Law. Robert Jerry encouraged my work in the early phases, and felt particularly strongly about the juvenile justice system. George Dawson as interim dean not only continued that strong support but also encouraged me to pursue a Fulbright in order to have more time to write and consider comparative insights. When I received word that I would have a Fulbright chair during the 2016–17 academic year, Dean Laura Rosenbury enthusiastically provided additional research leave so that I would be able to finish writing this book. That year to write was critical to being able to pull in the array of research that I had gathered since 2012, and the developmental model that I had developed along the way. The Fulbright enabled me to explore comparative and human rights perspectives at Lund University and the Raoul Wallenberg Institute of

Human Rights and Humanitarian Law, in the Distinguished Fulbright Chair jointly sponsored by those institutions, from January to June of 2017. I was supported by those institutions as a research scholar, and also taught Gender and Human Rights to a group of master's students who were further inspiration for my writing. I particularly benefitted from the unlimited support of Professor Eva Ryrstedt. The challenges of immigration and refugees in Sweden and Europe generally have reaffirmed my sense of the broad scope of hierarchies and inequalities among children, and the essential work to be done to support their development and equality not only in the United States but also globally.

I owe deep thanks to the librarians at UF, especially Loren Turner, formerly at the University of Florida and now at the University of Minnesota, for their expert assistance. Her research assistance was critical in particular to achieving my goal of exploring the interdisciplinary research on the life course of Black boys and youth, a task that was more difficult than expected. She helped me to accumulate a broad-ranging and comprehensive set of sources, and that research pathway was followed up and updated by her successor Rachel Purcell. It is the basis for the comprehensive bibliography in this book that I hope will be helpful to other scholars.

I benefitted from a series of research assistants, including Lauren Januzzi, Stephanie Galligan, Sarah Hensen, Jessica Harrison, Kevin Paule, and Joseph Cordova.

Florencia Alejandra Otegui provided able assistance in the preparation of the bibliography, which was very critical to my completion of the manuscript. Debbie Kelley provided invaluable support during the early years of my research, and Sherrice Smith did the same in the final year of work on the manuscript.

Rosemary Howard provided thorough, wonderful, final technical preparation of the manuscript, a marvelous full circle from her help with my very first book.

Portions of this volume were previously published in several law review articles, and are included here in edited form with the permission of the following law reviews, and with my appreciation for their work: "Black Boys Matter: Developmental Equality," 45 *Hofstra Law Review* 47–116 (2016); "Straight Out of Compton: Developmental Equality and a Critique of the Compton School Litigation," 45 *Capitol University Law*

Review 199–247 (2017); and "John Moore Jr: *Moore v City of East Cleveland* and Children's Constitutional Arguments," 85 *Fordham Law Review* 2603–13 (2017).

I have presented portions of this work to many workshops and conferences. Those audiences gave me valuable feedback that challenged my arguments and conclusions, for which I am very grateful. They included presentations at Fordham Law School, Emory Law School, Hofstra Law School, Capitol Law School, Duke Law School, the United Nations Convention on the Rights of the Child Conferences in Edinburgh and Bergen, the AALS Human Rights Program, Raoul Wallenberg Human Rights Institute, the Law Department of Lund University, Sligo Technical University (Ireland), and the Seventh World Congress on Family Law and Children's Rights in Dublin.

I particularly would like to thank, for reading, commenting, and inspiring, Barbara Woodhouse, Rachel Rebouché, Frank Rudy Cooper, Ann McGinley, Ursula Kilkelly, Martha Fineman, Stephanie Bornstein, Kenneth Nunn, Katheryn Russell-Brown, Joanna Grossman, Shani King, Barbara Stark, Jason Nance, Teresa Drake, James Bell, and Vinay Harpalani.

I have also had the support throughout of my family and friends, who understand my passion and always encourage me. My children Zoe and Zack are my inspiration for all that I do, and my cheering squad. My partner Paul has jumped on board enthusiastically and amazingly, in every possible way supporting this endeavor. His presence in my life, and his place in helping me finish this work, is beyond words. Even a leg broken on the ice in Sweden didn't get in the way. Thanks for getting me to the finish line. I dedicate this book to him.

August 25, 2017

BIBLIOGRAPHY

Abrams, Kathy. 2013. "Family Law History, Inside and Out." Review of *Inside the Castle: Law and the Family in Twentieth Century America*, by Joanna L. Grossman and Lawrence M. Friedman. *Michigan Law Review* 111:1001–20.

ACES Too High. 2016. Accessed January 7, 2017. www.acestoohigh.com.

Acevedo-Garcia, Dolores, Lindsay E. Rosenfeld, Erin Hardy, Nancy McArdle, and Theresa L. Osypuk. 2013. "Future Directions in Research on Institutional and Interpersonal Discrimination and Children's Health." *American Journal of Public Health* 103(10):1754–63.

Aguirre, Adalberto, Jr., and David V. Baker. 2008. *Structured Inequality in the United States: Critical Discussions on the Continuing Significance of Race, Ethnicity, and Gender.* Upper Saddle River, NJ: Pearson Education.

Aikens, Nikki L., and Oscar Barbarin. 2008. "Socioeconomic Difference in Reading Trajectories: The Contribution of Family, Neighborhood, and School Contexts." *Journal of Educational Psychology* 100(2):235–51.

Akbar, Na'im. 2004. "The Evolution of Human Psychology for African Americans." In Jones, *Black Psychology*, 17–40.

Alexander, Karl, Doris Entwisle, and Linda Olson. 2014. *The Long Shadow: Family Background, Disadvantaged Urban Youth, and the Transition to Adulthood.* New York: Russell Sage Foundation.

Alexander, Rudolph, Jr. 2010. "The Impact of Poverty on African American Children in the Child Welfare and Juvenile Justice Systems." In *Forum on Public Policy Online*, vol. 2010, no. 4. Urbana, IL: Oxford Round Table.

Alliman-Brissett, Annette E., and Sherri L. Turner. 2010. "Racism, Parent Support, and Math-Based Career Interests, Efficacy, and Outcome Expectations among African American Adolescents." *Journal of Black Psychology* 36:197–225.

Almond, Monica R. 2012. "The Black Charter School Effect: Black Students in American Charter Schools." *Journal of Negro Education* 81(4):354–65.

Alston, Doris N., and Nannette Williams. 1982. "Relationship between Father Absence and Self-Concept of Black Adolescent Boys." *Journal of Negro Education* 51(2):134–38.

Altschul, Inna, Daphna Oyserman, and Deborah Bybee. 2006. "Racial-Ethnic Identity in Mid-Adolescence: Content and Change as Predictors of Academic Achievement." *Child Development* 77(5):1155–69.

American Academy of Pediatrics. 2014. "Adverse Childhood Experiences and the Lifelong Consequences of Trauma." Accessed September 11, 2016. www.aap.org.

American Association of Pediatrics. 2017. "Health Equity Statement." Accessed April 4, 2017. www.aap.org.

American Civil Liberties Union. 2015. "Stop Solitary." Accessed October 3, 2016. www.juvjustice.org.

American Psychological Association. 2001. "APA Resolution on Racial/Ethnic Profiling and Other Racial/Ethnic Disparities in Law and Security Enforcement Activities." www.apa.org.

———. 2012a. "Ethnic and Racial Disparities in Education: Psychology's Contributions to Understanding and Reducing Disparities." www.apa.org.

———. 2012b. "Presidential Task Force on Preventing Discrimination and Promoting Diversity, Dual Pathways to a Better America: Preventing Discrimination and Promoting Diversity." www.apa.org.

Anda, Robert. 2009. "The Health and Social Impact of Growing Up with Alcohol Abuse and Related Adverse Childhood Experiences: The Human and Economic Costs of the Status Quo." National Association for Alcoholism and Drug Abuse Counselors. Available at www.naadac.org.

Anderson, Elijah. 1998. "The Social Ecology of Youth Violence." Crime and Justice 24:65–104.

———. 2013. "Emmet and Trayvon." Washington Monthly 45(1–2):31–33. www.washingtonmonthly.com.

Andretta, James R., Frank C. Worrell, Aaron M. Ramirez, Michael E. Barnes, Terri Odom, Successful Brim, and Malcolm H. Woodland. 2015. "The Effects of Stigma Priming on Forensic Screening in African American Youth." Counseling Psychologist 43(8):1162–89.

Ani, Amanishakete. 2013. "In Spite of Racism, Inequality, and School Failure: Defining Hope with Achieving Black Children." Journal of Negro Education 82(4):408–21.

Annang, Lucy, Lonnie Hannon, Faith E. Fletcher, Wendy Sykes Horn, and Disa Cornish. 2011. "Using Nominal Technique to Inform a Sexual Health Program for Black Youth." American Journal of Health Behavior 35(6):664–73.

Appell, Annette R. 1997. "Protecting Children or Punishing Mothers: Gender, Race, and Class in the Child Protection System [An Essay]." South Carolina Law Review 48:577–613.

Appleton, Susan Frelich. 2014. "Restating Childhood." Brooklyn Law Review 79:525–49.

Archer-Banks, Diane A. M., and Linda Behar-Horenstein. 2012. "Ogbu Revisited: Unpacking High-Achieving African American Girls' High School Experiences." Urban Education 47(1):198–223.

Armaline, William T. 2007. "Human Rights Abuses and Systemic Racism through the Criminalization of Survival: An Ethnographic Exploration of Juvenile Detention in a New England City." PhD dissertation, University of Connecticut.

Armistead, Lisa, Rex Forehand, Gene Brody, and Shira Maguen. 2002. "Parenting and Child Psychosocial Adjustment in Single-Parent African American Families: Is Community Context Important?" Behavior Therapy 33:361–75.

Armistead, Lisa, Deborah J. Jones, Rex Forehand, and Gene Brody. 2002. "Psychosocial Adjustment of African American Children in Single-Mother Families: A Test of Three Risk Models." *Journal of Marriage and Family* 64(1):105–15.

Aronson, Joshua, and Claude M. Steele. 2005. "Stereotypes and the Fragility of Academic Competence, Motivation and Self-Concept of Elliot." In *Handbook of Competence and Motivation*, edited by Andrew J. Elliot and Carol S. Dweck, 436–56. New York: Guilford.

Aronson, Robert E., Tony L. Whitehead, and Willie L. Baber. 2003. "Challenges to Masculine Transformation among Urban Low-Income African American Males." *American Journal of Public Health* 93(5):732–41.

Ashley, Wendy, and Jodi Constantine Brown. 2015. "Attachment tHAIRapy: A Culturally Relevant Treatment Paradigm for African American Foster Youth." *Journal of Black Studies* 46(6):587–604.

Atkins-Loria, Sasha, Heather Macdonald, and Courtney Mitterling. 2015. "Young African American Men and the Diagnosis of Conduct Disorder: The Neo-colonization of Suffering." *Clinical Social Work Journal* 43(4):431–41.

Austen-Smith, David, and Roland G. Fryer, Jr. 2005. "An Economic Analysis of 'Acting White.'" *Quarterly Journal of Economics* 120(2):551–83.

Baccara, Mariagiovanna, Allan Collard-Wexler, Leonardo Felli, and Leeat Yariv. 2014. "Child-Adoption Matching: Preferences for Gender and Race." *American Economic Journal: Applied Economics* 6(3):133–58.

Baggerly, Jennifer, and Max Parker. 2005. "Child-Centered Group Play Therapy with African American Boys at the Elementary School Level." *Journal of Counseling and Development* 83(4):387–96.

Baker, Claire E. 2014a. "African American Fathers' Contributions to Children's Early Academic Achievement: Evidence from Two-Parent Families from the Early Childhood Longitudinal Study-Birth Cohort." *Early Education and Development* 25(1):19–35.

———. 2014b. "Parenting and Cultural Socialization as Predictors of African American Children's Science and Social Studies Achievement." *Journal of African American Studies* 18:92–107.

Baker, Claire E., Claire E. Cameron, Sara E. Rimm-Kaufman, and David Grissmer. 2012. "Family and Sociodemographic Predictors of School Readiness among African American Boys in Kindergarten." *Early Education and Development* 23:833–54.

Baker, Claire E., and Iheoma U. Iruka. 2013. "Maternal Psychological Functioning and Children's School Readiness: The Mediating Role of Home Environments for African American Children." *Early Childhood Research Quarterly* 28:509–19.

Baldridge, Bianca J., Marc Lamont Hill, and James Earl Davis. 2011. "New Possibilities: (Re)engaging Black Male Youth within Community-Based Educational Spaces." *Race, Ethnicity and Education* 14:121–36.

Ball, Christopher, Kuo-Ting Huang, Shelia R. Cotton, R. V. Rikard, and LaToya O. Coleman. 2016. "Invaluable Values: An Expectancy-Value Theory Analysis of

Youths' Academic Motivations and Intentions." *Information Communication and Society* 19(5):618–38.

Banerjee, Meeta, Zaje A. T. Harrell, and Deborah J. Johnson. 2011. "Racial/Ethnic Socialization and Parental Involvement in Education as Predictors of Cognitive Ability and Achievement in African American Children." *Journal of Youth Adolescence* 40:595–605.

Banner, Kaitlin. 2015. "Breaking the School to Prison Pipeline: New Models for School Discipline and Community Accountable Schools." In Dowd, *New Juvenile Justice System*, 301–10.

Barbarin, Oscar A. 1993. "Coping and Resilience: Exploring the Inner Lives of African American Children." *Journal of Black Psychology* 19:478–92.

———. 2010. "Halting African American Boys' Progression from Pre-K to Prison: What Families, Schools, and Communities Can Do!" *American Journal of Orthopsychiatry* 80(1):81–88.

———. 2013a. "Development of Boys of Color: An Introduction." *American Journal of Orthopsychiatry* 83(2–3):143–44.

———. 2013b. "A Longitudinal Examination of Socioemotional Learning in African American and Latino Boys across the Transition from Pre-K to Kindergarten." *American Journal of Orthopyschiatry* 83(2–3):156–64.

Barbarin, Oscar A., Lisa Chinn, and Yamanda F. Wright. 2014. "Creating Developmentally Auspicious School Environments for African American Boys." *Role of Gender in Educational Contexts and Outcomes* 47:333–65.

Barbarin, Oscar A., Iheoma U. Iruka, Christine Harradine, Donna-Marie C. Winn, Marvin K. McKinney, and Lorraine C. Taylor. 2013. "Development of Social-Emotional Competence in Boys of Color: A Cross-Sectional Cohort Analysis from Pre-K to Second Grade." *American Journal of Orthopsychiatry* 83(2–3):145–55.

Barbarin, Oscar A., and Ester Jean-Baptiste. 2013. "The Relation of Dialogic, Control and Racial Socialization Practices to Early Academic and Social Competence: Effects of Gender, Ethnicity, and Family Socioeconomic Status." *American Journal of Orthopsychiatry* 83(2–3):201–17.

Barth, Joan M., Kristina L. McDonald, John E. Lochman, Carolyn Boxmeyer, Nicole Powell, Casey Dillion, and Meghann Sallee. 2013. "Racially Diverse Classrooms: Effects of Classroom Racial Composition on Interracial Peer Relationships." *American Journal of Orthopsychiatry* 83(2–3):231–43.

Beale, Sara Sun. 2009. "You've Come a Long Way, Baby: Two Waves of Juvenile Justice Reforms as Seen from Jena, Louisiana." *Harvard Civil Rights–Civil Liberties Law Review* 44:511–45.

Beatty, Alexandra, Ulric Neisser, William T. Trent, and Jay P. Heubert, eds. 2001. *Understanding Dropouts: Statistics, Strategies, and High-Stakes Testing*. Executive Summary, Committee on Educational Excellence and Testing Equity, National Research Council. Washington, DC: National Academy of Sciences.

Becares, Laia, and Naomi Priest. 2015. "Understanding the Influence of Race/Ethnicity, Gender, and Class on Inequalities in Academic and Non-academic Outcomes among Eighth-Grade Students: Findings from an Intersectionality Approach." *PLOS ONE* 10(10):0141363.

Belgrave, Faye Z., Anh B. Nguyen, Jessica L. Johnson, and Kristina Hood. 2011. "Who Is Likely to Help and Hurt? Profiles of African American Adolescents with Prosocial and Aggressive Behavior." *Journal of Youth and Adolescence* 40:1012–24.

Bell, James. 2015. "Child Well Being: Toward a Fair and Equitable Public Safety Strategy for the Twenty-First Century." In Dowd, *New Juvenile Justice System*, 22–24.

Bell, James, and Laura John Ridolfi. 2008. *Adoration of the Question: Reflections on the Failure to Reduce Racial and Ethnic Disparities in the Juvenile Justice System*. San Francisco: W. Haywood Burns Institute. www.burnsinstitute.org.

Benvenue, Anna L. 2008. "Comment, Turning Troubled Teens into Career Criminals: Can California Reform the System to Rehabilitate its Youth Offenders?" *Golden Gate University Law Review* 38:33–69.

Berry, Robert Q., III. 2005. "Voices of Success: Descriptive Portraits of Two Successful African American Male Middle School Mathematics Students." *Journal of African American Studies* 8(4):46–62.

Berry, Robert Q., III, Kateri Thunder, and Oren L. McClain. 2011. "Counter Narratives: Examining the Mathematics and Racial Identities of Black Boys Who Are Successful with School Mathematics." *Journal of African American Males in Education* 2(1):10–23.

Bertrand, Marianne, and Esther Duflo. 2016. "Field Experiments on Discrimination." Centre for Economic Policy Research Discussion Paper DP11123. www.cepr.org.

Biafora, Frank A., Jr., Dorothy L. Taylor, George J. Warheit, and William A. Vega. 1993. "Cultural Mistrust and Racial Awareness among Ethnically Diverse Black Adolescent Boys." *Journal of Black Psychology* 19(3):266–81.

Biafora, Frank A., Jr., George J. Warheit, Rick S. Zimmerman, Andres G. Gil, Eleni Apospori, Dorothy Taylor, and William A. Vega. 1993. "Racial Mistrust and Deviant Behaviors among Ethnically Diverse Black Adolescent Boys." *Journal of Applied Social Psychology* 23(11):891–910.

Bilchik, Shay. 2008. "Is Racial and Ethnic Equity Possible in Juvenile Justice?" *Reclaiming Children and Youth* 17(2):19–23.

———. 2011. "Redefining the Footprint of Juvenile Justice in America." In Dowd, *Justice for Kids*, 21–38.

Billson, Janet Mancini. 1996. *Pathways to Manhood: Young Black Males Struggle for Identity*. New Brunswick, NJ: Transaction.

Birckhead, Tamar R. 2012a. "Delinquent by Reason of Poverty." *Washington University Journal of Law and Policy* 38:53–107.

———. 2012b. "Juvenile Justice Reform 2.0." *Brooklyn Journal of Law and Policy* 19:15–62.

Black, Charles L., Jr. 1960. "The Lawfulness of the Segregation Decisions." *Yale Law Journal* 69:421–30.

———. 1986. "Further Reflections on the Constitutional Justice of Livelihood." *Columbia Law Review* 86(6):1103–17.

Black Lives Matter. 2016. Accessed December 7, 2016. www.blacklivesmatter.com.

Blake, Ira Kincade. 1994. "Language Development and Socialization in Young African-American Children." In *Cross-Cultural Roots of Minority Child Development*, edited by Patricia M. Greenfield and Rodney R. Cocking, 167–95. New York: Psychology Press.

Blasi, Gary. 2002. "Advocacy against the Stereotype: Lessons from Cognitive Social Psychology." *UCLA Law Review* 49(5):1241–81.

Blasi, Gary, and John T. Yost. 2006. "System Justification Theory and Research: Implications for Law, Legal Advocacy, and Social Justice." *California Law Review* 94(4):1119–68.

Blodgett, Christopher. 2012. "Adopting ACEs Screening and Assessment in Child Serving Systems." Washington State University. Accessed November 4, 2016. www.ext100.wsu.edu.

———. 2014. "ACEs in Head Start Children and Impact on Development." Washington State University. Accessed September 11, 2016. www.ext100.wsu.edu.

———. 2015. "No School Alone: How Community Risks and Assets Contribute to School and Youth Success." Washington State University, Office of Financial Management. Accessed September 11, 2016. www.ext100.wsu.edu.

Bogart, Laura M., Marc N. Eliott, David E. Kanouse, David J. Klein, Susan L. Davies, Paula M. Cuccaro, Stephen W. Banspach, Melissa F. Peskin, and Mark A. Schuster. 2013. "Association between Perceived Discrimination and Racial/Ethnic Disparities in Problem Behaviors among Preadolescent Youths." *American Journal of Public Health* 103(6):1074–81.

Bohnert, Amy M., Maryse Richards, Krista Kohl, and Edin Randall. 2009. "Relationships between Discretionary Time Activities, Emotional Experiences, Delinquency and Depressive Symptoms among Urban African American Adolescents." *Journal of Youth and Adolescence* 38:587–601.

Bolland, John M., Chalandra M. Bryant, Bradley E. Lian, Debra M. McCallum, Alexander T. Vazsonyi, and Joan M. Barth. 2007. "Development and Risk Behavior among African American, Caucasian, and Mixed-Race Adolescents Living in High Poverty Inner-City Neighborhoods." *American Journal of Community Psychology* 40:230–49.

Boone, Sherle L. 1991. "Aggression in African-American Boys: A Discriminant Analysis." *Genetic, Social and General Psychology Monographs* 117(2):205–28.

Borland, James H., Rachel Schnur, and Lisa Wright. 2000. "Economically Disadvantaged Students in a School for the Academically Gifted: A Postpositivist Inquiry into Individual and Family Adjustment." *Gifted Child Quarterly* 44(1):13–32.

Bornstein, Stephanie. 2017. "Reckless Discrimination." *California Law Review* 105:1055–1110.

Bowleg, Lisa, Devin English, Ana Maria del Rio-Gonzalez, Gary J. Burkholder, Michelle Teti, and Jeanne M. Tschann. 2016. "Measuring the Pros and Cons of What It Means to Be a Black Man: Development and Validation of the Black Men's Experiences Scale (BMES)." *Psychology of Men and Masculinity* 17(2):177–88.

Bowman, Barbara T. 1999. "Kindergarten Practices with Children from Low-Income Families." In *The Transition to Kindergarten*, edited by Robert C. Pianta and Martha J. Cox, 294–301. Baltimore: Brookes.

Bowman, Barbara, and Evelyn K. Moore, eds. 2006. *School Readiness and Social-Emotional Development: Perspectives on Cultural Diversity*. Silver Spring, MD: National Black Child Development Institute.

Boykin, A. Wade, and Caryn T. Baily. 2000. "The Role of Cultural Factors in School Relevant Cognitive Functioning: Synthesis of Findings on Cultural Contexts, Cultural Orientations, and Individual Differences." Report No. 42. Baltimore: Center for Research on the Education of Students Placed at Risk.

Braga, Anthony A., David Hureau, and Christopher Winship. 2008. "Losing Faith? Police, Black Churches, and the Resurgence of Youth Violence in Boston." *Ohio State Journal of Criminal Law* 6:141–72.

Brewster, Joe, Michele Stephenson, and Hilary Beard. 2013. *Promises Kept: Raising Black Boys to Succeed in School and in Life*. New York: Speigel and Grau.

Bridge, Jeffrey A., Lindsey Asti, Lisa M. Horowitz, Joel B. Greenhouse, Cynthia A. Fontanella, Arielle H. Sheftall, Kelly J. Kelleher, and John V. Campo. 2015. "Suicide Trends among Elementary School-Aged Children in the United States from 1993 to 2012." *Journal of the American Medical Association of Pediatrics* 169(7):673–77.

Bridges, George S., and Sara Steen. 1998. "Racial Disparities in Official Assessments of Juvenile Offenders: Attributional Stereotypes as Mediating Mechanisms." *American Sociological Review* 63(4):554–70.

Bright, Charlotte Lyn, and Melissa Jonson-Reid. 2008. "Onset of Juvenile Court Involvement: Exploring Gender-Specific Associations with Maltreatment and Poverty." *Children and Youth Services Review* 30:914–27.

Brittian, Aerika S. 2012. "Understanding African American Adolescents' Identity Development: A Relational Developmental Systems Perspective." *Journal of Black Psychology* 38(2):172–200.

Brodin, Mark S. 2016. "The Murder of Black Males in a World of Non-Accountability: The Surreal Trial of George Zimmerman for the Killing of Trayvon Martin." *Howard Law Journal* 59:765–85.

Brody, Gene H., Yi-Fu Chen, Velma McBride Murry, Ronald L. Simons, Xiaojia Ge, Frederick X. Gibbons, Meg Gerrard, and Carolyn E. Cutrona. 2006. "Perceived Discrimination and the Adjustment of African American Youth: A Five-Year Longitudinal Analysis with Contextual Moderation Effects." *Child Development* 77(5):1170–89.

Brody, Gene H., Velma McBride Murry, Sooyeon Kim, and Anita C. Brown. 2002. "Longitudinal Pathways to Competence and Psychological Adjustment among African American Children Living in Rural Single-Parent Households." *Child Development* 73(5):1505–16.

Bronfenbrenner, Urie. 1970. *Two Worlds of Childhood: U.S. and U.S.S.R.* New York: Russell Sage Foundation.

————. 1979. *The Ecology of Human Development: Experiments by Nature and Design.* Cambridge, MA: Harvard University Press.

————, ed. 2005. *Making Human Beings Human: Bioecological Perspectives on Human Development.* Thousand Oaks, CA: Sage.

Brookins, Craig C., and Tracy L. Robinson. 1995. "Rites-of-Passage as Resistance to Oppression." *Western Journal of Black Studies* 19(3):172–80.

Brookins, Geraldine Kearse, and Julie A. Hirsh. 2002. "Innocence Lost: Case Studies of Children in the Juvenile Justice System." *Journal of Negro Education* 71(3):205–17.

Brooks, Roy. 1995. "Analyzing Black Self-Esteem in the Post-*Brown* Era." *Temple Political and Civil Rights Law Review* 4:215–27.

Brooks, Roy L., and Kirsten Widner. 2010. "In Defense of the Black/White Binary: Reclaiming a Tradition of Civil Rights Scholarship." *Berkeley Journal of African-American Law and Policy* 12:107–44.

Brooks, Susan L., and Dorothy E. Roberts. 2002. "Social Justice and Family Court Reform." *Family Court Review* 40(4):453–59.

Brooks-Gunn, Jeanne, and Lisa B. Markman. "The Contribution of Parenting to Ethnic and Racial Gaps in School Readiness." *Future Child* 15(1):139–68.

Brown, Anthony. 2011. "'Same Old Stories:' The Black Male in Social Science and Educational Literature, 1930s to the Present." *Teachers College Record* 113(9):2047–79.

Brown, Anthony L., and Jamel K. Donnor. 2011. "Toward a New Narrative on Black Males, Education, and Public Policy." *Race Ethnicity and Education* 14(1):17–32.

Brown, Brené. 2010. *The Gifts of Imperfection.* Center City, MN: Hazelden.

Brown, Christia Spears, and Rebecca S. Bigler. 2005. "Children's Perceptions of Discrimination: A Developmental Model." *Child Development* 76(3):533–53.

Brown, Eleanor. 2000. "Black Like Me? 'Gangsta' Culture, Clarence Thomas, and Afrocentric Academies." *New York University Law Review* 75:308–53.

Brown, Jeffrey, Oscar Barbarin, and Kristin Scott. 2013. "Socioemotional Trajectories in Black Boys between Kindergarten and the Fifth Grade: The Role of Cognitive Skills and Family in Promoting Resiliency." *American Journal of Orthopsychiatry* 83(2–3):176–84.

Brown, Michael K., Martin Carnoy, Elliott Currie, Troy Duster, David B. Oppenheimer, Marjorie M. Schultz, and David Wellman. 2005. *Whitewashing Race: The Myth of a Colorblind Society.* Berkeley: University of California Press.

Bruce, Marino A. 2000. "Inequality and Delinquency: Sorting Out Some Class and Race Effects." *Race and Society* 2(2):133–48.

Brunson, Rod K., and Jody Miller. 2006. "Young Black Men and Urban Policing in the United States." *British Journal of Criminology* 46:613–40.

Bryan, Kevin A., and Leonardo Martinez. 2008. "On the Evolution of Income Inequality in the United States." *Economic Quarterly* 94(2):97–120.

Bryant, Alison L., and Marc A. Zimmerman. 2003. "Role Models and Psychosocial Outcomes among African American Adolescents." *Journal of Adolescent Research* 18(1):36–67.

Bryant, Wesley. 2011. "Internalized Racism's Association with African American Male Youth's Propensity for Violence." *Journal of Black Studies* 42(4):690–707.

Bulotsky-Shearer, Rebecca J., Patricia H. Manz, Julia L. Mendez, Christine M. McWayne, Yumiko Sekino, and John W. Fantuzzo. 2012. "Peer Play Interactions and Readiness to Learn: A Protective Influence for African American Preschool Children from Low-Income Households." *Child Development Perspectives* 6(3):225–31.

Burchinal, Margaret R., Frances A. Campbell, Donna M. Bryant, Barbara H. Wasik, and Craig T. Ramey. 1997. "Early Intervention and Mediating Processes in Cognitive Performance of Children of Low-Income African American Families." *Child Development* 68(5):935–54.

Burchinal, Margaret, Kathleen McCartney, Laurence Steinberg, Robert Crosnoe, Sarah L. Friedman, Vonnie McLoyd, Robert Pianta, and National Institute of Child Health and Human Development Early Child Care Research Network. 2011. "Examining the Black-White Achievement Gap among Low-Income Children Using the NICHD Study of Early Child Care and Youth Development." *Child Development* 82(5):1404–20.

Burrell, Sue. 2015. "Collateral Consequences of Juvenile Court: Boulders on the Road to Good Outcomes." In Dowd, *New Juvenile Justice System*, 332–34.

Bush, Lawson V., and Edward C. Bush. 2013. "God Bless the Child Who Got His Own: Toward a Comprehensive Theory for African-American Boys and Men." *Western Journal of Black Studies* 37(1):1–13.

Buss, Emily. 2009. "What the Law Should (and Should Not) Learn from Child Development Research." *Hofstra Law Review* 38(1):13–68.

Butler, Paul. 2006a. "Blogging at Blackprof." *Washington University Law Review* 84:1101–4.

———. 2006b. "Rehnquist, Racism, and Race Jurisprudence." *George Washington Law Review* 74:1019–42.

———. 2010a. "One Hundred Years of Race and Crime." *Journal of Criminal Law and Criminology* 100:1043–60.

———. 2010b. "White Fourth Amendment." *Texas Tech Law Review* 43:245–54.

———. 2013a. "Black Male Exceptionalism? The Problems and Potential of Black Male-Focused Interventions." *Du Bois Review* 10(2):485–511.

———. 2013b. "Poor People Lose: *Gideon* and the Critique of Rights." *Yale Law Journal* 122:2176–2204.

———. 2014. "Stop and Frisk and Torture-Lite: Police Terror of Minority Communities." *Ohio State Journal of Criminal Law* 12:57–69.

———. 2016. "The System Is Working the Way It Is Supposed To: The Limits of Criminal Justice Reform." *Georgetown Law Journal* 104:1419–78.

Butler-Barnes, Sheretta T., Tabbye M. Chavous, Noelle Hurd, and Fatima Varner. 2013. "African American Adolescents' Academic Persistence: A Strengths-Based Approach." *Journal of Youth and Adolescence* 42:1443–58.

Butler-Barnes, Sheretta T., Lorena Estrada-Martinez, Rosa J. Colin, and Brittni D. Jones. 2015. "School and Peer Influences on the Academic Outcomes of African American Adolescents." *Journal of Adolescence* 44:168–81.

Butler-Barnes, Sheretta T., Terrinieka T. Williams, and Tabbye M. Chavous. 2012. "Racial Pride and Religiosity among African American Boys: Implications for Academic Motivation and Achievement." *Journal of Youth and Adolescence* 41:486–98.

Byfield, Cheron. 2008. "The Impact of Religion on the Educational Achievement of Black Boys: A UK and USA Study." *British Journal of Sociology of Education* 29(2):189–99.

Bynum, Evita G., and Ronald I. Weiner. 2002. "Self-Concept and Violent Delinquency in Urban African-American Adolescent Males." *Psychological Reports* 90:477–86.

Bynum, Mia Smith, Candace Best, Sandra L. Barnes, and E. Thomoseo Burton. 2008. "Private Regard, Identity Protection and Perceived Racism among African American Males." *Journal of African American Studies* 12:142–55.

Byrd, Christy M., and Tabbye M. Chavous. 2009. "Racial Identity and Academic Achievement in the Neighborhood Context: A Multilevel Analysis." *Journal of Youth and Adolescence* 38:544–59.

Cabrera, Natasha J., Marjorie Beeghly, and Nancy Eisenberg. 2012. "Positive Development of Minority Children: Introduction to the Special Issue." *Child Development Perspectives* 6(3):207–9.

Cabrera, Natasha J., Sandra L. Hofferth, and Soo Chae. 2011. "Patterns and Predictors of Father-Infant Engagement across Race/Ethnic Groups." *Early Childhood Research Quarterly* 26:365–75.

Cahn, Edgar, and Cynthia Robbins. 2010. "An Offer They Can't Refuse: Racial Disparity in Juvenile Justice and Deliberate Indifference Meet Alternatives That Work." *University of the District of Columbia Law Review* 13:71–113.

Cahn, Naomi, and June Carbone. 2010. *Red Families v. Blue Families: Legal Polarization and the Creation of Culture*. New York: Oxford University Press.

California Courts. 2015. "Needs of Children at Different Ages." Accessed October 3, 2015. www.courts.ca.gov.

Cameron, Lindsey, Adam Rutland, and Rupert Brown. 2006. "Changing Children's Intergroup Attitudes toward Refugees: Testing Different Models of Extended Contact." *Child Development* 77(5):1208–19.

Campaign for Children. 2016. Accessed January 7, 2016. www.campaignforchildren.org.

Cannon, Yael, Michael Gregory, and Julie Waterstone. 2013. "A Solution Hiding in Plain Sight: Special Education and a Better Outcome for Children with Social, Emotional and Behavioral Challenges." *Fordham Urban Law Journal* 41(2):403–97.

Capers, I. Bennett. 2014. "Critical Race Theory and Criminal Justice." In Symposium: "Twenty-Plus Years of Critical Race Theory and Criminal Justice: Looking Backward, Looking Forward." *Ohio State Journal of Criminal Law* 12:1–7.

Carbado, Devon W., ed. 1999. *Black Men on Race, Gender and Sexuality: A Critical Reader*. New York: New York University Press.

———. 2000. "Men in Black." *Journal on Gender, Race and Justice* 3:427–38.

———. 2011. "Critical What What?" *Connecticut Law Review* 43:1593–1643.

Carbado, Devon W., and Mitu Gulati. 2013. *Acting White? Rethinking Race in Postracial America*. New York: Oxford University Press.

Cassidy, Elaine F., and Howard C. Stevenson, Jr. 2005. "They Wear the Mask: Hypervulnerability and Hypermasculine Aggression among African American Males in an Urban Remedial Disciplinary School." *Journal of Aggression, Maltreatment and Trauma* 11(4):53–74.

Catov, Janet M., MinJae Lee, James M. Roberts, Jia Xu, and Hyagriv N. Simhan. 2015. "Race Disparities and Decreasing Birth Weight: Are Babies Getting Smaller?" *American Journal of Epidemiology* 183(1):15–23.

Caughy, Margaret O'Brien, Patricia J. O'Campo, Saundra Murray Nettles, and Kimberly Fraleigh Lohrfink. 2006. "Neighborhood Matters: Racial Socialization of African American Children." *Child Development* 77(5):1220–36.

Centers for Disease Control and Prevention. 2015a. "Developmental Milestones." Accessed August 15, 2015. www.cdc.gov.

———. 2015b. "The Public Health Approach to Violence Prevention." Accessed March 25, 2015. www.cdc.gov.

———. 2015c. "Teenagers (15–17 Years of Age)." Accessed August 15, 2015. www.cdc.gov.

———. 2016a. "About the CDC-Kaiser ACE Study." Accessed September 11, 2016. www.cdc.gov.

———. 2016b. "Violence Prevention: Adverse Childhood Experiences (ACEs)." Accessed January 7, 2016. www.cdc.gov.

Center on the Developing Child. 2007. "A Science-Based Framework for Early Childhood Policy." www.developingchild.harvard.edu.

———. 2014. Excessive Stress Disrupts the Architecture of the Developing Brain. Working Paper No. 3, January.

———. 2016a. "Five Numbers to Remember about Early Childhood Development." Accessed September 19, 2016. www.perma.cc.

———. 2016b. "Three Core Concepts in Early Development." Accessed January 7, 2016. www.developingchild.harvard.edu.

Centre for Longitudinal Studies. 2007. "Millennium Cohort Study." www.cls.ioe.ac.uk.

Chapman, John F., Rani A. Desai, Paul R. Falzer, and Randy Borum. 2006. "Violence Risk and Race in a Sample of Youth in Juvenile Detention: The Potential to Reduce Disproportionate Minority Confinement." *Youth Violence and Juvenile Justice* 4(2):170–84.

Chemerinsky, Erwin. 1993. "Making the Right Case for a Constitutional Right to Minimum Entitlements." *Mercer Law Review* 44:525–41.

Chen, May S., and Vangie A. Foshee. 2015. "Stressful Life Events and the Perpetration of Adolescent Dating Abuse." *Journal of Youth and Adolescence* 44(3):696–707.

Chen, Wan-Yi. 2010. "Exposure to Community Violence and Adolescents' Internalizing Behaviors among African American and Asian American Adolescents." *Journal of Youth and Adolescence* 39:403–13.

Chetty, Raj, David Grusky, Maximilian Hell, Nathaniel Hendren, Robert Manducea, and Jimmy Narang. 2016. "The Fading American Dream: Trends in Absolute Income Mobility since 1940." *Science* 356(6336):398–406.

Chetty, Raj, Nathaniel Hendren, Patrick Kline, and Emmanuel Saez. 2014. "Where Is the Land of Opportunity? The Geography of Intergenerational Mobility in the United States." *Quarterly Journal of Economics* 129(4):1553–1623.

Chicago Tribune. 2015. "Laquan McDonald Police Reports Differ Dramatically from Video." December 5. www.chicagotribune.com.

Child Trends. 2013. "Adverse Experiences: Indicators on Children and Youth." Accessed September 11, 2016. www.childtrends.org.

Children's Defense Fund. 2015. "Children in the States Factsheets 2015." Accessed October 31, 2016. www.childrensdefense.org.

Chiu, Yueh-Hsiu Mathilda, Hsiao-Hsien Leon Hsu, Brent A. Coull, David C. Bellinger, Itai Kloog, Joel Schwartz, Robert O. Wright, and Rosalind J. Wright. 2016. "Prenatal Particulate Air Pollution and Neurodevelopment in Urban Children: Examining Sensitive Windows and Sex-Specific Associations." *Environment International* 87:56–65.

Cho, Sumi. 2008. "Embedded Whiteness: Theorizing Exclusion in Public Contracting." *Berkeley La Raza Law Journal* 19:5–26.

Christensenn, Anna. 1999. "Normative Patterns and the Normative Field: A Post-Liberal View on Law." In *From Dissonance to Sense: Welfare State Expectations, Privatisation, and Private Law*, edited by Thomas Wilhelmsson and Samuli Hurri, 83–98. Brookfield, VT: Ashgate.

———. 2000. "Protection of the Established Position: A Basic Normative Pattern." *Scandinavian Studies in Law* 40:285–324.

Christle, Christie A., Kristine Jolivette, and Michael Nelson. 2005. "Breaking the School to Prison Pipeline: Identifying School Risk and Protective Factors for Youth Delinquency." *Exceptionality* 13(2):69–88.

Chung, He Len, and Laurence Steinberg. 2006. "Relations between Neighborhood Factors, Parenting Behaviours, Peer Deviance, and Delinquency among Serious Juvenile Offenders." *Developmental Psychology* 42(2):319–31.

City-Data.com. 2016. "Compton California." Accessed April 25, 2016. www.city-data.com.

Clay, Andreana. 2003. "Keepin' It Real: Black Youth, Hip-Hop Culture, and Black Identity." *American Behavioral Scientist* 46(10):1346–58.

Clincy, Amanda R., and W. Roger Mills-Koonce. 2013. "Trajectories of Intrusive Parenting during Infancy and Toddlerhood as Predictors of Rural, Low-Income African American Boys' School-Related Outcomes." *American Journal of Orthopsychiatry* 83(2–3):194–206.

Coates, Ta-Nehisi. 2015. *Between the World and Me.* New York: Spiegel and Grau.

Cohen, Geoffrey L., Claude M. Steele, and Lee D. Ross. 1999. "The Mentor's Dilemma: Providing Critical Feedback across the Racial Divide." *Personality and Social Psychology Bulletin* 25:1302–17.

Collins, Patricia Hill. 1998. *Fighting Words: Black Women and the Search for Justice.* Minneapolis: University of Minnesota Press.

Compton Unified School District. 2016. Accessed April 25, 2016. www.compton.k12. ca.us.

Conchas, Gilberto Q., and Pedro A. Noguera. 2004. "Understanding the Exceptions: How Small Schools Support the Achievement of Academically Successful Black Boys." In Way and Chu, *Adolescent Boys*, 317–37.

Condron, Dennis J. 2009. "Social Class, School and Non-School Environments, and Black/White Inequalities in Children's Learning." *American Sociological Review* 74:683–708.

Conward, Cynthia. 2001. "Where Have All the Children Gone? A Look at Incarcerated Youth in America." *William Mitchell Law Review* 27(4):2435–64.

Cook, Philip J. 2010. "School Crime Control and Prevention." *Crime and Justice* 39:313–440.

Cook, Philip J., and John H. Laub. 1998. "The Unprecedented Epidemic in Youth Violence." *Crime and Justice* 24:27–64.

Cook, Philip J., and Jens Ludwig. 1998. "The Burden of 'Acting White': Do Black Adolescents Disparage Academic Achievement." In Jencks and Phillips, *Black-White Test Score Gap*, 375–400.

Cook, Rebecca. 2011. "Structures of Discrimination." *Macalester International* 28:33–60.

Cook, Rebecca, and Cornelia Weiss. 2016. "Gender Stereotyping in the Military: Insights from Court Cases." In *Stereotypes and Human Rights Law*, edited by Eva Brems and Alexandra Timmer, 175–98. Antwerp: Intersentia.

Cooler, Shauna M., and Vonnie C. McLoyd. 2011. "Racial Barrier Socialization and the Well-Being of African American Adolescents: The Moderating Role of Mother-Adolescent Relationship Quality." *Journal of Research on Adolescence* 21(4):895–903.

Cooper, Catherine R., Cynthia T. García Coll, W. Todd Bartko, Helen M. Davis, and Celina Chatman, eds. 2005. *Developmental Pathways through Middle Childhood: Rethinking Contexts and Diversity as Resources.* Mahwah, NJ: Lawrence Erlbaum.

Cooper, Frank Rudy. 2006. "Against Bipolar Black Masculinity: Intersectionality, Assimilation, Identity Performance, and Hierarchy." *University of California at Davis Law Review* 39:853–903.

———. 2009. "'Who's the Man?' Masculinities Studies, Terry Stops, and Police Training." *Columbia Journal of Gender and Law Review* 18(3):671–742.

———. 2013. "We Are Always Already Imprisoned: Hyper-incarceration and Black Male Identity Performance." *Boston University Law Review* 93:1185–1204.

———. 2015. "Always Already Suspect: Revising Vulnerability Theory." *North Carolina Law Review* 93:1339–79.

Cooper, Shauna M., Charity Brown, Isha Metzger, Yvette Clinton, and Barbara Guthrie. 2013. "Racial Discrimination and African American Adolescents' Adjustment: Gender Variation in Family and Community Social Support, Promotive and Protective Factors." *Journal of Child and Family Studies* 22:15–29.

Corprew, Charles S., and Michael Cunningham. 2012. "Educating Tomorrow's Men: Perceived School Support, Negative Youth Experiences, and Bravado Attitudes in African American Adolescent Males." *Education and Urban Society* 44(5):571–89.

Cossman, Brenda. 2005. "Contesting Conservatisms, Family Feuds and the Privatization of Dependency." *American University Journal of Gender, Social Policy and the Law* 13:415–509.

Coursen-Neff, Zama. 2015. "Discrimination against Palestinian Arabic Children in Israel." *New York University Journal of International Law and Politics* 36:101–62.

Cox, Judith A., and James Bell. 2001. "Addressing Disproportionate Representation of Youth of Color in the Juvenile Justice System." *Journal of the Center for Families, Children and the Courts* 3:31–43.

Crenshaw, Kimberlé. 2011. "Twenty Years of Critical Race Theory: Looking Back to Move Forward." *Connecticut Law Review* 43(5):1253–1352.

Crenshaw, Kimberlé, Neil Gotanda, Gary Peller, and Kendall Thomas, eds. 1995. *Critical Race Theory: The Key Writings That Formed the Movement.* New York: New Press.

Crenshaw, Kimberlé Williams, and Andrea J. Ritchie. 2015. "Say Her Name: Resisting Police Brutality against Black Women." African American Policy Forum. Accessed December 7, 2015. www.static1.squarespace.com.

Croke, Rhian, and Anne Crowley. 2011. "Human Rights and Child Poverty in the UK: Time for Change." In Invernizzi and Williams, *Human Rights of Children*, 264–86.

Cronholm, Peter F., Christine M. Forke, Roy Wade, Megan H. Bair-Merritt, Martha Davis, Mary Harkins-Schwarz, Lee M. Pachter, and Joel A. Fein. 2015. "Adverse Childhood Experiences: Expanding the Concept of Adversity." *American Journal of Preventative Medicine* 49(3):354–61.

Cross, Terry L. 2008. "Disproportionality in Child Welfare." *Child Welfare* 87(2):11–22.

Cross, William E., Jr. 1991. *Shades of Black: Diversity in African-American Identity.* Philadelphia: Temple University Press.

Culp, Jerome McCristal. 1999. "To the Bone: Race and White Privilege." *Minnesota Law Review* 83:1637–79.

Culp, Jerome M., Jr., Angela P. Harris, and Francisco Valdes. 2003. "Subject Unrest." *Stanford Law Review* 55:2435–52.

Cunningham, Michael. 1999. "African American Adolescent Males' Perception of Their Community Resources and Constraints: A Longitudinal Analysis." *Journal of Community Psychology* 27(5):569–88.

Cunningham, Michael, and Margaret Beale Spencer. 1996. "The Black Male Experiences Measure." In *Handbook of Tests and Measurements for Black Populations*, edited by Reginald L. Jones, 301–10. Hampton, VA: Cobb and Henry.

Cunningham, Michael, and Leah Newkirk Meunier. 2004. "The Influence of Peer Experiences on Bravado Attitudes among African American Males." In Way and Chu, *Adolescent Boys*, 219–32.

Cunningham, Michael, and Dena Phillips Swanson. 2010. "Educational Resilience in African American Adolescents." *Journal of Negro Education* 79(4):473–87.

Cunningham-Parmeter, Keith. 2013. "Men at Work, Fathers at Home: Uncovering the Masculine Face of Caregiver Discrimination." *Columbia Journal of Gender and Law* 24:253–301.

Curtis, Richard. 1998. "The Improbable Transformation of Inner City Neighborhoods: Crime, Violence, Drugs, and Youth in the 1990s." *Journal of Criminal Law and Criminology* 88:1233–76.

Curtis-Boles, Harriet. 2002. "The Application of Psychoanalytic Theory and Practice to African Americans." In *The Handbook of Multicultural Education, Research, Intervention, and Training*, edited by Elizabeth Davis-Russell, 193–209. San Francisco: Jossey-Bass.

Dailey, Anne C. 2011. "Children's Constitutional Rights." *Minnesota Law Review* 95:2099–2179.

———. 2016. "Children's Transitional Rights." *Law, Culture and the Humanities* 12(2):178–94.

Dallas, Constance M. 2015. "Paternal Involvement of Low Income African American Fathers with Children in Multiple Households." University of Illinois at Chicago, College of Nursing. Accessed August 15, 2015. www.nursing.uic.edu.

Dani, Anis A., and Arjan De Haan, eds. 2008. *Inclusive States: Social Policy and Structural Inequalities*. Washington, DC: World Bank.

Darity, William, Jr. 2009. "Stratification Economics: Context versus Culture and the Reparations Controversy." *Kansas Law Review* 57:795–811.

Darville, Sarah. 2016. "New York City Families Spend Millions of Hours Choosing High Schools, and Students from Poor Neighborhoods Finish Last: Report." *Chalkbeat*, May 11. www.chalkbeat.org.

Davis, Gwendolyn Y., and Howard C. Stevenson. 2006. "Racial Socialization Experiences and Symptoms of Depression among Black Youth." *Journal of Child and Family Studies* 15(3):303–17.

Davis, James Earl. 2003. "Early Schooling and Academic Achievement of African American Males." *Urban Education* 38(5):515–37.

———. 2006. "Research at the Margin: Mapping Masculinity and Mobility of African-American School Dropouts." *International Journal of Qualitative Studies in Education* 19(3):280–304.

Davis, Peggy Cooper. 2008. "*Moore v. East Cleveland*: Constructing the Suburban Family." In *Family Law Stories*, edited by Carol Sanger, 77–80. New York: Foundation Press.

Dawson-McClure, Spring, Esther Calzada, Keng-Yen Huang, Dimitra Kamboukos, Dana Rhule, Bukky Kolawole, Eva Petkova, and Laurie Miller Brotman. 2015. "A Population-Level Approach to Promoting Healthy Child Development and School Success in Low-Income, Urban Neighborhoods: Impact on Parenting and Child Conduct Problems." *Prevention Science* 16(2):279–90.

Deckha, Maneesha. 2008. "Intersectionality and Posthumanist Visions of Equality." *Wisconsin Journal of Law, Gender and Society* 23(2):249–67.

Deere, Stephen, and Koran Addo. 2015. "University of Missouri System President Becomes the Focus Amid Protests at Mizzou." *St. Louis Post Dispatch*, November 9. www.stltoday.com.

Delaney, Liam, and Orla Doyle. 2012. "Socioeconomic Differences in Early Childhood Time Preferences." *Journal of Economic Psychology* 33:237–47.

DeLuca, Stephanie, Susan Clampet-Lundquist, and Kathryn Edin. 2016. *Coming of Age in the Other America*. New York: Russell Sage Foundation.

Derezotes, Dennette M., John Poertner, and Mark F. Testa, eds. 2005. *Race Matters in Child Welfare: The Overrepresentation of African American Children in the System*. Washington, DC: CWLA Press.

Desmond, Mathew. 2016. "The Eviction Economy." *New York Times*, March 5. www.nytimes.com.

Dex, Shirley, and Heather Joshi. 2005. *Children of the 21st Century: From Birth to Nine Months*. Bristol, UK: Policy Press.

Dexter, Casey A., Kristyn Wong, Ann M. Stacks, Marjorie Beeghly, and Douglas Barnett. 2013. "Parenting and Attachment among Low-Income African American and Caucasian Preschoolers." *Journal of Family Psychology* 27(4):629–38.

Dickerson, Andy, and Gurleen Popli. 2012. "Persistent Poverty and Children's Cognitive Development: Evidence from the UK Millennium Cohort Study." Working paper, Centre for Longitudinal Studies, Institute of Education, University of London.

Dickerson, Niki. 2008. "Occupational and Residential Segregation: The Confluence of Two Systems of Inequality." *Labor Studies Journal* 33(4):393–411.

Dobbs, Will, and Roland G. Fryer, Jr. 2009. "Are High Quality Schools Enough to Close the Achievement Gap? Evidence from a Social Experiment in Harlem." Working paper, National Bureau of Economic Research.

———. 2010. "Are High-Quality Schools Enough to Increase Achievement among the Poor? Evidence from the Harlem Children's Zone." www.scholar.harvard.edu.

Dotterer, Aryn M., Katie Lowe, and Susan M. McHale. 2014. "Academic Growth Trajectories and Family Relationships among African American Youth." *Journal of Research on Adolescence* 24(4):734–47.

Dow, Dawn Marie. 2016. "The Deadly Challenges of Raising African American Boys: Navigating the Controlling Image of the 'Thug.'" *Gender and Society* 30(2):161–88.

Dowd, Nancy E. 1997. *In Defense of Single Parent Families*. New York: New York University Press.

———. 2010. *The Man Question: Male Subordination and Privilege*. New York: New York University Press.

———. 2011a. "Introduction." In Dowd, *Justice for Kids*, 1–18.

———, ed. 2011b. *Justice for Kids: Keeping Kids Out of the Juvenile Justice System*. New York: New York University Press.

———. 2013a. "Unfinished Equality: The Case of Black Boys." *Indiana Journal of Law and Social Equality* 2:36–61.

———. 2013b. "What Men? The Essentialist Error of the 'End of Men.'" *Boston University Law Review* 93:1203–36.

———, ed. 2015. *A New Juvenile Justice System: Total Reform for a Broken System*. New York: New York University Press.

———. 2016a. "Black Boys Matter: Developmental Equality." *Hofstra Law Review* 45:47–116.

———. 2016b. "A Developmental Equality Model for the Best Interests of Children." In *Implementing Article 3 of the United Nations Convention on the Rights of the Child: Best Interests, Welfare and Well-being*, edited by Elaine E. Sutherland and Lesley-Anne Barnes Macfarlane, 112–30. Cambridge: Cambridge University Press.

———. 2017a. "John Moore Jr: *Moore v. City of East Cleveland* and Children's Constitutional Arguments." *Fordham Law Review* 85:2603–13.

———. 2017b. "Straight Out of Compton: Developmental Equality and a Critique of the Compton School Litigation." *Capital Law Review* 45:199–247.

Dowd, Nancy E., Nancy Levit, and Ann C. McGinley. 2012. "Feminist Legal Theory Meets Masculinities Theory." In *Masculinities and the Law: A Multidimensional Approach*, edited by Frank Rudy Cooper and Ann McGinley, 25–50. New York: New York University Press.

Downey, Douglas B., and James W. Ainsworth-Darnell. 2002. "The Search for Oppositional Culture among Black Students." *American Sociological Review* 67(1):156–64.

Downey, Douglas B., Paul T. Von Hipple, and Beckett A. Broh. 2004. "Are Schools the Great Equalizer? Cognitive Inequality during the Summer Months and the School Year." *American Sociological Review* 69:613–35.

Downey, Douglas B., and Shana Pribesh. 2004. "When Race Matters: Teachers' Evaluations of Students' Classroom Behavior." *Sociology of Education* 77:267–82.

Doyle, James M. 2001. "Discounting the Error Costs: Cross-Racial False Alarms in the Culture of Contemporary Criminal Justice." *Psychology, Public Policy and Law* 7:253–62.

Drummond, Holli, John M. Bolland, and Waverly Ann Harris. 2011. "Becoming Violent: Evaluating the Mediating Effect of Hopelessness on the Code of the Street Thesis." *Deviant Behavior* 32(3):191–223.

Du Bois, W. E. B. 1903. *Souls of Black Folk*. Chicago: A.C. McClurg.

Dumas, Michael J. 2016. "My Brother as 'Problem': Neoliberal Governmentality and Interventions for Black Young Men and Boys." *Educational Policy* 30(1):94–113.

Dumas, Michael J., and Joseph Derrick Nelson. 2016. "(Re)imagining Black Boyhood: Toward a Critical Framework for Educational Research." *Harvard Educational Review* 86(1):27–47.

Dunbar, Keesha, and Richard P. Barth. 2007. "Racial Disproportionality, Race Disparity, and Other Race-Related Findings in Published Works Derived from the National Survey of Child and Adolescent Well-Being." Casey-CSSP Alliance for Racial Equity in Child Welfare. www.f2f.ca.gov.

Duncan, Greg J., and Katherine Magnuson. 2003. "Promoting the Healthy Development of Young Children." In Sawhill, *One Percent for the Kids*, 16–39.

———. 2014. "Early Childhood Interventions for Low-Income Children." *Focus* 31(2):1–5. Accessed September 11, 2016. www.irp.wisc.edu.

Dunham, Yarrow, Andrew Scott Baron, and Mahzarin R. Banji. 2006. "From American City to Japanese Village: A Cross-Cultural Investigation of Implicit Race Attitudes." *Child Development* 77(5):1268–81.

Dunn, Charlotte. 2010. "The Harlem Children's Zone: A Literature Review of Programs and Practices." Master's thesis, University of North Carolina, Wilmington. http://dl.uncw.edu.

Eamon, Mary Keegan. 2002. "Effects of Poverty on Mathematics and Reading Achievement of Young Adolescents." *Journal of Early Adolescence* 22(1):49–74.

Early, Diane M., Iheoma U. Iruka, Sharon Ritchie, Oscar A. Barbarin, Donna-Marie C. Winn, Gisele M. Crawford, Pamela M. Frome, Richard M. Clifford, Margaret Burchinal, Carolle Howes, Donna M. Bryant, and Robert C. Pianta. 2010. "How Do Pre-Kindergarteners Spend Their Time? Gender, Ethnicity, and Income as Predictors of Experiences in Pre-Kindergarten Classrooms." *Early Childhood Research Quarterly* 25:177–93.

Echenique, Federico, and Roland G. Freyer, Jr. 2007. "A Measure of Segregation Based on Social Interactions." *Quarterly Journal of Economics* 72:441–85.

Eddy, Melissa. 2015. "In Sweden, the Land of the Open Door, Anti-Muslim Sentiment Finds a Foothold." *New York Times*, January 2. www.nytimes.com.

Edelman, Peter B. 1987. "The Next Century of Our Constitution: Rethinking Our Duty to the Poor." *Hastings Law Journal* 39:1–61.

Edelman, Peter B., and Joyce Ladner, eds. 1991. *Adolescence and Poverty: Challenge for the 1990s*. Washington, DC: Center for National Policy Press.

Edin, Katheryn, and Timothy J. Nelson. 2013. *Doing the Best I Can: Fatherhood in the Inner City*. Berkeley: University of California Press.

Edin, Kathryn, Laura Tach, and Ronald Mincy. 2009. "Claiming Fatherhood: Race and the Dynamics of Paternal Involvement among Unmarried Men." *Annals of the American Academy of Political and Social Science* 621(1):149–77.

Editorial Board. 2015. "Affordable Housing, Racial Isolation." *New York Times*, June 29. www.nytimes.com.

Edsall, Thomas B. 2012. "Is Poverty a Kind of Robbery?" *New York Times*, September 16.

Eekelaar, John. 1986. "The Emergence of Children's Rights." *Oxford Journal of Legal Studies* 6:161–82.

Eichner, Maxine. 2010. *The Supportive State: Families, Government and America's Political Ideals*. New York: Oxford University Press.

Eisenberg, Theodore, and Sheri Lynn Johnson. 2008. "Implicit Racial Attitudes of Death Penalty Lawyers." In Parks, Jones, and Cardi, *Critical Race Realism*, 33–44.

Epps, Garrett. 2007. "Interpreting the Fourteenth Amendment: Two Don'ts and Three Dos." *William and Mary Bill of Rights Journal* 16:433–63.

Ernestus, Stephanie M., and Hazel M. Prelow. 2015. "Patterns of Risk and Resilience in African American and Latino Youth." *Journal of Community Psychology* 43(8):954–72.

Evans, Ashley B., Meeta Banerjee, Rika Meyer, Adriana Aldana, Monica Foust, and Stephanie Rowley. 2012. "Racial Socialization as a Mechanism for Positive Development among African American Youth." *Child Development Perspectives* 6(3):251–57.

Evans, Ashley B., Kristi Copping, Stephanie J. Rowley, and Beth Kurtz-Costes. 2010. "Academic Self-Concept in Black Adolescents: Do Race and Gender Stereotypes Matter?" *Self and Identity* 10:263–77.

Executive Office of the President. 2015. "The Economics of Early Childhood Investments." www.obamawhitehouse.archives.gov.

Fagan, Jeffrey, and Deanne L. Wilkinson. 1998. "Guns, Youth Violence, and Social Identity in Inner Cities." *Crime and Justice* 24:105–88.

Fantuzzo, John, Whitney LeBoeuf, Heather Rouse, and Chin-Chih Chen. 2012. "Academic Achievement of African American Boys: A City-Wide Community-Based Investigation of Risk and Resilience." *Journal of School Psychology* 50:559–79.

Farkas, George, Christy Lleras, and Steve Maczuga. 2002. "Does Oppositional Culture Exist in Minority and Poverty Peer Groups?" *American Sociological Review* 67(1):148–55.

Farkas, Lilla. 2014. "Report on Discrimination of Roma Children in Education." European Commission. www.ec.europa.eu.

Farmer, Sarah. 2010. "Criminality of Black Youth in Inner-City Schools: 'Moral Panic,' Moral Imagination, and Moral Formation." *Race Ethnicity and Education* 13(3):367–81.

Fashola, Olatokunbo S. 2003. "Developing the Talents of African American Male Students during the Nonschool Hours." *Urban Education* 38(4):398–430.

Fatal Force. 2015. Accessed January 20, 2017. www.washingtonpost.com.

———. 2016. Accessed January 20, 2017. www.washingtonpost.com.

———. 2017. Accessed April 25, 2017. www.washingtonpost.com

Feld, Barry C. 1999. *Bad Kids: Race and the Transformation of the Juvenile Court.* New York: Oxford University Press.

———. 2003. "The Politics of Race and Juvenile Justice: The 'Due Process Revolution' and the Conservative Reaction." *Justice Quarterly* 20(4):765–800.

Felitti, Vincent J. 2002. "The Relation between Adverse Childhood Experiences and Adult Health: Turning Gold into Lead." *Permanente Journal* 6:44–47.

Felitti, Vincent J., Robert F. Anda, Dale Nordenberg, David F. Williamson, Alison M. Spitz, Valerie Edwards, Mary P. Koss, and James S. Marks. 1998. "Relationship of Childhood Abuse and Household Dysfunction to Many of the Leading Causes of Death in Adults." *American Journal of Preventative Medicine* 14:245–58.

Ferguson, Ann Arnett. 2000. *Bad Boys: Public Schools in the Making of Black Masculinity.* Ann Arbor: University of Michigan Press.

Fineman, Martha Albertson. 2008. "The Vulnerable Subject: Anchoring Equality in the Human Condition." *Yale Journal of Law and Feminism* 20:1–23.

———. 2010. "The Vulnerable Subject and the Responsive State." *Emory Law Journal* 60:251–75.

Fineman, Martha Albertson, and Anna Grear, eds. 2013. *Vulnerability: Reflections on a New Ethical Foundation for Law and Politics.* Surrey: Ashgate.

Finkelhor, David, Anne Shattuck, Heather Turner, and Sherry Hamby. 2013. "Improving the Adverse Childhood Experiences Study Scale." *Journal of the American Medical Association of Pediatrics* 167(1):70–75.

Fisher, Celia B., Nancy A. Busch-Rossnagel, Daniel S. Jopp, and Joshua L. Brown. 2012. "Applied Developmental Science, Social Justice, and Socio-political Well-Being." *Applied Developmental Science* 16:54–64.

Fisher, Celia B., Scyatta A. Wallace, and Rose E. Fenton. 2000. "Discrimination Distress during Adolescence." *Journal of Youth and Adolescence* 29(6):679–95.

Fite, Paula J., Porche' Wynn, and Dustin A. Pardini. 2009. "Explaining Discrepancies in Arrest Rates between Black and White Male Juveniles." *Journal of Consulting and Clinical Psychology* 77(5):916–27.

Fitzpatrick, Kevin M. 1997. "Aggression and Environmental Risk among Low-Income African-American Youth." *Journal of Adolescent Health* 21(3):172–78.

Fitzpatrick, Kevin M., Akilah Dulin, and Bettina Piko. 2010. "Bullying and Depressive Symptomatology among Low-Income, African-American Youth." *Journal of Youth and Adolescence* 39:634–45.

Flagg, Barbara J. 1993. *Was Blind but Now I See: White Racial Consciousness and Law.* New York: New York University Press.

"Flint Water Crisis." 2017. *New York Times.* Accessed April 7, 2017. www.nytimes.com.

Florsheim, Paul, Patrick H. Tolan, and Deborah Gorman-Smith. 1996. "Family Processes and Risk for Externalizing Behavior Problems among African American and Hispanic Boys." *Journal of Consulting and Clinical Psychology* 64(6):1222–30.

Folk, Johanna B., Janice L. Zeman, Jennifer A. Poon, and Danielle H. Dallaire. 2014. "A Longitudinal Examination of Emotion Regulation: Pathways to Anxiety and Depressive Symptoms in Urban Minority Youth." *Child and Adolescent Mental Health* 19(4):243–50.

Fondacaro, Mark. 2015. "Why Should We Treat Juvenile Offenders Differently? It's Not Because the Pie Is Half Baked." In Dowd, *New Juvenile Justice System*, 128–39.

Fordham, Signithia. 1988. "Racelessness as a Factor in Black Students' School Success: Pragmatic Strategy or Pyrrhic Victory?" *Harvard Educational Review* 58:54–84.

———. 1999. "Dissin' the Standard: Ebonics and Guerrilla Warfare at Capital High." *Anthropology and Education Quarterly* 30(3):272–93.

———. 2008. "Beyond Capital High: On Dual Citizenship and the Strange Career of 'Acting White.'" *Anthropology and Education Quarterly* 39(3):227–93.

———. 2010. "Passin' for Black: Race, Identity, and Bone Memory in Postracial America." *Harvard Educational Review* 80:4–29.

Fordham, Signithia, and John U. Ogbu. 1986. "Black Students' School Success: Coping with the Burden of 'Acting White.'" *Urban Review* 18(3):176–206.

Forehand, Rex, Deborah J. Jones, Gene H. Brody, and Lisa Armistead. 2002. "African American Children's Adjustment: The Roles of Maternal and Teacher Depressive Symptoms." *Journal of Marriage and Family* 64:1012–23.

Forman, James, Jr. 2004. "Juries and Race in the Nineteenth Century." *Yale Law Journal* 113:895–938.

———. 2012. "Racial Critiques of Mass Incarceration: Beyond the New Jim Crow." *New York University Law Review* 87(1):21–69.

Fortunato, Stephen J., Jr. 2005. "Judges, Racism, and the Problem of Actual Innocence." *Maine Law Review* 57:481–518.

Forward through Ferguson. n.d. Accessed October 3, 2015. www.forwardthroughferguson.org.

Fottrell, Deidre, ed. 2000. *Revisiting Children's Rights: 10 Years of the UN Convention on the Rights of the Child.* Boston: Kluwer.

Foundation for Child Well Being Child and Youth Development Project. 2015. "Child and Youth Well-Being Index (CWI)." www.soc.duke.edu.

Fouts, Hillary N., Jaipaul L. Roopnarine, Michael E. Lamb, and Melanie Evans. 2012. "Infant Social Interactions with Multiple Caregivers: The Importance of Ethnicity and Socioeconomic Status." *Journal of Cross-Cultural Psychology* 43(2):328–48.

Fragile Families and Child Wellbeing Study. 2015. Accessed December 13, 2015. www.fragilefamilies.princeton.edu.

Franklin, Robert B., and Sherlon Pack-Brown. 2001. "Team Brothers: An Afrocentric Approach to Group Work with African American Male Adolescents." *Journal for Specialists in Group Work* 26(3):237–45.

Freeman, Michael. 2006. "The Future of Children's Rights." *Children and Society* 14(4):277–93.

———. 2010. "The Human Rights of Children." *Current Legal Problems* 63(1):1–44.

———, ed. 2011a. *Children's Rights: Progress and Perspectives.* Boston: Martinus Nijhoff.

———. 2011b. "The Value and Values of Children's Rights." In Invernizzi and Williams, *Human Rights of Children,* 21–36.

———. 2012. "Towards a Sociology of Children's Rights Law." In *Law and Childhood Studies: Current Legal Issues,* Vol. 14, edited by Michael Freeman, 29–38. Oxford: Oxford University Press.

Freiburger, Tina L., and Alison Burke. 2010. "Adjudication Decisions of Black, White, Hispanic, and Native American Youth in Juvenile Court." *Journal of Ethnicity in Criminal Justice* 8(4):231–47.

Freire, Paulo. 1990. *Pedagogy of the Oppressed.* Translated by Myra Bergman Ramos. New York: Continuum.

Freund, David M. P. 2016. "We Can't Forget How Racist Institutions Shaped Home-ownership in America." *Washington Post,* April 28. www.washingtonpost.com.

Friend, Christian A., Andrea G. Hunter, and Anne C. Fletcher. 2011. "Parental Racial Socialization and the Academic Achievement of African American Children: A Cultural-Ecological Approach." *Journal of African American Studies* 15:40–57.

Fryer, Roland G. 2006. "'Acting White': The Social Price Paid by the Best and Brightest Minority Students." *Education Next* 6(1):52–59.

Fryer, Roland G., Jr., and Steven D. Levitt. 2004. "Understanding the Black-White Test Score Gap in the First Two Years of School." *Review of Economics and Statistics* 86(2):447–64.

———. 2006. "The Black-White Test Score Gap through Third Grade." *American Law and Economics Review* 8(2):249–81.

———. 2013. "Testing for Racial Differences in the Mental Ability of Young Children." *American Economic Review* 103(2):981–1005.

Fryer, Roland G., and Paul Torelli. 2010. "An Empirical Analysis of 'Acting White.'" *Journal of Public Economics* 94(5):1–17.

Fultz, Michael, and Anthony Brown. 2008. "Historical Perspectives on African American Males as Subjects of Education Policy." *American Behavioral Scientist* 51(7):854–71.

Gabrieli, John. 2014. "The Promise of the Harlem Children's Zone." *Harvard Political Review*, June 11. www.harvardpolitics.com.

Gadsden, Vivian, Stanton Wortham, and Herbert M. Turner, III. 2003. "Situated Identities of Young, African American Fathers in Low-Income Urban Settings." *Family Court Review* 41(3):381–99.

Gagnon, Joseph C., and Brian R. Barber. 2011. "Preventing Incarceration through Special Education and Mental Health Collaboration for Students with Emotional and Behavioral Disorders." In Dowd, *Justice for Kids*, 82–106.

Gal, Tali. 2011. *Child Victims and Restorative Justice: A Needs-Rights Model*. New York: Oxford University Press.

Garbarino, James. 2000. *Lost Boys: Why Our Sons Turn Violent and How We Can Save Them*. New York: Free Press.

García Coll, Cynthia T. 1990. "Developmental Outcome of Minority Infants: A Process-Oriented Look into Our Beginnings." *Child Development* 61(2):270–89.

García Coll, Cynthia, Gontran Lamberty, Renee Jenkins, Harriet Pipes McAdoo, Keith Crnic, Barbara Hanna Wasik, and Heidie Vazquez-Garcia. 1996. "An Integrative Model for the Study of Developmental Competencies in Minority Children." *Child Development* 67(5):1891–1914.

García Coll, Cynthia T., and Katherine Magnuson. 2000. "Cultural Differences as Sources of Developmental Vulnerabilities and Resources: A View from Developmental Research." In *Handbook of Early Childhood Intervention*, edited by Jack P. Shonkoff and Samuel J. Meisels, 94–114. New York: Cambridge University Press.

García Coll, Cynthia, and Laura A. Szalacha. 2004. "The Multiple Contexts of Middle Childhood." *Future of Children* 14(2):80–97.

Gardner-Kitt, Donna L., and Frank C. Worrell. 2006. "Measuring Nigrescence Attitudes in School-Aged Adolescents." *Journal of Adolescence* 30(2):187–202.

Gardner-Neblett, Nicole, Elizabeth P. Pungello, and Iheoma U. Iruka. 2012. "Oral Narrative Skills: Implications for the Reading Development of African American Children." *Child Development Perspectives* 6(3):218–24.

Garibaldi, Antoine M. 1992. "Educating and Motivating African American Males to Succeed." *Journal of Negro Education* 61(1):4–11.

Garland, Brett E., Cassia Spohn, and Eric J. Wodahl. 2008. "Racial Disproportionality in the American Prison Population: Using the Blumstein Method to Address the Critical Race and Justice Issue of the 21st Century." *Justice Policy Journal* 5(2):1–42.

Gavazzi, Stephen M., Christiana M. Russell, and Atika Khurana. 2009. "Predicting Educational Risks among Court-Involved Black Males: Family, Peers, and Mental Health Issues." *Negro Educational Review* 60:99–114.

Gaylord-Harden, Noni K., Cynthia L. Campbell, and Christine M. Kesselring. 2010. "Maternal Parenting Behaviors and Coping in African American Children: The Influence of Gender and Stress." *Journal of Children and Family Studies* 19:579–87.

Geller, Joanna D., Bernadette Doykos, Krista Craven, Kimberly D. Bess, and Maury Nation. 2014. "Engaging Residents in Community Change: The Critical Role of Trust in the Development of a Promise Neighborhood." *Teachers College Record* 116:1–42.

Gelman, Andrew, Jeffrey Fagan, and Alex Kiss. 2007. "An Analysis of the New York City Police Department's 'Stop and Frisk' Policy in the Context of Claims of Racial Bias." *Journal of the American Statistical Association* 102(479):813–23.

Gibbs, Jewelle Taylor, ed. 1988. *Young, Black, and Male in America: An Endangered Species*. Westport, CT: Auburn House.

———. 1998. "High-Risk Behaviors in African American Youth: Conceptual and Methodological Issues in Research." In *Studying Minority Adolescents: Conceptual, Methodological, and Theoretical Issues*, edited by Vonnie C. McLoyd and Laurence Steinberg, 55–86. Mahwah, NJ: Lawrence Erlbaum.

Gilligan, James. 2001. *Preventing Violence*. New York: Thames and Hudson.

Girvan, Erik J. 2015. "Elevating Efficacy: On Using the Psychological Science of Implicit Bias to Advance Anti-discrimination Law." Draft paper on file with author.

Glennon, Theresa. 2002. "Knocking Against the Rocks: Evaluating Institutional Practice and the African-American Boy." *Journal of Health Care Law and Policy* 5:10–67.

———. 2011. "Looking for Air: Excavating Destructive and Racial Policies to Build Successful School Communities." In Dowd, *Justice for Kids*, 107–34.

Goff, Phillip Atiba, Matthew Christian Jackson, Carmen Marie Culotta, Brooke Allison Lewis Di Leone, and Natalie Ann DiTomasso. 2014. "The Essence of Innocence: Consequences of Dehumanizing Black Children." *Journal of Personality and Social Psychology* 106(4):526–45.

Goldhagen Jeffrey, and Raul Mercer. 2011. "Child Health Equity: From Theory to Reality." In Invernizzi and Williams, *Human Rights of Children*, 307–26.

Goldhagen, Jeffrey, Raul Mercer, Gary Robinson, Ernesto Duran, Elspeth Webb, and Jochen Ehrich. 2015. "Establishing a Child Rights, Health Equity, and Social Justice–Based Practice of Pediatrics." *Journal of Pediatrics* 166(4):1098–99.

Goldstein, Dana. 2016. "Bill de Blasio's Pre-K Crusade." *Atlantic*, September 7.

Goodkind, Sara, John M. Wallace, Jr., Jeffrey J. Shook, Jerald Bachman, and Patrick O'Malley. 2009. "Are Girls Really Becoming More Delinquent? Testing the Gender Convergence Hypothesis by Race and Ethnicity, 1976–2005." *Children and Youth Services Review* 31:885–95.

Gormley, William, Jr., Ted Gayer, Deborah Phillips, and Brittany Dawson. 2005. "The Effects of Universal Pre-K on Cognitive Development." *Developmental Psychology* 41(6):872–84.

Gould, Elise, and Hilary Wething. 2012. "U.S. Poverty Rates Higher, Safety Net Weaker Than in Peer Countries." Economic Policy Institute, July 24. www.epi.org.

Graff, Gilda. 2011. "Everything Has Changed, but Nothin' Has Changed: Shame, Racism, and a Dream Deferred." *Journal of Psychohistory* 34(4):346–58.

Graham, Sandra, and Brian S. Lowery. 2004. "Priming Unconscious Racial Stereotypes about Adolescent Offenders." *Law and Human Behavior* 28(5):483–504.

Grant, Kathryn E., Brian N. Katz, Kina J. Thomas, Jeffrey H. O'Koon, C. Manuel Meza, Anna-Marie DiPasquale, Vanessa O. Rodriguez, and Carrie Bergen. 2004. "Psychological Symptoms Affecting Low-Income Urban Youth." *Journal of Adolescent Research* 19:613–34.

Grant, Kathryn E., Aoife L. Lyons, Jo-Ann S. Finkelstein, Kathryn M. Conway, Linda K. Reynolds, Jeffrey H. O'Koon, Gregory R. Waitkoff, and Kira J. Hicks. 2004. "Gender Differences in Rates of Depressive Symptoms among Low-Income, Urban, African American Youth: A Test of Two Mediational Hypotheses." *Journal of Youth and Adolescence* 33(6):523–33.

Gray, Calonie M. K., Rona Carter, and Wendy K. Silverman. 2011. "Anxiety Symptoms in African American Children: Relations with Ethnic Pride, Anxiety Sensitivity, and Parenting." *Journal of Child and Family Studies* 20:205–13.

Gray-Little, Bernadette, and Adam R. Hafdahl. 2000. "Factors Influencing Racial Comparisons of Self-Esteem: A Quantitative Review." *Psychological Bulletin* 126(1):26–54.

Green, Tristin K. 2008. Review of *Critical Race Realism: Intersections of Psychology, Race, and Law,* by Gregory S. Parks, Shayne Jones, and W. Jonathan Cardi, eds. *Law and Society Review* 44:187–89.

Greene, Dwight L. 1994. "Naughty by Nurture: Black Male Joyriding—Is Everything Gonna Be Alright?" *Columbia Journal on Gender and Law* 4:73–125.

Greene, Melissa L., Niobe Way, and Kerstin Pahl. 2006. "Trajectories of Perceived Adult and Peer Discrimination among Black, Latino, and Asian American Adolescents: Patterns and Psychological Correlates." *Developmental Psychology* 42(2):218–38.

Greenwald, Anthony G., and Linda Hamilton Krieger. 2006. "Implicit Bias: Scientific Foundations." *California Law Review* 94(4):945–68.

Grimmett, Marc A. 2010. "Brothers in Excellence: An Empowerment Model for the Career Development of African American Boys." *Journal of Humanistic Counseling, Education and Development* 49:73–83.

Guggenheim, Martin. 2000. "Somebody's Children: Sustaining the Family's Place in Child Welfare Policy." Review of *Nobody's Children: Abuse and Neglect, Foster Drift, and the Adoption Alternative,* by Elizabeth Bartholet. *Harvard Law Review* 113(7):1716–50.

Guinier, Lani, and Gerald Torres. 2003. *The Miner's Canary: Enlisting Race, Resisting Power, Transforming Democracy.* Cambridge, MA: Harvard University Press.

Gump, Janice P. 2010. "Reality Matters: The Shadow of Trauma on African American Subjectivity." *Psychoanalytic Psychology* 27(1):42–54.

Gunn, Raymond. 2004. "Inner-City 'Schoolboy' Life." *Annals of the American Academy of Political and Social Science* 595:63–79.

Guthrie, Robert V. 1998. *Even the Rat Was White: A Historical View of Psychology.* Boston: Allyn & Bacon.

Haggerty, Robert J., Lonnie R. Sherrod, Norman Garmezy, and Michael Rutter, eds. 1994. *Stress, Risk, and Resilience in Children and Adolescents: Process, Mechanisms, and Interventions.* New York: Cambridge University Press.

Halgunseth, Linda C., Jean M. Ipsa, and Duane Rudy. 2006. "Parental Control in Latino Families: An Integrated Review of the Literature." *Child Development* 77(5):1282–97.

Hall, Diane M., Elaine F. Cassidy, and Howard C. Stevenson. 2008. "Acting 'Tough' in a 'Tough' World: An Examination of Fear among Urban African American Adolescents." *Journal of Black Psychology* 34(3):381–98.

Hall, Horace R. 2006. *Mentoring Young Men of Color: Meeting the Needs of African American and Latino Students.* Lanham, MD: Rowman & Littlefield.

Hall, Vernon C., John W. Huppertz, and Alan Levi. 1977. "Attention and Achievement Exhibited by Middle- and Lower-Class Black and White Elementary School Boys." *Journal of Educational Psychology* 69(2):115–20.

Hamer, Jennifer F. 1997. "The Fathers of 'Fatherless' Black Children." *Families in Society* 78(6):564–78.

Hamm, Jill V., Kerrylin Lambert, Charlotte A. Agger, and Thomas W. Farmer. 2013. "Promotive Peer Contexts of Academic and Social Adjustment among Rural African American Early Adolescent Boys." *American Journal of Orthopsychiatry* 83(2–3):278–88.

Hammack, Phillip L., Maryse H. Richards, Zupei Luo, Emily S. Edlynn, and Kevin Roy. 2010. "Social Support Factors as Moderators of Community Violence Exposure among Inner-City African American Young Adolescents." *Journal of Clinical Child and Adolescent Psychology* 33(3):450–62.

Hammond, Wizdom P., and Jacqueline S. Mattis. 2005. "Being a Man about It: Manhood Meaning among African American Men." *Psychology of Men and Masculinity* 6(2):114–26.

Haney-Lopez, Ian. 2010a. "Freedom, Mass Incarceration, and Racism in the Age of Obama." *Alabama Law Review* 62:1005–21.

———. 2010b. "Post-Racial Racism: Racial Stratification and Mass Incarceration in the Age of Obama." *California Law Review* 98(3):1023–73.

Hannah-Jones, Nicole. 2016. "Choosing a School for My Daughter in a Segregated City." *New York Times*, June 9. www.nytimes.com.

Hansen, Kirstine, Heather Joshi, and Shirley Dex. 2010. *Children of the 21st Century.* Bristol, UK: Policy Press.

Hanson, Danielle. 2013. "Assessing the Harlem Children's Zone." Heritage Foundation, March 6. www.heritage.org.

Hanson, Karl, and Olga Nieuwenhuys, eds. 2013. *Reconceptualizing Children's Rights in International Development: Living Rights, Social Justice, Translations*. Cambridge: Cambridge University Press.

Harden, Brenda Jones, Heather Sandstrom, and Rachel Chazen-Cohen. 2012. "Early Head Start and African American Families: Impacts and Mechanisms of Childhood Outcomes." *Early Childhood Research Quarterly* 27:572–81.

Harmon, Amy. 2017. "Beyond 'Hidden Figures': Nurturing New Black and Latino Math Whizzes." *New York Times*, February 17. www.nytimes.com.

Harper, Frederic D., Linda M. Terry, and Rashida Twiggs. 2009. "Counseling Strategies with Black Boys and Black Men: Implications for Policy." *Journal of Negro Education* 78(3):216–32.

———. 2012. "Black Male Students Success in Higher Education: A Report from the National Black Male College Achievement Study." University of Pennsylvania, Center for the Study of Race and Equality in Education.

Harper, Shaun R. 2015. "Success in These Schools? Visual Counternarratives of Young Men of Color and Urban High Schools They Attend." *Urban Education* 50(2):139–69.

Harper, Shaun R., and Charles H. F. Davis, III. 2012. "They (Don't) Care about Education: A Counternarrative on Black Male Students' Responses to Inequitable Schooling." *Educational Foundations* 26:103–20.

Harrell, Shelly P. 2000. "A Multidimensional Conceptualization of Racism-Related Stress: Implications for the Well-Being of People of Color." *American Journal of Orthopsychiatry* 70(1):42–57.

Harris, Angela P. 2000. "Gender, Violence, Race and Criminal Justice." *Stanford Law Review* 52:778–806.

Harris, Cheryl I. 1993. "Whiteness as Property." *Harvard Law Review* 106(8):1707–91.

Harris, Elizabeth A. 2016a. "Connecticut to Appeal Decision in Schools Funding Case." *New York Times*, September 15. www.nytimes.com.

———. 2016b. "Judge, Citing Inequality, Orders Connecticut to Overhaul Its School System." *New York Times*, September 7. www.nytimes.com.

Harris, Leslie Joan. 2011. "Challenging the Overuse of Foster Care and Disrupting the Path to Delinquency and Prison." In Dowd, *Justice for Kids*, 61–63.

Harris, Shanette M. 1992. "Black Male Socialization Theory and Concepts: Black Male Masculinity and Same-Sex Friendships." *Western Journal of Black Studies* 16(2):74–81.

———. 1995. "Psychosocial Development and Black Male Masculinity: Implications for Counseling Economically Disadvantaged African American Male Adolescents." *Journal of Counseling and Development* 73(3):279–87.

Harris, Toni, John Sideris, Zewelanji Serpell, Margaret Burchinal, and Chloe Pickett. 2014. "Domain-Specific Cognitive Stimulation and Maternal Sensitivity as Predictors of Early Academic Outcomes among Low-Income African American Preschoolers." *Journal of Negro Education* 83(1):15–28.

Hart, Betty, and Todd R. Risley. 2003. "The Early Catastrophe: The 30 Million Word Gap by Age 3." *American Educator* 27(1):4–9. www.aft.org.

Hartocollis, Anemona, and Jess Bidgood. 2015. "Racial Discrimination Protests Ignite at Colleges across the U.S." *New York Times*, November 11. www.nytimes.com.

Harvey, Aminifu R., and Robert B. Hill. 2004. "Africentric Youth and Family Rites of Passage Program: Promoting Resilience among At-Risk African American Youths." *Social Work* 49(1):65–74.

Hatcher, Daniel L. 2013. "Forgotten Fathers." *Boston University Law Review* 93:897–920.

———. 2016. *The Poverty Industry: The Exploitation of America's Most Vulnerable Citizens*. New York: New York University Press.

Haynie, Dana L., Harald E. Weiss, and Alex Piquero. 2008. "Race, the Economic Maturity Gap, and Criminal Offending in Young Adulthood." *Justice Quarterly* 25(4):595–622.

Hemmings, Annette. 1998. "The Self-Transformations of African American Achievers." *Youth and Society* 29(3):330–68.

Henfield, Malik S. 2011. "Black Male Adolescents Navigating in a Traditionally White Middle School: A Qualitative Study." *Journal of Multicultural Counseling and Development* 39:141–55.

Henry, Jessica S., Sharon F. Lambert, and Mia Smith Bynum. 2015. "The Protective Role of Maternal Racial Socialization for African American Adolescents Exposed to Community Violence." *Journal of Family Psychology* 29(4):548–57.

Herz, Denise C., Joseph P. Ryan, and Shay Bilchik. 2010. "Challenges Facing Crossover Youth: An Examination of Juvenile Justice Decision Making and Recidivism." *Family Court Review* 48:305–21.

Hill, Hope M., Monique Levermore, James Twaite, and Lauren Jones. 1996. "Exposure to Community Violence and Social Support as Predictors of Anxiety and Social and Emotional Behavior among African American Children." *Journal of Child and Family Studies* 5(4):399–414.

Hill, Hope M., and Serge Madhere. 1996. "Exposure to Community Violence and African American Children: A Multidimensional Model of Risks and Resources." *Journal of Community Psychology* 24:26–43.

Hills, John. 2003. "The Blair Government and Child Poverty: An Extra One Percent for Children in the United Kingdom." In Sawhill, *One Percent for the Kids*, 156–65.

Hines, Erik M., and Cheryl Holcomb-McCoy. 2013. "Parental Characteristics, Ecological Factors, and the Academic Achievement of African American Males." *Journal of Counseling and Development* 91:68–77.

Hinshelwood, R. D. 2007. "Intolerance and the Intolerable: The Case of Racism." *Psychoanalysis, Culture and Society* 12:1–20.

Hinton, KaaVonia. 2005. "Affirming African American Boys." *Book Links* 14(3):59–63.

Hitlin, Steven, J. Scott Brown, and Glen H. Elder, Jr. 2006. "Racial Self-Categorization in Adolescence: Multiracial Development and Social Pathways." *Child Development* 77(5):1298–1308.

Hobbs, Steven H., and Shenavia Baity. 2006. "Tending to the Spirit: A Proposal for Healing the Hearts of Black Children in Poverty." *Boston College Third World Law Journal* 26:107–29.

Hood, Kristina, Joshua Brevard, Anh Bao Nguyen, and Faye Belgrave. 2013. "Stress among African American Emerging Adults: The Role of Family and Cultural Factors." *Journal of Child and Family Studies* 22:76–84.

hooks, bell. 1989. *Talking Back*. Boston: South End Press.

Hope, Elan C., Alexandra B. Skoog, and Robert J. Jagers. 2015. "'It'll Never Be the White Kids, It'll Always Be Us': Black High School Students' Evolving Critical Analysis of Racial Discrimination and Inequity in Schools." *Journal of Adolescent Research* 30(1):83–112.

Howard, Donna E. 1996. "Searching for Resilience among African-American Youth Exposed to Community Violence: Theoretical Issues." *Journal of Adolescent Health* 18:254–62.

Howard, J. H. 1980. "Toward a Social Psychology of Colonialism." In Jones, *Black Psychology*, 367–75.

Howard, Lionel C., Oscar A. Barbarin, and Jason C. Rose. 2013. "Raising African American Boys: An Exploration of Gender and Racial Socialization Practices." *American Journal of Orthopsychiatry* 83(2–3):218–30.

Howard, Tyrone C. 2008. "Who Really Cares? The Disenfranchisement of African American Males in PreK–12 Schools: A Critical Race Theory Perspective." *Teachers College Record* 10(5):954–85.

Howarth, Joan. 1997. "Representing Black Male Innocence." *Journal of Gender, Race and Justice* 1:97–140.

Hrabowski, Freeman A., III, Kenneth I. Maton, and Geoffrey L. Greif. 1998. *Beating the Odds: Raising Academically Successful African American Males*. New York: Oxford University Press.

Hudley, Cynthia, and Sandra Graham. 1993. "An Attributional Intervention to Reduce Peer-Directed Aggression among African-American Boys." *Child Development* 64(1):124–38.

Huebner, G., N. Boothby, J. L. Aber, G. L. Darmstadt, A. Diaz, A. S. Mastern, H. Yoshikawa, I. Redlener, A. Emmel, M. Pitt, L. Arnold, B. Barber, B. Berman, R. Blum, M. Canavera, J. Eckerle, N. A. Fox, J. L. Gibbons, S. W. Hargarten, C. Landers, C. A. Nelson III, S. D. Pollak, V. Rauh, M. Samson, F. Ssewamala, N. St Clair, L. Stark, R. Waldman, M. Wessells, S. L. Wilson, and C. H. Zeanah. 2016. "Beyond Survival: The Case for Investing in Young Children Globally." Discussion paper, National Academy of Medicine. www.nam.edu.

Hughes, Diane, Niobe Way, and Deborah Rivas-Drake. 2011. "Stability and Change in Private and Public Ethnic Regard among African American, Puerto Rican, Dominican, and Chinese American Adolescents." *Journal of Research on Adolescence* 21:861–70.

Hughes, Jan N., Jiun-Yu Wu, Oi-man Kwok, Victor Villarreal, and Audrea Y. Johnson. 2011. "Indirect Effects of Child Reports of Teacher-Student Relationship on Achievement." *Journal of Educational Psychology* 104(2):350–65.

Hughes-Hassell, Sandra, Elizabeth Koehler, and Ernie J. Cox. 2011. "Through Their Eyes: The Development of Self-Concept in Young African American Children through Board Books." *Children and Libraries* 9(2):36–41.

Huizinga, David, Terence Thornberry, Kelly Knight, and Peter Lovegrove. 2007. "Disproportionate Minority Contact in the Juvenile Justice System: A Study of Differential Minority Arrest/Referral to Court in Three Cities." Accessed April 21, 2017. www.ncjrs.gov.

Hunt, Kristin L., Patricia M. Martens, and Harolyn M. E. Belcher. 2011. "Risky Business: Trauma Exposure and Rate of Posttraumatic Stress Disorder in African American Children and Adolescents." *Journal of Traumatic Stress* 24(3):365–69.

Hunter, Andrea G., and James Earl Davis. 1992. "Constructing Gender: An Exploration of Afro-American Men's Conceptualization of Manhood." *Gender and Society* 6(3):464–79.

Huntington, Clare. 2006. "Rights Myopia in Child Welfare." *UCLA Law Review* 53:637–99.

———. 2014. *Failure to Flourish: How Law Undermines Family Relationships*. New York: Oxford University Press.

Hurd, Noelle M., Fatima A. Varner, and Stephanie J. Rowley. 2013. "Involved-Vigilant Parenting and Socio-Emotional Well-Being among Black Youth: The Moderating Influence of Natural Mentoring Relationships." *Journal of Youth Adolescence* 42:1538–95.

Hurder, Alex. 2014. "Left Behind with No 'IDEA': Children with Disabilities without Means." *Boston College Journal of Law and Social Justice* 34:283–310.

Hutchinson, Darren Lenard. 2002. "New Complexity Theories: From Theoretical Innovation to Doctrinal Reform." *University of Missouri–Kansas City Law Review* 71:431–45.

———. 2003. "'Unexplainable on Grounds Other Than Race': The Inversion of Privilege and Subordination in Equal Protection Jurisprudence." *University of Illinois Law Review* 2003:615–700.

———. 2004. "Critical Race Histories: In and Out." *American University Law Review* 53:1187–1215.

Hutchinson, Earl Ofari. 1996. *The Assassination of the Black Male Image*. New York: Simon & Schuster.

Hyman, David A. 2005. "The Poor State of Health Care Quality in the U.S.: Is Malpractice Liability Part of the Problem or Part of the Solution." *Cornell Law Review* 90:893–993.

Institute for Work and Health. 2016. "What Researchers Mean by . . . Primary, Secondary and Tertiary Prevention." Accessed September 11, 2016. www.iwh.on.ca.

Invernizzi, Antonella, and Jane Williams, eds. 2011. *The Human Rights of Children: From Visions to Implementation*. New York: Routledge.

Inzlicht, Michael, and Toni Schmader. 2012. *Stereotype Threat: Theory, Process, and Application*. New York: Oxford University Press.

Irby, Decoteau J. 2014. "Revealing Racial Purity Ideology: Fear of Black-White Intimacy as a Framework for Understanding School Discipline in Post-*Brown* Schools." *Educational Administration Quarterly* 50(5):783–95.

Iruka, Iheoma U., Margaret Burchinal, and Karen Cai. 2010. "Long-Term Effect of Early Relationships for African American Children's Academic and Social Development: An Examination from Kindergarten to Fifth Grade." *Journal of Black Psychology* 36(2):144–71.

Iruka, Iheoma U., Stephanie M. Curenton, and Shari Gardner. 2015. "How Changes in Home and Neighborhood Environment Factors Are Related to Change in Black Children's Academic and Social Development from Kindergarten to Third Grade." *Journal of Negro Education* 84(3):282–97.

Iruka, Iheoma U., Nicole Gardner-Neblett, J. S. Matthews, and Donna-Marie C. Winn. 2014. "Preschool to Kindergarten Transition Patterns for African American Boys." *Early Childhood Research Quarterly* 29:106–17.

Jackson, Aurora P., Jeong-Kyun Choi, and Peter M. Bentler. 2009. "Parenting Efficacy and the Early School Adjustment of Poor and Near-Poor Black Children." *Journal of Family Issues* 30:1339–55.

Jackson, Iesha, Yolanda Sealey-Ruiz, and Wanda Watson. 2014. "Reciprocal Love: Mentoring Black and Latino Males through an Ethos of Care." *Urban Education* 49(4):394–417.

Jackson, Kara, and Jonee Wilson. 2012. "Supporting African American Students' Learning of Mathematics: A Problem of Practice." *Urban Education* 47(2):354–98.

Jackson, Melissa Faye, Joan M. Barth, Nicole Powell, and John E. Lochman. 2006. "Classroom Contextual Effects of Race on Children's Peer Nominations." *Child Development* 77(5):1325–37.

Jacobs, Lynne. 2014. "Circumstances of Birth: Life on the Color Line." *Psychoanalytic Inquiry* 34:746–58.

Jarrett, Robin L. 1997. "Resilience among Low-Income African American Youth: An Ethnographic Perspective." *Ethos* 25(2):218–29.

Jarrett, Robin L., Kevin M. Roy, and Linda M. Burton. 2013. "'Fathers in the 'Hood': Insights from Qualitative Research on Low-Income African American Men." In *Handbook of Father Involvement: Multidisciplinary Perspectives*, edited by Catherine S. Tamis-LeMondal and Natasha Cabrera, 211–42. Mahwah, NJ: Lawrence Erlbaum.

Jaschik, Scott. 2015. "Yale Police Aim Gun at Columnist's Son, Turn Spotlight on Racial Profiling on Campus." *PBS NewsHour*, January 26. www.pbs.org.

Jencks, Christopher, and Meredith Phillips, eds. 1998. *The Black-White Test Score Gap*. Washington, DC: Brookings Institution Press.

Johnson, Deborah J., Elizabeth Jaeger, Suzanne M. Randolph, Ana Mari Cauce, Janie Ward, and National Institute of Child Health and Human Development Early Child Care Research Network. 2003. "Studying the Effects of Early Child Care Experiences on the Development of Children of Color in the United States: Toward a More Inclusive Research Agenda." *Child Development* 74(5):1227–44.

Johnson, Latrise P. 2015. "The Writing on the Wall: Enacting Place Pedagogies in Order to Reimagine Schooling for Black Male Youth." *Discourse* 36(6):908–19.

Johnson, Odis, Jr. 2010. "Assessing Neighborhood Racial Segregation and Macro-economic Effects in the Education of African Americans." *Review of Education Research* 80:527–75.

———. 2014. "Race-Gender Inequality across Residential and School Contexts: What Can Policy Do?" In Moore and Lewis, *African American Male Students in PreK–12 Schools*, 343–74.

Johnson, Olatunde C. A. 2007. "Disparity Rules." *Columbia Law Review* 107(2):374–425.

Johnson, Sheri Lynn. 1998. "Respectability, Race Neutrality, and Truth." Review of *Race, Crime and the Law*, by Randall Kennedy. *Yale Law Journal* 107:2619–59.

Johnson, Waldo E., Jr. 2010. *Social Work with African American Males: Health, Mental Health, and Social Policy.* Oxford: Oxford University Press.

Jones, Martin H., and James M. Ford. 2014. "Social Achievement Goals, Efficacious Beliefs, and Math Performance in a Predominately African American High School." *Journal of Black Psychology* 40(3):239–62.

Jones, Nikki. 2014. "'The Regular Routine': Proactive Policing and Adolescent Development among Young, Poor Black Men." *New Directions in Child and Adolescent Development* 143:33–54.

Jones, Reginald L., ed. 2004. *Black Psychology.* Hampton, VA: Cobb and Henry.

Jones, Trina. 2000. "Shades of Brown: The Law of Skin Color." *Duke Law Journal* 49:1487–1557.

Kahn, Jonathan. 2008. "Race, Genes, and Justice: A Call to Reform the Presentation of Forensic DNA Evidence in Criminal Trials." *Brooklyn Law Review* 74(1):325–75.

Kang, Jerry. 2005. "Trojan Horses of Race." *Harvard Law Review* 118(5):1489–1593.

Kang, Jerry, and Mahzarin Banaji. 2006. "Fair Measures: A Behavioral Realist Revision of Affirmative Action." *California Law Review* 94(4):1063–1118.

Katner, David. 2015. "Delinquency, Due Process and Mental Health: Presuming Youth Incompetency." In Dowd, *New Juvenile Justice System*, 104–28.

Katznelson, Ira. 2006. *When Affirmative Action Was White: An Untold History of Racial Inequality in Twentieth-Century America.* New York: Norton.

Keels, Micere. 2009. "Ethnic Group Differences in Early Head Start Parents' Parenting Beliefs and Practices and Links to Children's Early Cognitive Development." *Childhood Research Quarterly* 24(4):381–97.

Kelly, Joan B., and Michael E. Lamb. 2005. "Using Child Development Research to Make Appropriate Custody and Access Decisions for Young Children." *Family and Conciliation Courts Review* 38(3):297–311.

Kennedy, David. 2011. *Don't Shoot: One Man, a Street Fellowship, and the End of Violence in Inner-City America.* New York: Bloomsbury.

Khadka, Susan. 2013. "Social Rights and the United Nations—Child Rights Convention (UN-CRC): Is the CRC a Help or Hindrance for Developing Universal and Egalitarian Social Policies for Children's Wellbeing in the 'Developing World'?" *International Journal of Children's Rights* 21:616–28.

Khalifa, Muhamad A., and Felecia Briscoe. 2015. "A Counternarrative Autoethnography Exploring School Districts' Role in Reproducing Racism: Willful Blindness to Racial Inequities." *Teachers College Record* 117(8):1–34.

Kiang, Lisa, Tiffany Yip, Melinda Gonzales-Backen, Melissa Witkow, and Andrew J. Fuligni. 2006. "Ethnic Identity and the Daily Psychological Well-Being of Adolescents from Mexican and Chinese Backgrounds." *Child Development* 77(5):1338–50.

Kids Count Data Center. 2015. "Children in Single-Parent Families by Race." Accessed December 13, 2015. www.datacenter.kidscount.org.

Kilgore, Kim, James Snyder, and Chris Lentz. 2000. "The Contribution of Parental Discipline, Parental Monitoring, and School Risk to Early-Onset Conduct Problems in African American Boys and Girls." *Developmental Psychology* 36(6):835–45.

Kilkelly, Ursula. 2011. "Using the Convention on the Rights of the Child in Law and Policy: Two Ways to Improve Compliance." In Invernizzi and Williams, *Human Rights of Children*, 179–98.

Kilpatrick, Mary. 2014. "Tamir Rice's Family Remembers 12-Year-Old at Memorial Service." *Cleveland.com*, December 3. www.cleveland.com.

Kim, Catherine Y., Daniel J. Losen, and Damon T. Hewitt. 2010. *The School-to-Prison Pipeline: Structuring Legal Reform*. New York: New York University Press.

King, Anthony E. O. 1997. "Understanding Violence among Young African American Males: An Afrocentric Perspective." *Journal of Black Studies* 28(1):79–96.

Kistner, Janet A., Corinne F. David-Ferdon, Cristina M. Lopez, and Stephanie B. Dunkel. 2007. "Ethnic and Sex Differences in Children's Depressive Symptoms." *Journal of Clinical Child and Adolescent Psychology* 36(2):171–81.

Klonoff, Elizabeth A., and Hope Landrine. 1999. "Cross-Validation of the Schedule of Racist Events." *Journal of Black Psychology* 25(2):231–54.

Knight, George P., and Gustavo Carlo. 2012. "Prosocial Development among Mexican American Youth." *Child Development Perspectives* 6(3):258–63.

Koblinsky, Sally A., Katherine A. Kuvalanka, and Suzanne M. Randolph. 2006. "Social Skills and Behavior Problems of Urban, African American Preschoolers: Role of Parenting Practices, Family Conflict, and Maternal Depression." *American Journal of Orthopsychiatry* 76(4):554–63.

Kreader, J. Lee, Daniel Ferguson, and Sharmila Lawrence. 2005. "Infant and Toddler Child Care Quality." *Child Care and Early Education Research-to-Policy Connections* 2:1–8.

Krieger, Linda Hamilton. 1995. "The Content of Our Categories: A Cognitive Bias Approach to Discrimination and Equal Employment Opportunity." *Stanford Law Review* 47:1161–1248.

Krieger, Linda Hamilton, and Susan T. Fiske. 2006. "Behavioral Realism in Employment Discrimination Law: Implicit Bias and Disparate Treatment." *California Law Review* 94:997–1062.

Kroger, Jane. 2004. *Identity in Adolescence: The Balance between Self and Other*. New York: Routledge.

Kunesh, Claire E., and Amity Noltemeyer. 2015. "Understanding Disciplinary Disproportionality: Stereotypes Shape Pre-service Teachers' Beliefs about Black Boys Behavior." *Urban Education*. http://journals.sagepub.com.

Kuriloff, Peter, and Michael C. Reichert. 2003. "Boys of Class, Boys of Color: Negotiating the Academic and Social Geography of an Elite Independent School." *Journal of Social Issues* 59(4):751–69.

Kymlicka, Will. 1995. *Multicultural Citizenship: A Liberal Theory of Minority Rights.* Oxford: Clarendon.

Ladson-Billings, Gloria. 2011. "Race . . . to the Top, Again: Comments on the Genealogy of Critical Race Theory." *Connecticut Law Review* 43:1439–57.

Land, A'Lesia, Jason R. Mixon, Jennifer Butcher, and Sandra Harris. 2014. "Stories of Six Successful African American Males High School Students: A Qualitative Study." *National Association of Secondary School Principals Bulletin* 98(2):142–62.

Land, Kenneth C. 2017. "Child and Youth Well-Being Index." Accessed April 25, 2017. Available at www.soc.duke.edu.

Landa, Melissa Hare. 2012. "Deconstructing Black History Month: Three African American Boys' Exploration of Identity." *Multicultural Perspectives* 14(1):11–17.

La Paro, Karen M., Bridget K. Hamre, Jennifer Locasale-Crouch, Robert C. Pianta, Donna Bryant, Dianne Early, Richard Clifford, Oscar Barbarin, Carollee Howes, and Margaret Burchinal. 2009. "Quality in Kindergarten Classrooms: Observational Evidence for the Need to Increase Children's Learning Opportunities in Early Education Classrooms." *Early Education and Development* 20(4):657–92.

Lareau, Annette. 2003. *Unequal Childhood: Class, Race, and Family Life.* Berkeley: University of California Press.

Last, Cynthia G., and Sean Perrin. 1993. "Anxiety Disorders in African-American and White Children." *Journal of Abnormal Child Psychology* 21(2):153–64.

Latzman, Robert D., James A. Naifeh, David Watson, Jatin G. Vaidya, Laurie J. Heiden, John D. Damon, Terry L. Hight, and John Young. 2011. "Racial Differences in Symptoms of Anxiety and Depression among Three Cohorts of Students in the Southern United States." *Psychiatry—Interpersonal and Biological Processes* 74:332–48.

Lawrence, Charles. 1995. "The Id, the Ego, and Equal Protection: Reckoning with Unconscious Racism." In Crenshaw et al., *Critical Race Theory*, 235–57.

———. 2001. "Segregation Misunderstood: The Miliken Decision Revisited." In Powell, Kearney, and Kay, *In Pursuit of a Dream Deferred*, 183–203.

Lawrence, Keith O., ed. 2011. *Race, Crime and Punishment: Breaking the Connection in America.* Washington, DC: Aspen Institute Roundtable on Community Change.

Leary, Joy DeGruy. 2005. *Post Traumatic Slave Syndrome: America's Legacy of Enduring Injury and Healing.* Portland, OR: Joy DeGruy.

Lee, Cynthia Kwei Yung. 1996. "Race and Self-Defense: Toward a Normative Conception of Reasonableness." *Minnesota Law Review* 81:367–500.

Lee, Felicia A., Rhonda K. Lewis, Jamilia R. Sly, Chakema Carmack, Shani R. Roberts, and Polly Basore. 2011. "Promoting Positive Youth Development by Examining the Career and Educational Aspirations of African American Males: Implications for

Designing Educational Programs." *Journal of Prevention and Intervention in the Community* 39(4):299–309.

Lee, Kyunghee. 2009. "The Bidirectional Effects of Early Poverty on Children's Reading and Home Environment Scores: Associations and Ethnic Differences." *Social Work Research* 33:79–94.

Leff, Stephen S., Nicki R. Crick, Jennifer Angelucci, Kisha Haye, Abbas F. Jawad, Michael Grossman, and Thomas J. Power. 2006. "Social Cognition in Context: Validating a Cartoon-Based Attributional Measure for Urban Girls." *Child Development* 77(5):1351–58.

Leiber, Michael J., and Joseph D. Johnson. 2008. "Being Young and Black: What Are Their Effects in Juvenile Justice Decision Making?" *Crime and Delinquency* 54(4):560–81.

Lenhardt, Robin A. 2011a. "Equality Innovators." *Stanford Journal of Civil Rights and Civil Liberties* 7:265–92.

———. 2011b. "Race Audits." *Hastings Law Journal* 62:1527–77.

———. 2016. Presentation at the Fordham Law Review Family Law Symposium: Moore Kinship, October 14.

———. 2017. Email to author regarding John Moore Jr.

Leventhal, Tama, and Jeanne Brooks-Gunn. 2000. "The Neighborhoods They Live In: The Effects of Neighborhood Residence on Child and Adolescent Outcomes." *Psychological Bulletin* 126(2):309–37.

Leventhal, Tama, Yange Xue, and Jeanne Brooks-Gunn. 2006. "Immigrant Differences in School-Age Children's Verbal Trajectories: A Look at Four Racial/Ethnic Groups." *Child Development* 77(5):1359–74.

Li, Susan Tinsley, Karin M. Nussbaum, and Maryse H. Richards. 2007. "Risk and Protective Factors for Urban African-American Youth." *American Journal of Community Psychology* 39(1–2):21–35.

Li-Grining, Christine Pajunar. 2012. "The Role of Cultural Factors in the Development of Latino Preschoolers' Self-Regulation." *Child Development Perspectives* 6(3):210–17.

Lindsey, Michael A., Sean Joe, and Von Nebbitt. 2010. "Family Matters: The Role of Mental Health Stigma and Social Support on Depressive Symptoms and Subsequent Help Seeking among African American Boys." *Journal of Black Psychology* 36(4):458–82.

Lo, Ya-yu, and Gwendolyn Cartledge. 2006. "FBA and BIP: Increasing the Behavior Adjustment of African American Boys in Schools." *Behavioral Disorders* 31(1):147–61.

Love, John M., Ellen Eliason Kisker, Christine Ross, Jill Constantine, Kimberly Boller, Rachel Chazan-Cohen, Christy Brady-Smith, Allison Sidle Fuligni, Helen Raikes, Jeanne Brooks-Gunn, Louisa Banks Tarullo, Peter Z. Schochet, Diane Paulsell, and Cheri Vogel. 2005. "The Effectiveness of Early Head Start for 3-Year-Old Children and Their Parents: Lessons for Policy and Programs." *Developmental Psychology* 41(6):885–901.

Ludwig, Jens. 2003. "Improving Neighborhoods for Poor Children." In Sawhill, *One Percent for the Kids*, 136–55.

Luster, Tom, and Harriette Pipes McAdoo. 1995. "Factors Related to Self-Esteem among African American Youths: A Secondary Analysis of the High/Scope Perry Preschool Data." *Journal of Research on Adolescence* 5(4):451–67.

Luthar, Suniya S., and Shawn J. Latendresse. 2002. "Adolescent Risk: The Costs of Affluence." *New Directions for Youth Development* 95:101–21.

Madkour, Aubrey Spriggs, Kristina Jackson, Heng Wang, Thomas T. Miles, Frances Mather, and Arti Shankar. 2015. "Perceived Discrimination and Heavy Episodic Drinking among African-American Youth: Differences by Age and Reason for Discrimination." *Journal of Adolescent Health* 57(5):530–36.

Madyun, Na'im, and Moosung Lee. 2010. "Effects of Religious Involvement on Parent-Child Communication regarding Schooling: A Study of Black Youth in the United States." *Journal of Negro Education* 79(3):295–307.

Maguin, Eugene, Rolf Loeber, and Paul G. LeMahieu. 1993. "Does the Relationship between Poor Reading and Delinquency Hold for Males of Different Age and Ethnic Groups?" *Journal of Emotional and Behavioral Disorders* 1(2):88–100.

Majd, Katayoon. 2011. "Students of the Mass Incarceration Nation." *Howard Law Journal* 54(2):343–95.

Major, Brenda, Shannon K. McCoy, Toni Schmader, Richard H. Gramzow, Shana Levin, and Jim Sidanius. 2002. "Perceiving Personal Discrimination: The Role of Group Status and Legitimizing Ideology." *Journal of Personality and Social Psychology* 82(3):269–82.

Majors, Richard, and Janet Mancini Billson. 1992. *Cool Pose: The Dilemmas of Black Manhood in America*. New York: Simon & Schuster.

Majors, Richard, and Susan Wiener. 1995. *Programs That Serve African American Male Youth*. Washington, DC: Urban Institute.

Maldonado, Solangel. 2005. "Beyond Economic Fatherhood: Encouraging Divorced Fathers to Parent." *University of Pennsylvania Law Review* 153:921–1009.

———. 2014. "Shared Parenting and Never Married Families." *Family Court Review* 52(4):632–38.

Mandara, Jelani, and Carolyn B. Murray. 2006. "Father's Absence and African American Adolescent Drug Use." *Journal of Divorce and Remarriage* 46:1–12.

Mandara, Jelani, Carolyn B. Murray, James M. Telesford, Fatima A. Varner, and Scott B. Richman. 2012. "Observed Gender Differences in African American Mother-Child Relationships and Child Behaviors." *Family Relations* 61(1):129–41.

Mann, Tammy L., Nancy E. Hill, and Hiram E. Fitzgerald, eds. 2011. *African American Children and Mental Health, Volume 2: Prevention and Social Policy*. Santa Barbara, CA: Praeger.

Martin, Don, Magy Martin, Suzanne Semivan Gibson, and Jonathan Wilkins. 2007. "Increasing Prosocial Behavior and Academic Achievement among Adolescent African American Males." *Adolescence* 42(168):689–98.

Masi, Alessandria. 2015. "France's Secularism Is Driving Young Muslims Out of School, Work and French Culture." *International Business Times*, January 21. www.ibtimes.com.

Massey, Douglas S. 2007. *Categorically Unequal: The American Stratification System*. New York: Russell Sage Foundation.

Massey, Douglas S., and Nancy A. Denton. 1993. *American Apartheid: Segregation and the Making of the Underclass*. Cambridge, MA: Harvard University Press.

Matsuda, Mari J. 1991. "Beside My Sister, Facing the Enemy: Legal Theory Out of Co-alition." *Stanford Law Review* 43(6):1183–92.

Matthews, J. S., Karmen T. Kizzie, Stephanie J. Rowley, and Kai Cortina. 2010. "African Americans and Boys: Understanding the Literacy Gap, Tracing Academic Trajectories, and Evaluating the Role of Learning-Related Skills." *Journal of Educational Psychology* 102(3):757–71.

Mayeri, Serena. 2006. "The Strange Career of Jane Crow: Sex Segregation and the Transformation of Anti-Discrimination Discourse." *Yale Journal of Law and the Humanities* 18:187–272.

Mazama, Ama, and Garvey Lundy. 2012. "African American Homeschooling as Racial Protection." *Journal of Black Studies* 43(7):723–48.

McCabe, Kristen M., Rodney Clark, and Douglas Barnett. 1999. "Family Protective Factors among Urban African American Youth." *Journal of Clinical Child Psychology* 28(2):137–50.

McCarthy, Kyle, and Betina Jean-Louis. 2017. "Harlem Children's Zone." Friends of Evidence Case Study, Center for the Study of Social Policy. Accessed February 2, 2017. www.cssp.org.

McGee, Ebony O., and F. Alvin Pearman II. 2014. "Risk and Protective Factors in Mathematically Talented Black Male Students Snapshots from Kindergarten through Eighth Grade." *Urban Education* 49(4):363–93.

McGinley, Ann C. 2015. "Policing and the Clash of Masculinities." *Howard Law Journal* 59:221–70.

McGlothlin, Heidi, and Melanie Killen. 2006. "Intergroup Attitudes of European American Children Attending Ethnically Homogenous Schools." *Child Development* 77(5):1375–86.

McHale, Susan M., Ann C. Crouter, Ji-Yeon Kim, Linda M. Burton, Kelly D. Davis, Aryn M. Dotterer, and Dena P. Swanson. 2006. "Mothers' and Fathers' Racial Socialization in African American Families: Implications for Youth." *Child Development* 77(5):1387–1402.

McIntosh, Peggy. 2013. "White Privilege and Male Privilege: A Personal Account of Coming to See Correspondences through Work in Women's Studies." In *Race, Class and Gender*, edited by Margaret L. Anderson and Patricia Hill Collins, 73–79. Boston: Cengage.

McKernan, Signe-Mary, Caroline Ratcliffe, C. Eugene Steuerle, and Sisi Zhang. 2013. "Less Than Equal: Racial Disparities in Wealth Accumulation." Urban Institute. Available at www.urban.org.

McLoyd, Vonnie C. 1990. "The Impact of Economic Hardship on Black Families and Children: Psychological Distress, Parenting, and Socioemotional Development." *Child Development* 61(2):311–46.

———. 2006a. "The Legacy of Child Development's 1990 Special Issue on Minority Children: An Editorial Retrospective." *Child Development* 77(5):1142–48.

———. 2006b. "The Role of African American Scholars in Research on African American Children: Historical Perspectives and Personal Reflections." *Monographs of the Society for Research in Child Development* 71(1):121–44.

McLoyd, Vonnie C., and Suzanne M. Randolph. 1984. "The Conduct and Publication of Research on Afro-American Children: A Content Analysis." *Human Development* 27:65–75.

———. 1985. "Secular Trends in the Study of Afro-American Children: A Review of Child Development, 1936–1980." *Monographs of the Society for Research in Child Development* 50:78–92.

McMahon, Susan D., and Roderick J. Watts. 2002. "Ethnic Identity in Urban African American Youth: Exploring Links with Self-Worth, Aggression, and Other Psychosocial Variables." *Journal of Community Psychology* 30(4):411–31.

McMillian, M. Monique, Henry T. Frierson, and Frances A. Campbell. 2011. "Do Gender Differences Exist in the Academic Identification of African American Elementary School-Aged Children?" *Journal of Black Psychology* 37(1):78–98.

Mead, Sara. 2012. "Quality Pre-K: Starting Early to Close Achievement Gaps and Boost Student Achievement." Stand for Children Leadership Center. Available at www.standleadershipcenter.org.

Meehan, Albert J., and Michael C. Ponder. 2002. "Race and Place: The Ecology of Racial Profiling African American Motorists." *Justice Quarterly* 19(3):399–430.

Melish, Tara J. "Maximum Feasible Participation of the Poor: New Governance, New Accountability, and a 21st Century War on the Sources of Poverty." *Yale Human Rights and Development Law Journal* 13:1–134.

Mendel, Richard A. 2011. *No Place for Kids: The Case for Reducing Juvenile Incarceration*. Baltimore: Annie E. Casey Foundation.

Menzel, Kristina. 2010. "The School-to-Prison Pipeline: How Schools Are Failing to Properly Identify and Service Their Special Education Students and How One Probation Department Has Responded to the Crisis." *Loyola Public Interest Law Reporter* 3:198–207.

Mercy, James A., and Janet Saul. 2009. "Creating a Healthier Future through Early Intervention for Children." *Journal of the American Medical Association* 301:2262–64.

Metzger, Isha, Shauna M. Cooper, Nicole Zarrett, and Kate Flory. 2013. "Culturally Sensitive Risk Behavior Prevention Programs for African American Adolescents: A Systematic Analysis." *Clinical Children Family Psychological Review* 16:187–212.

Michelman, Frank I. 1968. "Protecting the Poor through the Fourteenth Amendment." *Harvard Law Review* 83:7–37.

Mickelson, Roslyn Arlin. 2006. "Segregation and the SAT." *Ohio State Law Journal* 67:157–99.

Milam, Adam J., C. Debra Furr-Holden, Damiya Whitaker, Mieka Smart, Philip Leaf, and Michele Cooley-Strickland. 2012. "Neighborhood Environment and Internalizing Problems in African American Children." *Community Mental Health Journal* 48:39–44.

Miller, Jerome G. 2011. *Search and Destroy: African-American Males in the Criminal Justice System*. Cambridge: Cambridge University Press.

Miller-Wilson, Laval S. 2006. "Law and Adolescence: Examining the Legal and Policy Implications of Adolescent Development Research for Youth Involved in the Child Welfare, Juvenile Justice, or Criminal Justice System." *Temple Law Review* 79(2):317–24.

Mills, Steve. 2015. "Chicago Police Reports Conflict with Video of Laquan McDonald Shooting." *Los Angeles Times*, December 6. www.latimes.com.

Mincy, Ronald B., ed. 1994. *Nurturing Young Black Males: Challenges to Agencies, Programs, and Social Policy*. Washington, DC: Urban Institute Press.

Mincy, Ronald B., and Hillard Pouncy. 2009. "The Impoverished 'Culture vs. Structure' Debate on the Woes of Young Black Males and Its Remedy." In *The Expanding Boundaries of Black Politics*, edited by Georgia A. Persons, 195–206. New Brunswick, NJ: Transaction.

Mitchell, Anthony B., and James B. Steward. 2013. "The Efficacy of All-Male Academies: Insights from Critical Race Theory (CRT)." *Sex Roles* 69:382–92.

Mitchell, Colter, John Hobcraft, Sara S. McLanahan, Susan Rutherford Siegel, Arthur Berg, Jeanne Brooks-Gunn, Irwin Garfinkel, and Daniel Notterman. 2014. "Social Disadvantage, Genetic Sensitivity, and Children's Telomere Length." *Proceedings of the National Academy of Sciences* 111(16):5944–49.

Mizell, C. Andre. 1999. "African American Men's Personal Sense of Mastery: The Consequences of the Adolescent Environment, Self-Concept, and Adult Achievement." *Journal of Black Psychology* 25(2):210–30.

Moffitt, William. 2000. "Race and the Criminal Justice System." *Gonzaga Law Review* 36(2):305–13.

Moiduddin, Emily M. 2008. "Understanding the Sources of Racial and Gender Disparities in Early Childhood Aggression." PhD dissertation, Princeton University, Woodrow Wilson School of Public Policy and International Affairs.

Monroe, Carla R. 2006. "African American Boys and the Discipline Gap: Balancing Educators' Uneven Hand." *Educational Horizons* 84(2):102–11.

Moore, James L., III, and Chance W. Lewis, eds. 2014. *African American Male Students in PreK–12 Schools: Informing Research Policy and Practice*. Bingley, UK: Emerald.

Moore, Sharo. 1995. "Adolescent Black Males' Drug Trafficking and Addiction: Three Theoretical Perspectives." *Journal of Black Studies* 26(2):99–116.

Moran, Rachel F. 2005. "Whatever Happened to Racism?" *St. John's Law Review* 79(4):899–927.

Moriearty, Perry L. 2010. "Framing Justice: Media, Bias, and Legal Decisionmaking." *Maryland Law Review* 69(4):849–909.

Morris, Edward W. 2005. "'Tuck in That Shirt!' Race, Class, Gender, and Discipline in an Urban School." *Sociological Perspectives* 48(1):25–48.

Moynihan, Daniel P. 1965. *The Negro Family: The Case for National Action.* Washington, DC: U.S. Department of Labor, Office of Policy Planning and Research.

Murry, Kantahyanee W., Denise L. Haynie, Donna E. Howard, Tina L. Cheng, and Bruce Simmons-Morton. 2010. "Perceptions of Parenting Practices as Predictors of Aggression in a Low-Income, Urban, Predominately African American Middle School Sample." *Journal of School Violence* 9:174–93.

Murry, Velma McBride. 2001. "Challenges and Life Experiences of Black American Families." In *Families and Change: Coping with Stressful Events and Transitions,* 2nd ed., edited by Patrick C. McKenry and Sharon J. Price, 333–58. Thousand Oaks, CA: Sage.

Murry, Velma McBride, Mia S. Bynum, Gene H. Brody, Amanda Willert, and Dionne Stephens. 2001. "African American Single Mothers and Children in Context: A Review of Studies on Risk and Resilience." *Clinical Child and Family Psychology Review* 4(2):133–55.

Mutua, Athena D., ed. 2006. *Progressive Black Masculinities.* New York: Routledge.

Nakazawa, Donna Jackson. 2016. "7 Ways Childhood Adversity Changes a Child's Brain." *ACES Too High,* September 8. www.acestoohigh.com.

Nance, Jason P. 2013. "Students, Security, and Race." *Emory Law Review* 63:1–57.

———. 2015. "Students, Police, and the School-to-Prison Pipeline." *Washington University Law Review* 93(4):919–87.

———. 2016. "Dismantling the School to Prison Pipeline: Tools for Change." *Arizona State Law Journal* 48:313–72.

National Center for Education Statistics. 1993. "Statistics in Brief. Readiness for Kindergarten: Parent and Teacher Beliefs." U.S. Department of Education, Office of Educational Research and Improvement.

National Child Traumatic Stress Network. 2016. "Complex Trauma." Accessed April 17, 2016. www.nctsn.org.

National Commission for Quality Assurance. n.d. Accessed January 8, 2016. www.ncqa.org.

National Institutes of Health. 2001. "Teenage Brain: A Work in Progress." Publication No. 01–4929.

National Public Radio. 2015. "Stories about Charleston Shooting." Accessed December 8, 2015. www.npr.org.

National Research Council and Institute of Medicine. 2000. "From Neurons to Neighborhoods." Washington, DC: National Academies Press.

National Scientific Council on the Developing Child. 2007. "A Science-Based Framework for Early Childhood Policy: Using Evidence to Improve Outcomes in Learning, Behavior, and Health for Vulnerable Children." Harvard University Center on the Developing Child. Accessed September 11, 2016. www.developingchild.harvard.edu.

———. 2014. "Excessive Stress Disrupts the Architecture of the Developing Brain." Harvard University Center on the Developing Child. www.developingchild. harvard.edu.

National Urban League. 2007. "The State of Black American 2007: Portrait of the Black Male." New York: National Urban League.

Neal, Angela M., and Heather Knisley. 1995. "What Are African American Children Afraid Of? Part II: A Twelve-Month Follow-Up." *Journal of Anxiety Disorders* 9(2):151–61.

Neal, Angela M., Roy S. Lilly, and Sandra Zakis. 1993. "What Are African American Children Afraid Of? A Preliminary Study." *Journal of Anxiety Disorders* 7:129–39.

Neal, Angela M., and Leslie Nagle. 1995. "Fears in African-American Sibling and Non-sibling Pairs." *Journal of the National Medical Association* 87(1):48–50.

Neal, Mark Anthony. 2005. *New Black Men*. New York: Routledge.

Neal-Barnett, Angela. 2004. "Orphans No More: A Commentary on Anxiety and African American Youth." *Journal of Clinical Child and Adolescent Psychology* 33(2):276–78.

Nebbitt, Von. 2009. "Self-Efficacy in African American Adolescent Males Living in Urban Public Housing." *Journal of Black Psychology* 35(3):295–316.

Neblett, Enrique W., Jr., Deborah Rivas-Drake, and Adrianna J. Umana-Taylor. 2012. "The Promise of Racial and Ethnic Protective Factors in Promoting Ethnic Minority Youth Development." *Child Development Perspectives* 6(3):295–303.

Neff, Zama. 2005. "Discrimination against Palestinian Arab Children in the Israeli Education System." Human Rights Watch. www.hrw.org.

New York Civil Liberties Union. 2014. "Stop-and-Frisk Data." www.nycluorg.

New York City Office of the Mayor, Bill de Blasio, New York City Center for Innovation through Data Intelligence. 2016. "Disparity Report." www.politico.com.

Nobel, Richard, III, and Crystal Hill Morton. 2013. "African Americans and Mathematics Outcomes on National Assessment of Educational Progress: Parental and Individual Influences." *Journal of Child and Family Studies* 22:30–37.

Nobles, Wade W. 2007. "African American Family Life: An Instrument of Culture." In *Black Families*, edited by Harriet Pipes McAdoo, 83–93. Thousand Oaks, CA: Sage.

Noguera, Pedro A. 2003. "The Trouble with Black Boys: The Role and Influence of Environmental Cultural Factors on the Academic Performance of African American Males." *Urban Education* 38:431–59.

———. 2008. *The Trouble with Black Boys and Other Reflections on Race, Equity, and the Future of Public Education*. San Francisco: Jossey-Bass.

———. 2012. "Saving Black and Latino Boys: What Schools Can Do to Make a Difference." *Phi Delta Kappan* 93(5):8–12.

Numhauser-Henning, Ann, and Mia Ronnmar, eds. 2013. *Normative Patterns and Legal Developments in the Social Dimension of the EU*. Portland, OR: Hart.

Nunn, Kenneth B. 2002. "The Child as Other: Race and Differential Treatment in the Juvenile Justice System." *DePaul Law Review* 51:679–714.

Nyborg, Vanessa M., and John F. Curry. 2003. "The Impact of Perceived Racism: Psychological Symptoms among African American Boys." *Journal of Clinical Child and Adolescent Psychology* 32(2):258–66.

Obama, Barack. 1995. *Dreams from My Father: A Story of Race and Inheritance*. New York: Crown.

Ogbu, John U. 1981. "Origins of Human Competence: A Cultural-Ecological Perspective." *Child Development* 52(2):413–29.

———. 2004. "Collective Identity and the Burden of 'Acting White' in Black History, Community, and Education." *Urban Review* 36(1):1–35.

Ogbu, John U., and Herbert D. Simons. 1998. "Voluntary and Involuntary Minorities: A Cultural-Ecological Theory of School Performance with Some Implications for Education." *Anthropology and Education Quarterly* 29(2):155–88.

Ogletree, Charles J. 2010. *The Presumption of Guilt: The Arrest of Henry Louis Gates, Jr. and Race, Class, and Crime in America*. New York: St. Martin's Griffin.

Ohlheiser, Abby, and Abby Phillip. 2015. "'I Will Light You Up!' Texas Officer Threatened Sandra Bland with Taser During Traffic Stop." *Washington Post*, July 22. www.washingtonpost.com.

Okundaye, Joshua Nosa, Llewellyn J. Cornelius, and Maxwell Manning. 2001. "Drug Trafficking among African American Youth: Risk Factors for Future Incarceration." *Journal of African American Men* 5(4):39–63.

Onwuachi-Willig, Angela. 2009. "Celebrating Critical Race Theory at 20." *Iowa Law Review* 94:1497–1504.

Opportunity Mapping Initiative and Project Listing. 2017. Accessed April 8, 2017. http://kirwaninstitute.osu.edu.

Oregon Judicial Department. 2016. "Sample Parenting Plans." Accessed October 3, 2016. www.courts.oregon.gov.

Orfield, Gary, ed. 2004. *Dropouts in America: Confronting the Graduating Rate Crisis*. Cambridge, MA: Harvard Education Press.

Orfield, Gary, and Chungmei Lee. 2004. "*Brown* at 50: King's Dream or Plessy's Nightmare?" Civil Rights Project. Accessed September 11, 2016. www.civilrightsproject.ucla.edu.

———. 2007. "Historic Reversals, Accelerating Resegregation, and the Need for New Integration Strategies." www.civilrightsproject.ucla.edu.

Organisation for Economic Co-operation and Development. 2001. "Starting Strong I." www.oecd.org.

———. 2006. "Starting Strong II: Early Childhood Education and Care." www.oecd.org.

———. 2007. "Babies and Bosses: Reconciling Work and Family Life—A Synthesis for OECD Countries." www.oecd.org.

———. 2008. "Growing Unequal: Income Distribution and Poverty in OECD Countries." www.oecd.org.

———. 2009a. "Childhood Decides: How Can We Do Better for Our Children." Available at www.oecd.org.

———. 2009b. "Doing Better for Children." www.oecd.org.

———. 2012. "Starting Strong III—A Quality Toolbox for Early Childhood Education and Care." www.oecd.org.

———. 2015a. "In It Together: Why Less Inequality Benefits All." www.oecd.org.

———. 2015b. "Starting Strong IV: Monitoring Quality in Early Childhood Education and Care." www.oecd.org.

———. 2016. "Multilingual Summaries PISA 2015 Results (Volume I). Excellence and Equity in Education." www.oecd.org.

Owens, Timothy J., Sheldon Stryker, and Norman Goodman. 2001. *Extending Self-Esteem Theory and Research: Sociological and Psychological Currents.* Cambridge: Cambridge University Press.

Oyserman, Daphna, Daniel Brickman, Deborah Bybee, and Aaron Celious. 2006. "Fitting in Matters—Markers of In-Group Belonging and Academic Outcomes." *Psychological Science* 17:854–61.

Page, Emily E., and Alayna M. Stone. 2010. "From Harlem Children's Zone to Promise Neighborhoods: Creating the Tipping Point for Success." Paper presented at the Family Impact Seminar, Georgetown Public Policy Institute. www.purdue.edu.

Pahl, Kerstin, and Niobe Way. 2006. "Longitudinal Trajectories of Ethnic Identity among Urban Black and Latino Adolescents." *Child Development* 77(5):1403–15.

Pancsofar, Nadya, Lynne Vernon-Feagans, Erika C. Odom, and Family Life Project Investigators. 2013. "Work Characteristics and Fathers' Vocabulary to Infants in African American Families." *Journal of Applied Developmental Psychology* 34:73–81.

Parham, Thomas A., Adisa Ajamu, and Joseph L. White. 2011. *The Psychology of Blacks: Centering Our Perspectives in the African Consciousness.* Boston: Prentice Hall.

Park, Nan S., Beom S. Lee, Fei Sun, Alexander T. Vazsonyi, and John M. Bolland. 2010. "Pathways and Predictors of Antisocial Behaviors in African American Adolescents from Poor Neighborhoods." *Children and Youth Services Review* 32:409–15.

Parker, Karen F., and Scott R. Maggard. 2009. "Making a Difference: The Impact of Traditional Male Role Models on Drug Sale Activity and Violence Involving Black Urban Youth." *Journal of Drug Issues* 39(3):715–39.

Parker, Karen F., and Amy Reckdenwald. 2008. "Concentrated Disadvantage, Traditional Male Role Models, and African-American Juvenile Violence." *Criminology* 46(3):711–30.

Parks, Brad. 2015. "How to Fix America's Mass Incarceration Problem." *New York Post*, November 1. www.nypost.com.

Parks, Gregory Scott. 2008. "Toward a Critical Race Realism." *Cornell Journal of Law and Public Policy* 17:683–745.

Parks, Gregory S., Shayne Jones, and W. Jonathan Cardi, eds. 2008. *Critical Race Realism: Intersections of Psychology Race and Law.* New York: New Press.

Parsons-Pollard, Nicolle, ed. 2011. *Disproportionate Minority Contact: Current Issues and Policies.* Durham, NC: Carolina Academic Press.

Patten, Eileen, and Jens Manual Krogstad. 2015. "Black Poverty Rate Holds Steady Even as Other Groups Decline." Pew Research Center, July 14. Accessed October 10, 2015. www.pewresearch.org.

Pattillo, Mary. 2005. "Black Middle-Class Neighborhoods." *Annual Review of Sociology* 31:305–29.

Pattison, Brent. 1998. "Minority Youth in Juvenile Correctional Facilities: Cultural Differences and the Right to Treatment." *Law and Inequality* 16:573–99.

Patton, Desmond U., and David W. Johnson. 2010. "Exposure to Community Violence and Social Capital: African American Students in the Critical Transition to High School." *Harvard Journal of African American Public Policy* 16:53–72.

Payne, Macheo. 2010. "Educational Lynching: Critical Race Theory and the Suspension of Black Boys." www.files.eric.ed.gov.

Payne, Yasser Arafat, and Tara M. Brown. 2010. "The Educational Experiences of Street-Life-Oriented Black Boys: How Black Boys Use Street Life as a Site of Resilience in High School." *Journal of Contemporary Criminal Justice* 26(3):316–38.

Peralta, Eyder, and Bill Chappell. 2014. "Ferguson Jury: No Charges for Officer in Michael Brown's Death." National Public Radio, November 24. www.npr.org.

Perenyi, Agnes, Joanne S. Katz, Tzipporah Sklar, and Peter Flom. 2011. "Neurodevelopmental Outcome and Risk Factors for Impaired Development of African American Infants in an Underserved Urban Population: A Population-Based Study." *Journal of Health Care for the Poor and Underserved* 22:983–994.

Perkins, Danielle E. K. 2013. "Challenges to Traditional Clinical Definitions of Depression in Young Black Men." *American Journal of Men's Health* 8(1):74–81.

Perry, Bruce D. 1999. "Memories of Fear: How the Brain Stores and Retrieves Physiologic States, Feelings, Behaviors and Thoughts from Traumatic Events." Child Trauma Academy. Accessed November 3, 2016. www.childtrauma.org.

———. 2007. "Stress, Trauma and Post-traumatic Stress Disorders in Children." Child Trauma Academy. Accessed September 11, 2016. www.childtrauma.org.

Perry, Bruce D., Ronnie A. Pollard, Toi L. Blakley, William L. Baker, and Domenico Vigilante. 1995. "Childhood Trauma, the Neurobiology of Adaptation, and 'Use-Dependent' Development of the Brain: How 'States' Become 'Traits.'" *Infant Mental Health Journal* 16(4):271–91.

Peters, Marie F., and Grace Massey. 1983. "Mundane Extreme Environmental Stress in Family Stress Theories: The Case of Black Families in White America." In *Social Stress and the Family: Advances and Developments in Family Stress Therapy and Research*, edited by Hamilton I. McCubbin, Marvin B. Sussman, and Joan M. Patterson, 193–217. New York: Routledge.

Peterson, Dana, Finn-Aage Esbensen, Terrance J. Taylor, and Adrienne Freng. 2007. "Youth Violence in Context: The Roles of Sex, Race and Community in Offending." *Youth Violence and Juvenile Justice* 5(4):385–410.

Phinney, Jean S. 1989. "Stages of Ethnic Identity Development in Minority Group Adolescents." *Journal of Early Adolescence* 9:34–49.

———. 1993. "A Three-Stage Model of Ethnic Identity Development in Adolescence." In *Ethnic Identity: Formation and Transmission among Hispanics and Other Minorities*, edited by Martha E. Bernal and George P. Knight, 61–79. Albany: State University of New York Press.

Phinney, Jean S., and Anthony D. Ong. 2007. "Conceptualization and Measurement of Ethnic Identity: Current Status and Future Directions." *Journal of Counseling Psychology* 54:271–81.

Phoenix, Ann. 2003. "Neoliberalism and Masculinity: Racialization and the Contradictions of Schooling for 11- to 14-Year-Olds." *Youth and Society* 36(2):227–46.

Piketty, Thomas, and Emmanuel Saez. 2013. "Top Incomes and the Great Recession: Recent Evolutions and Policy Implications." *IMF Economic Review* 61(3):456–78.

Pinckney, Harrison P., Corliss Outley, Jamilia J. Blake, and Brandy Kelly. 2011. "Promoting Positive Youth Development of Black Youth: A Rites of Passage Framework." *Journal of Park and Recreational Administration* 29(1):98–112.

Piquero, Alex R. 2008. "Disproportionate Minority Contact." *Future of Children* 18(2):59–79.

Pitre, Abul, Esrom Pitre, Ruth Ray, and Twana Hilton-Pitre, eds. 2009. *Educating African American Students: Foundations, Curriculum and Experiences*. New York: Rowman & Littlefield.

Poindexter, LaShaunda Michelle. 2000. "Roads to Resiliency for Low Income, Urban African American Adolescents." PhD dissertation, DePaul University.

Polite, Vernon C. 1994. "The Method in the Madness: African American Males, Avoidance Schooling, and Chaos Theory." *Journal of Negro Education* 63(4):588–601.

Polite, Vernon C., and James Earl Davis. 1999. *African American Males in School and Society*. New York: Teachers College Press.

Porter, Judith D. R. 1971. *Black Child, White Child: The Development of Racial Attitudes*. Cambridge, MA: Harvard University Press.

Povich, Deborah, Brandon Roberts, and Mark Mather. 2014. "Low-Income Working Families: The Racial/Ethnic Divide." Working Poor Families Project. Available at www.workingpoorfamilies.org.

Powell, John A., Gavin Kearney, and Vina Kay, eds. 2001. *In Pursuit of a Dream Deferred: Linking Housing and Education Policy*. New York: Peter Lang.

Pratt-Clarke, Menah A. E. 2010. *Critical Race, Feminism, and Education: A Social Justice Model*. New York: Palgrave Macmillan.

Pratto, Felicia, Jim Sidanius, and Shana Levin. 2006. "Social Dominance Theory and the Dynamics of Intergroup Relations: Taking Stock and Looking Forward." *European Review of Social Psychology* 17:271–320.

Prelow, Hazel M., Sharon Danoff-Burg, Rebecca R. Swenson, and Dana Pulgiano. 2004. "The Impact of Ecological Risk and Perceived Discrimination on the Psychological Adjustment of African American and European American Youth." *Journal of Community Psychology* 32(4):375–89.

Preski, Sally, and Deborah Shelton. 2001. "The Role of Contextual, Child, and Parent Factors in Predicting Criminal Outcomes in Adolescence." *Issues in Mental Health Nursing* 22:197–205.

Price, Jeremy N. 2000. *Against the Odds: The Meaning of School and Relationships in the Lives of Six Young African-American Men.* Stamford, CT: Ablex.

Project Implicit. 2017. Accessed August 22, 2017. http://projectimplicit.net.

Pruitt, Lisa R. 2010. "Spatial Inequality as Constitutional Infirmity: Equal Protection, Child Poverty, and Place." *Montana Law Review* 71:1–114.

Public Counsel. 2015. "Historic Ruling in Landmark Complaint on Unique Learning Needs of Children Affected by Trauma." September 30. Accessed September 11, 2016. www.publiccounsel.org.

Quintana, Stephen M., Ruth K. Chao, William E. Cross, Jr., Diane Hughes, Sharon Nelson-Le Gall, Frances E. Aboud, Josefina Contreras-Grau, Cynthia Hudley, Lynn S. Liben, and Deborah L. Vietze. 2006. "Race, Ethnicity, and Culture in Child Development: Contemporary Research and Future Directions." *Child Development* 77(5):1129–41.

Rabiner, David L., John D. Coie, Shari Miller-Johnson, Anne-Sylvie M. Boykin, and John E. Lochman. 2005. "Predicting the Persistence of Aggressive Offending of African American Males from Adolescence into Adulthood: The Importance of Peer Relations, Aggressive Behavior, and ADHD Symptoms." *Journal of Emotional and Behavioral Disorders* 13(3):131–40.

Raghavan, Ramesh, Derek S. Brown, Benjamin T. Allaire, Lauren D. Garfield, Raven E. Ross, and Lonnie R. Snowden. 2014. "Racial/Ethnic Differences in Medical Expenditures on Psychotropic Medications among Maltreated Children." *Child Abuse and Neglect* 38:1002–10.

Rainville, Laura A. 2011. "Fighting to Grow: A Developmental Approach to Aggression among Inner City, African American Adolescent Boys." PhD dissertation, California Institute of Integral Studies.

Randolph, Suzanne M., Sally A. Koblinsky, Martha A. Beemer, Debra D. Roberts, and Bethany L. Letiecq. 2000. "Behavior Problems of African American Boys and Girls Attending Head Start Programs in Violent Neighborhoods." *Early Education and Development* 11(3):339–56.

Ready, Douglas D. 2010. "Socioeconomic Disadvantage, School Attendance, and Early Cognitive Development: The Differential Effects of School Exposure." *Sociology of Education* 83(4):271–86.

Reardon, Sean F. 2011. "The Widening Academic Achievement Gap between the Rich and the Poor: New Evidence and Possible Explanations." In *Whither Opportunity? Rising Inequality, Schools, and Children's Life Chances,* edited by Greg J. Duncan and Richard J. Murnane, 91–111. New York: Russell Sage Foundation.

Rebell, Michael A. 2009. *Courts and Kids: Pursuing Educational Equity through the State Courts.* Chicago: University of Chicago Press.

Rebouché, Rachel. 2011. "Parental Involvement Laws and New Governance." *Harvard Journal of Law and Gender* 34:175–223.

Rebouché, Rachel, and Scott Burris. 2015. "The Social Determinants of Health." In *Oxford Handbook on United States Healthcare Law*, edited by I. Glenn Cohen, Allison K. Hoffman, and William M. Sage, 1097–1112. New York: Oxford University Press.

Redding, Richard E. 2015. "Lost in Translation No More: Marketing Evidence-Based Policies for Reducing Juvenile Crime." In Dowd, *New Juvenile Justice System*, 138–40.

Rein, Kristen, and Roberta Bernstein. 2015. "Dueling Princeton Student Petitions Argue Legacy of Woodrow Wilson." *USA Today*, November 25. www.college.usatoday.com.

Repetto, Paula B., Cleopatra H. Caldwell, and Marc A. Zimmerman. 2004. "Trajectories of Depressive Symptoms among High Risk African-American Adolescents." *Journal of Adolescent Health* 35:468–77.

Reskin, Barbara. 2012. "The Race Discrimination System." *Annual Review of Sociology* 38:17–35.

Reynolds, Rema. 2010. "'They Think You're Lazy,' and Other Messages Black Parents Send Their Black Sons: An Exploration of Critical Race Theory in the Examination of Educational Outcomes for Black Males." *Journal of African American Males in Education* 1(2):144–63.

Rich, Camille Gear. 2014. "Angela Harris and the Racial Politics of Masculinity: Trayvon Martin, George Zimmerman, and the Dilemmas of Desiring Whiteness." *California Law Review* 102:1027–52.

Rich, John A. 2000. "The Health of African American Men." *Annals of the American Academy of Political and Society Sciences* 569:149–59.

Rich, John A., and Courtney Grey. 2005. "Pathways to Recurrent Trauma among Young Black Men: Traumatic Stress, Substance Use, and the 'Code of the Street.'" *American Journal of Public Health* 95(5):816–21.

Richardson, Bridget L., Tamarie A. Macon, Faheemah N. Mustafaa, Erin D. Bogan, Yasmin Cole-Lewis, and Tabbye M. Chavous. 2015. "Associations of Racial Discrimination and Parental Discrimination Coping Messages with African American Adolescent Racial Identity." *Journal of Youth and Adolescence* 44(6):1301–17.

Richardson, Joseph B., Jr., and Christopher St. Vil. 2016. "'Rolling Dolo': Desistance from Delinquency and Negative Peer Relationships over the Early Adolescent Life-Course." *Ethnography* 17(1):47–71.

Richardson, L. Soong. 2015. "Police Racial Violence: Lessons from Social Psychology." *Fordham Law Review* 83:2961–76.

Richardson, L. Soong, and Philip Atiba Goff. 2014. "Interrogating Racial Violence." *Ohio State Journal of Criminal Law* 12:115–52.

Rios, Victor M. 2009. "The Consequences of the Criminal Justice Pipeline on Black and Latino Masculinity." *Annals of the American Academy of Political and Social Science* 623:150–62.

———. 2011. *Punished: Policing the Lives of Black and Latino Boys*. New York: New York University Press.

Rivas-Drake, Deborah, Carol Markstrom, Moin Syed, Richard M. Lee, Adriana J. Umana-Taylor, Tiffany Yip, Eleanor K. Seaton, Stephen Quintana, Seth J. Schwartz, Sabine French, and Ethnic and Racial Identity in the 21st Century Study Group. 2014. "Ethnic and Racial Identity in Adolescence: Implications for Psychosocial, Academic, and Health Outcomes." *Child Development* 85:40–57.

Roberts, A. L., Stephen E. Gilman, Joshua Breslau, Naomi Breslau, and K. C. Koenen. 2011. "Race/Ethnic Differences in Exposure to Traumatic Events, Development of Post-traumatic Stress Disorder, and Treatment-Seeking for Post-traumatic Stress Disorder in the United States." *Psychological Medicine* 41(1):71–83.

Roberts, Dorothy E. 1994. "The Value of Black Mothers' Work." *Connecticut Law Review* 26:871–78.

———. 2001. *Shattered Bonds: The Color of Child Welfare.* New York: Basic Civitas Books.

———. 2012. "Prison, Foster Care, and the Systemic Punishment of Black Mothers." *UCLA Law Review* 59:1474–1500.

Roberts-Douglass, Karisman, and Harriet Curtis-Boles. 2013. "Exploring Positive Masculinity Development in African American Men: A Retrospective Study." *Psychology of Men and Masculinity* 14(1):7–15.

Robinson, Russell K. 2008. "Perceptual Segregation." *Columbia Law Review* 108:1093–1180.

Robinson-English, Tracey. 2006. "Saving Black Boys: Is Single-Sex Education the Answer?" *Ebony* 62(2):52–58.

Rocque, Michael, and Raymond Paternoster. 2011. "Understanding the Antecedents of the 'School to Jail' Link: The Relationship between Race and School Discipline." *Journal of Criminal Law and Criminology* 101:633–65.

Roderick, Melissa. 2003. "'What's Happening to the Boys?' Early High School Experiences and School Outcomes among African American Male Adolescents in Chicago." *Urban Education* 38:538–607.

Rodney, H. Elaine, and Robert Mupier. 1999. "Behavioral Differences between African American Male Adolescents with Biological Fathers and Those without Biological Fathers in the Home." *Journal of Black Studies* 30(1):45–61.

Roettger, Michael E., and Raymond R. Swisher. 2011. "Associations of Fathers' History of Incarceration with Sons' Delinquency and Arrest among Black, White, and Hispanic Males in the United States." *Criminology* 49:1109–47.

Rogers, Leoandra Onnie, Kristina M. Zosuls, May Ling Halim, Diane Ruble, Diane Hughes, and Andres Fuligni. 2012. "Meaning Making in Middle Childhood: An Exploration of the Meaning of Ethnic Identity." *Cultural Diversity and Ethnic Minority Psychology* 18(2):99–108.

Roithmayr, Daria. 2000. "Barriers to Entry: A Market Lock-In Model of Discrimination." *Virginia Law Review* 86:727–99.

———. 2014. *Reproducing Racism: How Everyday Choices Lock in White Advantage.* New York: New York University Press.

Rome, Dennis. 2004. *Black Demons: The Media's Depiction of the African American Male Criminal Stereotype*. Westport, CT: Praeger.

Rose, Henry. 2010. "The Poor as a Suspect Class under the Equal Protection Clause: An Open Constitutional Question." *Nova Law Review* 34:407–21.

Rosenberg, Morris, and Leonard I. Pearlin. 1978. "Social Class and Self-Esteem among Children and Adults." *American Journal of Sociology* 84(1):53–77.

Ross, Janell. 2015. "Why You Should Know What Happened in Freddie Gray's Life—Long Before His Death." *Washington Post*, December 19. www.washingtonpost.com.

Ross, Marlon B. 2004. *Manning the Race: Reforming Black Men in the Jim Crow Era*. New York: New York University Press.

Ross, Richard. 2012. *Juvenile in Justice*. Santa Barbara, CA: Richard Ross Photography.

Rothstein, Richard. 2015. "The Racial Achievement Gap, Segregated Schools, and Segregated Neighborhoods: A Constitutional Insult." *Race and Social Problems* 7:21–30.

Roy, Kevin M. 2006. "Father Stories: A Life Course Examination of Paternal Identity among Low-Income African American Men." *Journal of Family Issues* 27(1):31–54.

Royster, Deirde A. 2007. "What Happens to Potential Discouraged? Masculinity Norms and the Contrasting Institutional and Labor Market Experiences of Less Affluent Black and White Men." *Annals of the American Academy of Political and Social Sciences* 609:153–80.

Rudd, Tom. 2014. "Racial Disproportionality in School Discipline." Kirwan Institute. www.kirwaninstitute.osu.edu.

Rush, Sharon Elizabeth. 1999. "Sharing Space: Why Racial Goodwill Isn't Enough." *Connecticut Law Review* 32:1–71.

Rush, Sharon Elizabeth, Joe R. Feagin, and Jacqueline Johnson. 2000. "Doing Anti-Racism: Making an Egalitarian Future." *Contemporary Sociology* 29:95–110.

Russell-Brown, Katheryn. 2017. "Making Implicit Bias Explicit: Black Men and the Police." In *Policing the Black Man: Arrest, Prosecution and Prison*, edited by Angela J. Davis, 136–61. New York: Knopf Doubleday.

Ryan, Joseph P., Denise Herz, Pedro M. Hernandez, and Jane Marie Marshall. 2007. "Maltreatment and Delinquency: Investigating Child Welfare Bias in Juvenile Justice Processing." *Children and Youth Services Review* 29:1035–50.

Ryan, Joseph P., Mark F. Testa, and Fuhua Zhai. 2008. "African American Males in Foster Care and the Risk of Delinquency: The Value of Social Bonds and Permanence, Child Welfare League of America." *Child Welfare* 87(1):115–40.

Saez, Emmanuel, and Gabrial Zucman. 2016. "Wealth Inequality in the United States since 1913: Evidence from Capitalized Income Tax Data." *Quarterly Journal of Economics* 131(2):519–78.

Saleem, Farzana T., and Sharon F. Lambert. 2016. "Differential Effects of Racial Socialization Messages for African American Adolescents: Personal versus Institutional Racial Discrimination." *Journal of Child and Family Studies* 25(5):1385–96.

Sanders, Kay. 2005. "It Takes a Village: Early Race Socialization of African American and Latino Children in Child Care." PhD dissertation, University of California, Los Angeles.

Sanders, Kay E., Amy Diehl, and Amy Kyler. 2007. "DAP in the 'Hood: Perceptions of Child Care Practices by African American Child Care Directors Caring for Children of Color." *Early Childhood Research Quarterly* 22:394–406.

Sanders-Smith, Stephanie. 2015. "Early Childhood Education Scholar Says NYC's Universal Preschool Program Must Be Flexible, Adaptive." University of Illinois, September 10. www.education.illinois.edu.

Santos, Carlos E., Kathrine Galligan, Erin Pahlke, and Richard A. Fabes. 2013. "Gender-Typed Behaviors, Achievement, and Adjustment among Racially and Ethnically Diverse Boys during Early Adolescence." *American Journal of Orthopsychiatry* 83(2–3):252–64.

Satz, Ani B. 2008. "Disability, Vulnerability, and the Limits of Antidiscrimination." *Washington Law Review* 83:513–68.

Sawhill, Isabel, ed. 2003. *One Percent for the Kids: New Policies, Brighter Futures for America's Children.* Washington, DC: Brookings Institution Press.

#SayHerName. Accessed January 7, 2016. www.aapf.org.

Schott Foundation for Public Education. 2015. "Black Lives Matter: The Schott 50 State Report on Public Education and Black Males." www.blackboysreport.org.

Schwartz, Nelson D. 2016. "Poorest Areas Have Missed Out on Boons of Recovery, Study Finds." *New York Times*, February 24. www.nytimes.com.

Scott, Daryl Michael. 1997. *Contempt and Pity: Social Policy and the Image of the Damaged Black Psyche, 1879–1997.* Chapel Hill: University of North Carolina Press.

Scott, Elizabeth S., and Laurence D. Steinberg. 2008. *Rethinking Juvenile Justice.* Cambridge, MA: Harvard University Press.

Scott, Kristin M., Oscar A. Barbarin, and Jeffrey M. Brown. 2013. "From Higher Order Thinking to Higher Order Behavior: Exploring the Relationship between Early Cognitive Skills and Social Competence in Black Boys." *American Journal of Orthopsychiatry* 83(2–3):185–93.

Scott, Lionel D., Jr., and Laura E. House. 2005. "Relationship of Distress and Perceived Control to Coping with Perceived Racial Discrimination among Black Youth." *Journal of Black Psychology* 31(3):254–72.

Scott, Lionel D., Jr., J. Curtis McMillen, and Lonnie R. Snowden. 2015. "Informal and Formal Help Seeking among Older Black Male Foster Care Youth and Alumni." *Journal of Child and Family Studies* 24(2):264–77.

Seaton, Eleanor K., Cleopatra H. Caldwell, Robert M. Sellers, and James S. Jackson. 2008. "The Prevalence of Perceived Discrimination among African American and Caribbean Black Youth." *Developmental Psychology* 44(5):1288–97.

Seaton, Eleanor K., Krista Maywalt Scottham, and Robert M. Sellers. 2006. "The Status Model of Racial Identity Development in African American Adolescents: Evidence of Structure, Trajectories, and Well-Being." *Child Development* 77(5):1416–26.

Seaton, Gregory. 2007. "Toward a Theoretical Understanding of Hypermasculine Coping among Urban Black Adolescent Males." *Journal of Human Behavior in the Social Environment* 15(2–3):367–90.

Sellers, Robert M., Nikeea Copeland-Linder, Pamela P. Martin, and R. L'Hereux Lewis. 2006. "Racial Identity Matters: The Relationship between Racial Discrimination and Psychological Functioning in African American Adolescents." *Journal of Research on Adolescence* 16(2):187–216.

Sellers, Robert M., Stephanie A. J. Rowley, Tabbye M. Chavous, J. Nicole Shelton, and Mia A. Smith. 1997. "Multidimensional Inventory of Black Identity: A Preliminary Investigation of Reliability and Construct Validity." *Journal of Personality and Social Psychology* 73(4):805–15.

The Sentencing Project. Accessed December 8, 2015. www.sentencingproject.org.

Sethi, Jasmin. 2010. "Lessons for Social Scientists and Politicians: An Analysis of Welfare Reform." *Georgetown Journal on Poverty Law and Policy* 17:5–32.

Sharkey, Patrick. 2012. "An Alternative Approach to Addressing Selection Into and Out of Social Settings: Neighborhood Change and African American Children's Economic Outcomes." *Sociological Methods and Research* 41(2):251–93.

———. 2013. *Stuck in Place: Urban Neighborhoods and the End of Progress toward Racial Equality*. Chicago: University of Chicago Press.

Shedd, Carla. 2015. *Unequal City: Race, Schools, and Perceptions of Injustice*. New York: Russell Sage Foundation.

Sheng, Feng, and Shihui Han. 2012. "Manipulations of Cognitive Strategies and Intergroup Relationships Reduce the Racial Bias in Empathic Neural Responses." *NeuroImage* 61:786–97.

Shin, Richard Q., Larisa Buhin, Melissa L. Morgan, Tikana J. Truitt, and Elizabeth M. Vega. 2010. "Expanding the Discourse on Urban Youth of Color." *Cultural Diversity and Ethnic Minority Psychology* 16:421–26.

Silva, Janelle M., Regina Day Langhout, Danielle Kohfeldt, and Edith Gurrola. 2015. "'Good' and 'Bad' Kids? A Race and Gender Analysis of Effective Behavioral Support in an Elementary School." *Urban Education* 50(7):787–811.

Simons, Ronald L., Velma Murry, Vonnie McLoyd, and Kuei-Hsiu Lin. 2002. "Discrimination, Crime, Ethnic Identity, and Parenting as Correlates of Depressive Symptoms among African American Children: A Multilevel Analysis." *Development and Psychopathology* 14:371–93.

Sith, Robert J., Justin D. Levinson, and Zoe Robinson. 2015. "Implicit White Favoritism in the Criminal Justice System." *Alabama Law Review* 66:872–923.

Sleath, Betsy, Marisa E. Domino, Elizabeth Wiley-Exley, Bradley Martin, Shirley Richards, and Tim Carey. 2010. "Antidepressant and Antipsychotic Use and Adherence among Medicaid Youths: Differences by Race." *Community Mental Health Journal* 46:265–72.

Smalls, Ciara, Rhonda White, Tabbye Chavous, and Robert Sellers. 2007. "Racial Ideological Beliefs and Racial Discrimination Experiences as Predictors of Academic Engagement among African American Adolescents." *Journal of Black Psychology* 33(3):299–330.

Smith, Carolyn, and Marvin D. Krohn. 1995. "Delinquency and Family Life among Male Adolescents: The Role of Ethnicity." *Journal of Youth and Adolescence* 24(1):69–93.

Smith, Jocelyn R., and Desmond U. Patton. 2016. "Posttraumatic Stress Symptoms in Context: Examining Trauma Responses to Violent Exposures and Homicide Death among Black Males in Urban Neighborhoods." *American Journal of Orthopsychiatry* 86(2):212–23.

Smith-Bynum, Mia A., Sharon F. Lambert, Devin English, and Nicholas S. Ialongo. 2014. "Associations between Trajectories of Perceived Racial Discrimination and Psychological Symptoms among African American Adolescents." *Development and Psychopathology* 26(4):1049–65.

Snowden, Lonnie R., Mary C. Masland, Kya Fawley, and Neal Wallace. 2009. "Ethnic Differences in Children's Entry into Public Mental Health Care via Emergency Mental Health Services." *Journal of Child and Family Studies* 18:512–19.

Soler, Mark, Dana Schoenberg, and Marc Schindler. 2009. "Juvenile Justice: Lessons for a New Era." *Georgetown Journal on Poverty Law and Policy* 16:483–540.

Solman, Paul. 2013. "It Pays to Invest in Early Education Says a Nobel Economist Who Boosts Kids' IQ." *PBS NewsHour*, February 22. Accessed November 4, 2016. www.pbs.org.

Somers, Cheryl L., Lisa M. Chiodo, Jina Yoon, Hilary Ratner, Elizabeth Barton, and Virginia Delaney-Black. 2011. "Family Disruption and Academic Functioning in Urban, Black Youth." *Psychology in the Schools* 48(4):357–70.

Spano, Richard. 2012. "First Time Gun Carrying and the Primary Prevention of Youth Gun Violence for African American Youth Living in Extreme Poverty." *Aggression and Violent Behavior* 17:83–88.

Spencer, Margaret Beale. 1994. "Old Issues and New Theorizing about African-American Youth: A Phenomenological Variant of Ecological Systems Theory." In *African American Youth: Their Social and Economic Status in the United States*, edited by Ronald L. Taylor, 36–38. Westport, CT: Praeger.

———. 2001a. "Identity, Achievement Orientation, and Race: 'Lessons Learned' about the Normative Developmental Experiences of African American Males." In *Race and Education: The Role of History and Society in Educating African American Students*, edited by William H. Watkins, James H. Lewis, and Victoria Chou, 100–127. Boston: Allyn & Bacon.

———. 2001b. "Resilience and Fragility Factors Associated with the Contextual Experiences of Low Resource Urban African American Male Youth and Families." In *Does It Take a Village? Community Effects on Children, Adolescents, and Families*, edited by Alan Booth and Ann C. Crouter, 51–57. Mahwah, NJ: Lawrence Erlbaum.

———. 2006. "Revisiting the 1990 *Special Issue on Minority Children*: An Editorial Perspective 15 Years Later." *Child Development* 77(5):1149–54.

Spencer, Margaret Beale, Geraldine Kearse Brookins, and Walter Recharde Allen, eds. 1985. *Beginnings: The Social and Affective Development of Black Children*. Hillsdale, NJ: Lawrence Erlbaum.

Spencer, Margaret Beale, Blanch Dobbs, and Dena Phillips Swanson. 1988. "African American Adolescents: Adaptational Processes and Socioeconomic Diversity in Behavioural Outcomes." *Journal of Adolescence* 11:117–37.

Spencer, Margaret Beale, Davido Dupree, and Dena Phillips Swanson. 1997. "Parental Monitoring and Adolescents' Sense of Responsibility for Their Own Learning: An Examination of Sex Differences." *Journal of Negro Education* 65(1):30–43.

Spencer, Margaret B., Suzanne G. Fegley, and Vinay Harpalani. 2003. "A Theoretical and Empirical Examination of Identity as Coping: Linking Coping Resources to the Self Processes of African American Youth." *Applied Developmental Science* 7(3):181–88.

Spencer, Margaret Beale, Suzanne Fegley, Vinay Harpalani, and Gregory Seaton. 2004. "Understanding Hypermasculinity in Context: A Theory-Driven Analysis of Urban Adolescent Males' Coping Responses." *Research in Human Development* 1(4):229–57.

Spencer, Margaret Beale, and Vinay Harpalani. 2004. "Nature, Nurture, and the Question of 'How?' A Phenomenological Variant of Ecological Systems Theory." In *Nature and Nurture: The Complex Interplay of Genetic and Environmental Influences on Human Behavior and Development*, edited by Cynthia García Coll, Elaine L. Bearer, and Richard M. Lerner, 53–77. Mahwah, NJ: Lawrence Erlbaum.

———. 2008. "What does 'Acting White' Actually Mean? Racial Identity, Adolescent Development, and Academic Achievement among African American Youth." In *Minority Status, Oppositional Culture, and Schooling*, edited by John U. Ogbu, 222–39. New York: Routledge.

Spencer, Margaret Beale, and Carol Markstrom-Adams. 1990. "Identity Processes among Racial and Ethnic Minority Children in America." *Child Development* 61(2):290–310.

Stanley-Becker, Isaac. 2015. "Minority Students at Yale Give List of Demands to University President." *Washington Post*, November 13. www.washingtonpost.com.

St. Clair, Stacy, Steve Mills, and Todd Lighty. 2015. "Video Shows Philip Coleman's Death in Chicago Police Custody." *Chicago Tribune*, December 8. www.chicagotribune.com.

Steele, Claude M. 1988. "The Psychology of Self-Affirmation: Sustaining the Integrity of the Self." *Advances in Experimental Social Psychology* 21:261–302.

———. 1997. "A Threat in the Air: How Stereotypes Shape Intellectual Identity and Performance." *American Psychologist* 52(6):613–29.

———. 1999a. "Expert Report of Claude M. Steele." *Michigan Journal of Race and Law* 5:439–50.

———. 1999b. "Thin Ice: Stereotype Threat and Black College Students." *Atlantic*, August. www.theatlantic.com.

———. 2003. "Through the Back Door to Theory." *Psychological Inquiry* 14(3–4):314–17.

———. 2004a. "Kenneth B. Clark's Context and Mine: Toward a Context-Based Theory of Social Identity Threat." In *Racial Identity in Context: The Legacy of Kenneth B. Clark*, edited by Gina Philogene, 61–76. Washington, DC: American Psychological Association.

———. 2004b. "Not Just a Test." *Nation*, April 15. www.thenation.com.

Steele, Claude M., and Joshua Aronson. 1995. "Stereotype Threat and the Intellectual Test Performance of African Americans." *Journal of Personality and Social Psychology* 69:797–811.

———. 1998. "Stereotype Threat and the Test Performance of Academically Successful African Americans." In Jencks and Phillips, *Black-White Test Score Gap*, 401–27.

———. 2004. "Stereotype Threat Does Not Live by Steele and Aronson (1995) Alone." *American Psychologist* 59(1):48–49.

Steele, Claude M., and Paul G. Davies. 2003. "Stereotype Threat and Employment Testing: A Commentary." *Human Performance* 16(3):311–26.

Steele, Claude, and David A. Sherman. 1999. "The Psychological Predicament of Women on Welfare." In *Cultural Divides: Understanding and Overcoming Group Conflict*, edited by Deborah A. Prentice and Dale T. Miller, 393–428. New York: Russell Sage Foundation.

Steele, Claude M., Steven J. Spencer, and Joshua Aronson. 2002. "Contending with Group Image: The Psychology of Stereotype and Social Identity Threat." *Advances in Experimental Social Psychology* 34:379–44.

Stevens, Tia, and Merry Morash. 2015. "Racial/Ethnic Disparities in Boys' Probability of Arrest and Court Actions in 1980 and 2000: The Disproportionate Impact of 'Getting Tough' on Crime." *Youth Violence and Juvenile Justice* 13(1):77–95.

Stevenson, Howard C. 1997. "Missed, Dissed, and Pissed: Making Meaning of Neighborhood Risk, Fear, and Anger Management in Urban Black Youth." *Cultural Diversity and Mental Health* 3(1):37–52.

———. 2004. "Boys in Men's Clothing: Racial Socialization and Neighborhood Safety as Buffers to Hypervulnerability in African American Adolescent Males." In Way and Chu, *Adolescent Boys*, 59–77.

Stevenson, Howard C., Rick Cameron, Teri Herrero-Taylor, and Gwendolyn Y. Davis. 2002a. "Development of the Teenager Experience of Racial Socialization Scale: Correlates of Race-Related Socialization Frequency from the Perspective of Black Youth." *Journal of Black Psychology* 28(2):84–106.

Stevenson, Howard C., Jr., and Gwendolyn Y. David. 2004. "Racial Socialization." In Jones, *Black Psychology*, 353–82.

Stevenson, Howard C., Teri Herrero-Taylor, Rick Cameron, and Gwendolyn Y. Davis. 2002b. "'Mitigation Instigation': Cultural Phenomenological Influences of Anger and Fighting Among 'Big-Boned' and 'Baby-Faced' African American Youth." *Journal of Youth and Adolescence* 31(6):473–85.

Stevenson, Howard C., Jr., Derek McNeil, Teresa Herrero-Taylor, and Gwendolyn Y. Davis. 2005. "Influence of Perceived Neighborhood Diversity and Racism Experience on the Racial Socialization of Black Youth." *Journal of Black Psychology* 31:273–90.

Stevenson, Howard C., Jocelyn Reed, Preston Bodison, and Angela Bishop. 1997. "Racism Stress Management: Racial Socialization Beliefs and the Experience of Depression and Anger in African American Youth." *Youth and Society* 29(2):197–222.

Stewart, Anna, Michael Livingston, and Susan Dennison. 2008. "Transitions and Turning Points: Examining the Link between Child Maltreatment and Juvenile Offending." *Child Abuse and Neglect* 32:51–66.

St. Jean, Yanick, and Joe R. Feagin. 1998. "The Family Costs of White Racism: The Case of African American Families." *Journal of Comparative Family Studies* 29(2):297–312.

Stopford, Annie. 2015. "There's No Trust at All in Anything: Psychosocial Perspectives on Trauma in a Distressed African American Neighborhood." In *Fragments of Trauma and the Social Production of Suffering: Trauma, History, and Memory*, edited by Michael O'Loughlin and Marilyn Charles, 221–42. Lanham, MD: Rowman & Littlefield.

Sullivan, Terri N., Sarah W. Helms, Wendy Kliewer, and Kimberly L. Goodman. 2010. "Associations between Sadness and Anger Regulation Coping, Emotional Expression, and Physical and Relational Aggression among Urban Adolescents." *Social Development* 9(1):31–51.

Suplee, Patricia D., Marcia Gardner, and Lynne Borucki. 2014. "Low-Income, Urban Minority Women's Perceptions of Self- and Infant Care during the Postpartum Period." *Journal of Obstetric, Gynecologic, and Neonatal Nursing* 43(6):803–12.

Supple, Andrew J., Sharon R. Ghazarian, James M. Frabutt, Scott W. Plunkett, and Tovah Sands. 2006. "Contextual Influences on Latino Adolescent Ethnic Identity and Academic Outcomes." *Child Development* 77(5):1427–33.

Supplee, Lauren H., Emily Moye Skuban, Daniel S. Shaw, and Joanna Prout. 2009. "Emotion Regulation Strategies and Later Externalizing Behavior among European American and African American Children." *Development and Psychopathology* 21:393–415.

Swanson, Dena Phillips, Michael Cunningham, and Margaret Beale Spencer. 2003. "Black Males' Structural Conditions, Achievement Patterns, Normative Needs, and 'Opportunities.'" *Urban Education* 38(5):608–33.

Swanson, Dena Phillips, Margaret Beale Spencer, Vinay Harpalani, Davido Dupree, Elizabeth Noll, Sofia Ginzburg, and Gregory Seaton. 2003. "Psychosocial Development in Racially and Ethnically Diverse Youth: Conceptual and Methodological Challenges in the 21st Century." *Development and Psychopathology* 15:743–71.

Tamis-LeMonda, Catherine S., Lulu Song, Ashley Leavell Smith, Ronit Kahana Kalman, and Hirokazu Yoshikawa. 2012. "Ethnic Differences in Mother-Infant Language and Gestural Communications Are Associated with Specific Skills in Infants." *Developmental Science* 15:384–97.

Tamis-LeMonda, Catherine S., Irene Nga-Lam Sze, Florrie Fei-Yin Ng, Ronit Kahana-Kalman, and Hirokazu Yoshikawa. 2013. "Maternal Teaching during Play with Four-Year-Olds: Variation by Ethnicity and Family Resources." *Merrill-Palmer Quarterly Journal of Developmental Psychology* 59:361–98.

Tanner, Jeffrey C., Tara Candland, and Whitney S. Odden. 2015. "Later Impacts of Early Childhood Interventions: A Systematic Review." Working Paper No. 3, World Bank Group. Accessed September 11, 2016. www.ieg.worldbankgroup.org.

Tapia, Michael. 2010. "Untangling Race and Class Effects on Juvenile Arrests." *Journal of Criminal Justice* 38:255–65.

Taylor, Alan. 2015. "The Mediterranean Migrant Crisis: Risking Everything for a Chance at a Better Life." *Atlantic*, May 11. www.theatlantic.com.

Tesliuc, Emil. 2006. "Social Safety Nets in OECD Countries." Accessed September 11, 2016. http://documents.worldbank.org.

Thomas, Duane E., Tiffany G. Townsend, and Faye Z. Belgrave. 2003. "The Influence of Cultural and Racial Identification on the Psychosocial Adjustment of Inner-City African American Children in School." *American Journal of Community Psychology* 32(3):217–28.

Thomas, W. John, Dorothy E. Stubbe, and Geraldine Pearson. 1999. "Race, Juvenile Justice and Mental Health: New Dimensions in Measuring Pervasive Bias." *Journal of Criminal Law and Criminology* 89:615–69.

Thompson, Aisha R., and Anne Gregory. 2011. "Examining the Influence of Perceived Discrimination during African American Adolescents' Early Years of High School." *Education and Urban Society* 43(1):3–25.

Tilly, Charles. 1998. *Durable Inequality*. Berkeley: University of California Press.

Todd, Andrew R., Kelsey C. Thiem, and Rebecca Neel. 2016. "Does Seeing Faces of Young Black Boys Facilitate the Identification of Threatening Stimuli?" *Psychological Science* 27(3):384–93.

Todres, Jonathan, Mark E. Wojcik, and Cris R. Revaz, eds. 2006. *The United Nations Convention on the Rights of the Child: An Analysis of Treaty Provisions and Implications of U.S. Ratification*. Ardsley, NY: Transnational.

Tolan, Patrick H., Deborah Gorman-Smith, and David B. Henry. 2003. "The Developmental Ecology of Urban Males' Youth Violence." *Developmental Psychology* 39(2):274–91.

Toldson, Ivory A., and Chance W. Lewis. 2012. *Challenge the Status Quo: Academic Success among School-Age African-American Males*. Washington, DC: Congressional Black Caucus Foundation.

Tough, Paul. 2008. *Whatever It Takes: Geoffrey Canada's Quest to Change Harlem and America*. New York: Houghton Mifflin.

Trask-Tate, Angelique J., and Michael Cunningham. 2010. "Planning Ahead: The Relationship among School Support, Parental Involvement, and Future Academic Expectations in African American Adolescents." *Journal of Negro Education* 79(2):137–50.

Trauma and Learning. Accessed December 8, 2015. www.traumaandlearning.org.

Triffleman, Elisa G., and Nnamdi Pole. 2010. "Future Directions in Studies of Trauma among Ethnoracial and Sexual Minority Samples: Commentary." *Journal of Consulting and Clinical Psychology* 78(4):490–97.

Tseng, Vivian. 2006. "Unpacking Immigration in Youths' Academic and Occupational Pathways." *Child Development* 77(5):1434–45.

Tsesis, Alexander. 2016. "The Declaration of Independence and Constitutional Interpretation." *Southern California Law Review* 89:359–98.

Tudge, Jonathan, Jacquelyn T. Gray, and Diane M. Hogan. 2008. "Ecological Perspectives in Human Development: A Comparison of Gibson and Bronfenbrenner." In *Comparisons in Human Development: Understanding Time and Context*, edited by Jonathan Tudge, Michael J. Shanahan, and Jaan Valsiner, 72–103. New York: Cambridge University Press.

Tudge, Jonathan, Irina Mokrova, Bridget Hatfield, and Rachana Karnit. 2009. "Uses and Misuses of Bronfenbrenner's Bioecological Theory of Human Development." *Journal of Family Theory and Review* 1(4):198–210.

Tudge, Jonathan R. H., Dolphine Odero, Cesar A. Piccini, Fabienne Doucet, Tania M. Sperb, and Rita S. Lopes. 2006. "A Window into Different Cultural Worlds: Young Children's Everyday Activities in the United States, Brazil, and Kenya." *Child Development* 77(5):1446–69.

Tulman, Joseph B. 2003. "Disability and Delinquency: How Failures to Identify, Accommodate, and Serve Youth with Education-Related Disabilities Leads to Their Disproportionate Representation in the Delinquency System." *Whittier Journal of Child and Family Advocacy* 3:3–76.

Tuminello, Elizabeth R., and Denise Davidson. 2011. "What the Face and Body Reveal: In-Group Emotion Effects and Stereotyping of Emotion in African American and European American Children." *Journal of Experimental Child Psychology* 110:258–74.

Turner, Bryan S. 2006. *Vulnerability and Human Rights*. University Park: Pennsylvania State University Press.

Turner, Cory. 2015. "Ruling in Compton Case: Trauma Could Cause Disability." National Public Radio, October 1. Accessed December 8, 2015. www.npr.org.

Twenge, Jean M., and Jennifer Crocker. 2002. "Race and Self-Esteem: Meta-Analyses Comparing Whites, Blacks, Hispanics, Asians, and American Indians and Comment on Gray-Little and Hafdahl (2000)." *Psychological Bulletin* 128(3):371–408.

UNICEF. 2000. "Children's Rights Bibliography." www.unicef.org.

———. 2005. "The State of the World's Children 2006: Excluded and Invisible." www.unicef.org.

———. 2009. "OECD and the European Commission." May. http://oecd.org.

———. 2015. "A Fair Chance for Every Child." www.unicef.org.

UNICEF Office of Research. 2010. "Innocenti Report Card 9: The Children Left Behind: A League Table of Inequality in Child Well Being the World's Rich Countries." www.unicef.org.

———. 2016. "Innocenti Report Card 13: Fairness for Children: A League Table of Inequality in Child Well-Being in Rich Countries." www.unicef-irc.org.

United Nations. 2015. "Millennium Development Goals and Beyond 2015." www.un.org.

United Nations Convention on the Rights of the Child. 1990. November 20. 1577 UNTS 3.

Urban Child Institute. 2017. "Baby's Brain Begins Now: Conception to Age 3." Accessed April 25, 2017. www.urbanchildinstitute.org.

U.S. Commission on Civil Rights. 1999. "The Crisis of the Young African American Male in the Inner Cities: A Consultation of the United States Commission on Civil Rights."

U.S. Department of Education. 2015. "Office of Elementary and Secondary Education, Report to Congress on the Elementary and Secondary Education Act."

U.S. Department of Health and Human Services. 2007. "Assessing Promising Approaches in Child Welfare: Strategies for State Legislators."

———. 2013. "Implementing Early Intervention Program for Adolescent Mothers." www.homvee.acf.hhs.gov.

U.S. Department of Justice. 2017. "Overview of Title VI of the Civil Rights Act of 1964." Accessed April 25, 2017. www.justie.gov.

U.S. House of Representatives. 2003. "Black Men and Boys in the District of Columbia and Their Impact on the Future of the Black Family." Committee on Government Reform, U.S. House of Representatives.

Valverde, Jennifer Rosen. 2013. "A Poor Idea: Statute of Limitations Decisions Cement Second-Class Remedial Scheme for Low-Income Children with Disabilities in the Third Circuit." *Fordham Urban Law Journal* 41:599–668.

Vazsonyi, Alexander T., Lloyd E. Pickering, and John M. Bolland. 2006. "Growing Up in a Dangerous Developmental Milieu: The Effects of Parenting Processes on Adjustment in Inner-City African American Adolescents." *Journal of Community Psychology* 34(1):47–73.

Votruba, Mark Edward, and Jeffrey R. Kling. 2009. "Effects of Neighborhood Characteristics on the Mortality of Black Male Youth: Evidence from Gautreaux, Chicago." *Social Science and Medicine* 68:814–23.

Wade, Jay C. 2006. "African American Fathers and Sons: Social, Historical, and Psychological Considerations." In *Impacts of Incarceration on the African American Family*, edited by Othello Harris and R. Robin Miller, 141–55. New Brunswick, NJ: Transaction.

Wade, Jay C., and Aaron B. Rochlen. 2012. "Introduction: Masculinity, Identity, and the Health and Well-Being of African American Men." *Psychology of Men and Masculinity* 14(1):1–6.

Wade, Roy, Jr., Judy A. Shea, David Rubin, and Joanne Wood. 2014. "Adverse Childhood Experiences of Low-Income Urban Youth." *Pediatrics* 134:13–20. Accessed November 4, 2016. www.pediatrics.aappublications.org.

Ward, Geoff K. 2012. *The Black Child Savers: Racial Democracy and Juvenile Justice*. Chicago: University of Chicago Press.

Ward, L. Monique, Kayla M. Day, and Khia A. Thomas. 2010. "Confronting the Assumptions: Exploring the Nature and Predictors of Black Adolescents' Media Use." *Journal of Broadcasting and Electronic Media* 54(1):69–86.

Warner, Tara D., and Raymond R. Swisher. 2015. "Adolescent Survival Expectations: Variations by Race, Ethnicity and Nativity." *Journal of Health and Social Behavior* 56:478–94.

Way, Niobe, and Judy Y. Chu, eds. 2004. *Adolescent Boys: Exploring Diverse Cultures of Boyhood*. New York: New York University Press.

Way, Niobe, Maria G. Hernandez, Leoandra Onnie Rogers, and Diane L. Hughes. 2013. "'I'm Not Going to Become No Rapper': Stereotypes as a Context of Ethnic and Racial Identity Development." *Journal of Adolescent Research* 28:407–30.

Weber, Mark C. 2012. "Common-Law Interpretation of Appropriate Education: The Road Not Taken in Rowley." *Journal of Law and Education* 41:95–128.

Weithorn, Lois A. 2005. "Envisioning Second-Order Change in America's Responses to Troubled and Troublesome Youth." *Hofstra Law Review* 33:1305–1506.

Wellman, David. 2009. "Reconfiguring the Color Line: Racializing Inner-City Youth and Rearticulating Class Hierarchy in Black America." *Transforming Anthropology* 17(2):131–46.

West, Robin. 2011. "Tragic Rights: The Rights Critique in the Age of Obama." *William and Mary Law Review* 53:713–46.

Western, Bruce. 2002. "The Impact of Incarceration on Wage Mobility and Inequality." *American Sociological Review* 67(4):526–46.

West-Olatunji, Circie, Tiffany Sanders, Sejal Mehta, and Linda Behar-Horenstein. 2010. "Parenting Practices among Low-Income Parents/Guardians of Academically Successful Fifth Grade African American Children." *Multicultural Perspectives* 12(3):138–44.

White, Joseph L. 2004. "Toward a Black Psychology." In Jones, *Black Psychology*, 5–16.

Whitehurst, Grover J., and Michelle Croft. 2010. "The Harlem Children's Zone, Promise Neighborhoods, and the Broader, Bolder Approach to Education." Brown Center on Education Policy at Brookings, July 20. www.brookings.edu.

Whitesell, Nancy Rumbaugh, Christina M. Mitchell, Carol E. Kaufman, Paul Spicer, and Voices of Indian Teens Project Team. 2006. "Developmental Trajectories of Personal and Collective Self-Concept among American Indian Adolescents." *Child Development* 77(5):1487–1503.

Wildman, Stephanie. 2004. "Privilege, Gender, and the Fourteenth Amendment: Reclaiming Equal Protection of the Laws." *Temple Political and Civil Rights Law Review* 13:707–32.

Wilkinson, Deanne L., Chauncey C. Beaty, and Regina M. Lurry. 2009. "Youth Violence Crime or Self-Help? Marginalized Urban Males' Perspectives on the Limited Efficacy of the Criminal Justice System to Stop Youth Violence." *Annals of the American Academy of Political and Social Science* 623:25–38.

Williams, David R., and Ruth Williams-Morris. 2000. "Racism and Mental Health: The African American Experience." *Ethnicity and Health* 5(3–4):243–68.

Williams, Joanna Lee, Patrick H. Tolan, Myles I. Durkee, Amir G. Francois, and Riana E. Anderson. 2012. "Integrating Racial and Ethnic Identity Research into Developmental Understanding of Adolescents." *Child Development Perspectives* 6(3):304–11.

Wilson, Emily. 2012. "ACEs, ACEs Everywhere . . . But Are We on the Brink?" Health Federation of Philadelphia. Accessed November 3, 2016. www.instituteforsafefamilies.org.

Wilson, Travis, and Philip C. Rodkin. 2011. "African American and European American Children in Diverse Elementary Classrooms: Social Integration, Social Status, and Social Behavior." *Child Development* 82(5):1454–69.

Wilson, William Julius. 1987. *The Truly Disadvantaged: The Inner City, the Underclass, and Public Policy*. Chicago: University of Chicago Press.

———. 2009. *More Than Just Race: Being Black and Poor in the Inner City*. New York: Norton.

———. 2011a. "Being Poor, Black, and American: The Impact of Political, Economic, and Cultural Forces." *American Educator* 35:10–46.

———. 2011b. "The Declining Significance of Race: Revisited and Revised." *Daedalus* 140(2):55–69.

———. 2011c. "More Than Just Race: A Response to William Darity, Jr. and Mark Gould." *Du Bois Review: Social Science Research on Race* 8(2):489–95.

Wolfe, Barbara, and Scott Scrivner. 2003. "Providing Universal Preschool for Four-Year-Olds." In Sawhill, *One Percent for the Kids*, 113–35.

Wong, Alia, and Adrienne Green. 2016. "Campus Politics: A Cheat Sheet." *Atlantic*, January 19. www.theatlantic.com.

Wong, Carol A., Jacquelynne S. Eccles, and Arnold Sameroff. 2003. "The Influence of Ethnic Discrimination and Ethnic Identification on African American Adolescents' School and Socioemotional Adjustment." *Journal of Personality* 71(6):1197–1232.

Wood, Dana, Beth Kurtz-Costes, and Kristine E. Copping. 2011. "Gender Differences in Motivational Pathways to College for Middle Class African American Youths." *Developmental Psychology* 47(4):961–68.

Woodhouse, Barbara Bennett. 2005. "Ecogenerism: An Environmental Approach to Protecting Endangered Children." *Virginia Journal of Social Policy and Law* 12:409–47.

———. 2008a. *Hidden in Plain Sight: The Tragedy of Children's Rights from Ben Franklin to Lionel Tate*. Princeton, NJ: Princeton University Press.

———. 2008b. "Individualism and Early Childhood in the U.S.: How Culture and Tradition Have Impeded Evidence-Based Reforms." *Journal of Korean Law* 8:135–60.

———. Forthcoming. *The Ecology of Childhood: Small Worlds in Peril*. Manuscript on file with author.

Wright, Brian L. 2009. "Racial-Ethnic Identity, Academic Achievement, and African American Males: A Review of Literature." *Journal of Negro Education* 78(2):123–34.

Wright, Cecile, Uvanney Maylor, and Sophie Becker. 2016. "Young Black Males: Resilience and the Use of Capital to Transform School 'Failure.'" *Critical Studies in Education* 57(1):21–34.

Wright, Cecile, Penny Standen, and Tina Patel. 2010. *Black Youth Matters: Transitions from School to Success*. New York: Routledge.

Xie, Hongling, Molly Dawyes, Tabitha J. Wurster, and Bing Shi. 2013. "Aggression, Academic Behaviors, and Popularity Perceptions among Boys of Color during the Transition to Middle School." *American Journal of Orthopsychiatry* 83(2–3):265–77.

Yakin, Jeanne A., and Susan D. McMahon. 2003. "Risk and Resiliency: A Test of a Theoretical Model for Urban, African-American Youth." *Journal of Prevention and Intervention in the Community* 26(1):5–19.

Yinusa-Nayahkoon, Leanne S., Ellen S. Cohn, Dharma E. Cortes, and Barbara G. Bokhour. 2010. "Ecological Barriers and Social Forces in Childhood Asthma Management: Examining Routines of African American Families Living in the Inner-City." *Journal of Asthma* 47:701–10.

Yip, Tiffany, Robert M. Sellers, and Eleanor K. Seaton. 2006. "African American Racial Identity across the Lifespan: Identity Status, Identity Content, and Depressive Symptoms." *Child Development* 77(5):1504–17.

Zalot, Alecia, Deborah J. Jones, Carlye Kincaid, and Tasia Smith. 2009. "Hyperactivity, Impulsivity, Inattention (HIA) and Conduct Problems among African American Youth: The Roles of Neighborhood and Gender." *Journal of Abnormal Child Psychology* 37:535–49.

Zero to Three. 2016. National Center for Infants Toddlers and Families. Accessed January 7, 2017. www.zerotothree.org.

Zuberi, Tukufu. 2011. "Critical Race Theory of Society." *Connecticut Law Review* 43:1573–91.

CASES

Arias v. Arizona, No. 15–9044 (U.S. October 31, 2016) (mem.).

Bellotti v. Baird, 443 U.S. 622 (1979).

Brock v. International Union of Operating Engineers, 2015 WL 6039734 (E.D. Penn. October 15, 2015).

Brown v. Board of Education, 347 U.S. 483 (1954).

Carey v. Population Services International, 431 U.S. 678 (1977).

City of Akron v. Akron Center for Reproductive Health, 462 U.S. 416 (1983).

City of Richmond v. J.A. Croson Co., 488 U.S. 469 (1989).

Civil Rights Cases, 109 U.S. 3 (1883).

Connecticut Coalition for Justice in Education Funding v. Rell, September 7, 2016, Memorandum Decision, Judicial District of Hartford, Docket No. X 07HHD-CV-14–5037565-S. www.jud.ct.gov.

DeShaney v. Winnebago County Department of Social Services, 489 U.S. 189 (1989).

DeShaw v. Arizona, No. 15–9057 (U.S. October 31, 2016) (mem.).

Graham v. Florida, 560 U.S. 48 (2010).

Hazelwood School District v. United States, 433 U.S. 299 (1977).

Hodgson v. Minnesota, 497 U.S. 419 (1990).

Korematsu v. United States, 323 U.S. 214 (1944).

McCleskey v. Kemp, 481 U.S. 279 (1987).

McDonald v. Chicago, 561 U.S. 742 (2010).

Michael H. v. Gerald D., 491 U.S. 110 (1989).

Miller v. Alabama, 132 S. Ct. 2455 (2012).

Montgomery v. Louisiana, No. 14–280, 577 U.S., slip opinion (January 25, 2016).

Moore v. City of East Cleveland, 431 U.S. 494 (1977).

Najar v. Arizona, No. 15–8878 (U.S. October 31, 2016) (mem.).

Newark Branch, N.A.A.C.P. v. Town of Harrison, 940 F.2d 792 (3d Cir. 1991).

Obergefell v. Hodges, 135 S. Ct. 2584 (2015).

Palmer v. Thompson, 403 U.S. 217 (1971).

Palmore v. Sidoti, 466 U.S. 429 (1984).

Parents Involved in Community Schools v. Seattle School District No. 1, 551 U.S. 701 (2007).

Perry v. Schwarzenegger, 704 F. Supp. 2d 921 (N.D. Cal. 2010).

Personnel Administrator v. Feeney, 442 U.S. 256 (1979).

Planned Parenthood of Central Missouri v. Danforth, 428 U.S. 52 (1976).

Planned Parenthood of Kansas City v. Ashcroft, 462 U.S. 476 (1983).

Plessy v. Ferguson, 163 U.S. 537 (1896).

Plyler v. Doe, 457 U.S. 202 (1982).

P.P. v. Compton Unified School District, No. CV 15–3726-MWF (PLAx) (C.D. Cal. Filed May 18, 2015).

P.P. v. Compton Unified School District, No. CV 15–3726-MWF (PLAx), 2015 WL 5755964 (C.D. Cal. September 29, 2015).

P.P. v. Compton Unified School District, No. CV 15–3726-MWF, 2015 WL 5752770 (C.D. Cal. September 29, 2015) (Class Certification).

P.P. v. Compton Unified School District, 135 F. Supp. 3d 1098 (C.D. Cal. 2015) (Motion to Dismiss).

P.P. v. Compton Unified School District, 135 F. Supp. 3d. 1126 (C.D. Cal. 2015) (No. CV 15–3726-MWF) (Complaint).

Purcell v. Arizona, No. 15–8842 (U.S. October 31, 2016) (mem.).

Regents of University of California v. Bakke, 438 U.S. 265 (1978).

Roper v. Simmons, 543 U.S. 551 (2005).

Safford Unified School District No. 1 v. Redding, 557 U.S. 364 (2009).

San Antonio Independent School District v. Rodriguez, 411 U.S. 1 (1973).

Shelby County v. Holder, 133 S. Ct. 2612 (2013).

Slaughter-House Cases, 83 U.S. 36 (1872).

Strauder v. West Virginia, 100 U.S. 303 (1880).

Tatum v. Arizona, No. 15–8850 (U.S. October 31, 2016).

Troxel v. Granville, 530 U.S. 57 (2000).

United States v. Guest, 383 U.S. 745 (1966).

Washington v. Davis, 426 U.S. 229 (1976).

STATUTES/REGULATIONS

FLA. STAT. § 61.13(3) (a)–(m) (2006).

FLA. STAT. § 61.13 (2015).

Individuals with Disabilities Education Act (IDEA), 20 U.S.C. §1400 (2012).

Older Americans Act of 1965 (Pub. L. 89–73, 79 Stat. 218).

Rehabilitation Act of 1973, 29 U.S.C. §794 (2012).

Title VI of the Civil Rights Act of 1964, 42 U.S.C. §2000d (2012).

Title IX of the Education Amendments of 1972, 20 U.S.C. §1681 (2012).

INDEX

ABOUT THE AUTHOR

Nancy E. Dowd is Professor and David Levin Chair in Family Law at the University of Florida Levin College of Law. She researches and writes at the confluence of civil rights, feminist, and critical race theory about issues of children and youth, men and masculinities, juvenile justice, and nontraditional families. She is the author or editor of seven previous books, mostly with New York University Press, and is the series editor of Families, Law, and Society at New York University Press.